Nietzsche and the Vicious Circle

Nietzsche and the Vicious Circle

PIERRE KLOSSOWSKI

Translated by Daniel W. Smith

The University of Chicago Press

The University of Chicago Press, Chicago 60637

The Athlone Press, London, NW11 7SG

First published in France in 1969 by
Mercure de France, Paris as
Nietzsche et le Cercle Vicieux

Printed in Great Britain

06 05 04 03 02 01 00   2 3 4 5 6

ISBN: 0-226-44386-8 (cloth)
ISBN: 0-226-44387-6 (paperback)

Publisher's note
The publishers wish to record their thanks to the French
Ministry of Culture for a grant towards the cost of
translation.

Library of Congress Cataloging in Publication Data
Klossowski, Pierre.
   [Nietzsche et le cercle vicieux. English]
   Nietzsche and the vicious circle / Pierre Klossowski ;
translated by Daniel W. Smith.
      p.   cm.
   Includes bibliographical references and index.
   ISBN 0–226-44386-8 (cloth : alk. paper). —
   ISBN 0–226-44387-6 (pbk : alk. paper)
   1. Nietzsche, Friedrich Wilhelm, 1844–1900.   I. Title.
B3317.K6213   1997
193--dc21   97–14379
                                                          CIP

Contents

Translator's Preface   vii
Introduction   xiv

1   The Combat against Culture   1
2   The Valetudinary States at the Origin of a Semiotic
    of Impulses   15
3   The Experience of the Eternal Return   55
4   The Valetudinary States at the Origin of Four
    Criteria: Decadence, Vigour, Gregariousness,
    the Singular Case   74
5   Attempt at a Scientific Explanation of the
    Eternal Return   93
6   The Vicious Circle as a Selective Doctrine   121
7   The Consultation of the Paternal Shadow   172
8   The Most Beautiful Invention of the Sick   198
9   The Euphoria of Turin   208
10 Additional Note on Nietzsche's Semiotic   254

Notes   262
Index   274

To Gilles Deleuze

Translator's Preface

Pierre Klossowski's *Nietzsche and the Vicious Circle* ranks alongside Martin Heidegger's *Nietzsche* and Gilles Deleuze's *Nietzsche and Philosophy* as one of the most important and influential, as well as idiosyncratic, readings of Nietzsche to have appeared in Europe.[1] When it was originally published in 1969, Michel Foucault, who frequently spoke of his indebtedness to Klossowski's work, penned an enthusiastic letter to its author. 'It is the greatest book of philosophy I have read,' he wrote, 'with Nietzsche himself.'[2] *Nietzsche and the Vicious Circle* was in fact the result of a long apprenticeship. Under the influence of Georges Bataille, Klossowski first began reading Nietzsche in 1934, 'in competition with Kierkegaard'.[3] During the next three decades, he published a number of occasional pieces on Nietzsche: an article in a special issue of the journal *Acéphale* devoted to the question of 'Nietzsche and the Fascists' (1937); reviews of Karl Löwith's and Karl Jasper's books on Nietzsche (1939); an introduction to his own translation of *The Gay Science* (1954); and most importantly, a lecture presented to the Collège de Philosophie entitled 'Nietzsche, polytheism, and parody' (1957), which Deleuze later praised for having 'renewed the interpretation of Nietzsche'.[4]

It was not until the 1960s, however, that Klossowski seems to have turned his full attention to Nietzsche. *Nietzsche and the Vicious Circle* grew out of a paper entitled 'Forgetting and anamnesis in the lived experience of the eternal return of the same', which Klossowski presented at the famous Royaumont conference on Nietzsche in July 1964.[5] Over the next few years, Klossowski published a number of additional articles that were ultimately gathered together in *Nietzsche and the Vicious Circle* in 1969.[6] The primary innovation of the study lay in the importance it gave to Nietzsche's experience of the Eternal Return at Sils-Maria in August 1881, of which Klossowski provided a new and highly original interpretation. The book was one of the primary texts in the explosion of interest in Nietzsche that occurred in France around 1970,[7] and it exerted a profound influence on Deleuze and Guattari's *Anti-Oedipus* (1972) and Lyotard's *Libidinal Economy* (1975).[8] In July 1972, a second major conference on Nietzsche took place in France at Cerisy-la-Salle, which included presentations by Deleuze, Derrida, Lyotard, Nancy, Lacoue-Labarthe and Gandillac, among many others. Klossowski's contribution was a paper entitled 'Circulus vitiosus', which analysed what he called the 'conspiracy' (*complot*) of the eternal return. It was the last text he would write on Nietzsche.[9]

Klossowski is himself a rather idiosyncratic figure whose work on Nietzsche constitutes merely one aspect of an extraordinary and rather enigmatic career. The older brother of the painter Balthus, he was born in Paris in 1905 into an old Polish family, and in his youth was a close friend and disciple of Rainer Maria Rilke and André Gide. In the 1930s he participated in the Collège de Sociologie with Michel Leiris, Roger Callois and Georges Bataille, with whom he maintained a lifelong friendship. In 1939 he entered a Dominican seminary, where he studied scholasticism and theology, but then underwent a religious crisis during the Occupation. In 1947, after having participated in the French Resistance, he returned to the lay life, married, and wrote a now-famous study of the Marquis de Sade entitled *Sade My Neighbor*.[10] His first novel, *The Suspended Vocation* (1950), was a transposition of the vicissitudes of his religious crisis.[11] During the next decade, he wrote what is perhaps his most celebrated work, *The Laws of Hospitality*, a trilogy that includes *The Revocation of the Edict of Nantes* (1959), *Roberte, ce soir* (1954), and *Le Souffleur* (1960), and in which he created Roberte, the central sign of his entire oeuvre.[12] In 1965, he published *The Baphomet*, an allegorical version of the Eternal Return that received the coveted Prix des Critiques.[13] During this period, he also produced numerous translations of German and Latin texts, including works by Benjamin, Kafka, Kierkegaard, Heidegger, Hamaan, Wittgenstein, Rilke, Klee, Nietzsche, Suetonius and Virgil. Since the publication, in 1970, of *Living Currency*, an essay on the economy and the affects, Klossowski has devoted himself almost exclusively to painting.[14] His large 'compositions', as he calls them, executed in coloured pencils on paper, frequently transpose scenes from his novels, and have been exhibited in Paris, Zurich, Berne, Cologne, New York, Tokyo, Rome, Madrid and elsewhere.[15] Throughout all these endeavours, Klossowski has remained almost unclassifiable, singular. Novelist, essayist, translator, artist, he categorically refuses the designation 'philosopher'. 'Je suis un "maniaque",' he says. 'Un point, c'est tout.'[16] It is hoped that this translation of *Nietzsche and the Vicious Circle* will provoke renewed interest in Klossowski's remarkable work in the English-speaking world.

Klossowski describes his books on Nietzsche and Sade as 'essays devoted not to ideologies but to the *physiognomies* of problematic thinkers who differ greatly from each other'.[17] He has developed an idiosyncratic vocabulary to describe such physiognomies, and some of his terminological innovations deserve comment here.

(1) The term *fond* has a wide range of meanings in French ('bottom', 'ground', 'depth', 'heart', 'background' and so on), and has been translated uniformly here as 'depth'. Klossowski almost always uses it in the context of the expression *le fond inéchangeable* ('the unexchangeable depth') or *le fond unintelligible* ('the unintelligible depth'), which refers to the

'obstinate singularity' of the human soul that is by nature non-communicable.

(2) *Impulsion* has been rendered throughout as 'impulse', and its cognate *impulsionnel* as 'impulsive'. The term is related to the French *pulsion*, which translates the Freudian term *Triebe* ('drive'), but which Klossowski uses only in rare instances. Nietzsche himself had recourse to a varied vocabulary to describe what Klossowski summarizes in the term 'impulse': 'drive' (*Triebe*), 'desire' (*Begierden*), 'instinct' (*Instinke*), 'power' (*Mächte*), 'force' (*Kräfte*), 'impulse' (*Reize, Impulse*), 'passion' (*Leidenschaften*), 'feeling' (*Gefülen*), 'affect' (*Affekte*), 'pathos' (*Pathos*), and so on.[18] The essential point for Klossowski is that these terms refer to *intensive* states of the soul that are in constant fluctuation.

(3) Klossowski's use of the term 'soul' (*âme*) is in part derived from the theological literature of the mystics, for whom the unexchangeable depth of the soul was irreducible and uncreated; it eludes the exercise of the created intellect, and can be grasped only negatively.[19] If there is an apophaticism in Klossowski, however, it is related exclusively to the immanent movements of the soul's intensive affects, and not to the transcendence of God. Klossowski frequently employs the French term *tonalité* to describe these states of the soul's fluctuating intensities (their diverse tones, timbres and amplitudes). Since this use of the term is as unusual in French as it is in English, we have retained the English 'tonality' as its equivalent.

(4) *Phantasme* ('phantasm') and *simulacrum* ('simulacrum') are perhaps the most important terms in Klossowski's vocabulary. The former comes from the Greek *phantasia* (appearance, imagination), and was taken up in a more technical sense in psychoanalytic theory; the latter comes from the Latin *simulare* (to copy, represent, feign), and during the late Roman empire referred to the statues of the gods that lined the entrance to a city. In Klossowski, the term 'phantasm' refers to an obsessional image produced instinctively from the life of the impulses. 'My true themes', writes Klossowski

of himself, 'are dictated by one or more obsessional (or "obsidianal") instincts that seek to express themselves.'[20] A 'simulacrum', by contrast, is a willed reproduction of a phantasm (in a literary, pictorial, or plastic form) that simulates this invisible agitation of the soul. 'The simulacrum, in its *imitative* sense, is the actualization of something in itself incommunicable and nonrepresentable: the *phantasm* in its obsessional constraint.'[21] If *Nietzsche and the Vicious Circle* is primarily an interpretation of Nietzsche's physiognomy, it is because it attempts to identify the impulses or powers that exercised their constraint on Nietzsche (notably those associated with his valetudinary states), the phantasms they produced (notably the phantasm of the Eternal Return that Nietzsche experienced at Sils-Maria in August 1881), and the various simulacra Nietzsche created to express them.

(5) Simulacra stand in a complex relationship to what Klossowski, in his later works, calls a *stéréotype* ('stereo-type').[22] On the one hand, the invention of simulacra always presupposes a set of prior stereotypes – what he here calls 'the code of everyday signs' – that express the gregarious aspect of a lived experience in a form schematized by the habitual usages of feeling and thought. In this sense, the code of everyday signs, by making them intelligible, necessarily inverts and falsifies the singularity of the soul's intensive movements: 'How can one give an account of an irreducible depth of sensibility except by acts that betray it?'[23] On the other hand, Klossowski also speaks of a 'science of stereotypes' in which the stereotype, by being 'accentuated' to the point of excess, can itself bring about a critique of its own gregarious interpretation of the phantasm: 'Practiced advisedly, the institutional stereotypes (of syntax) provoke the presence of what they circumscribe; their circumlocutions conceal the incongruity of the phantasm but at the same time trace the outline of its opaque physiognomy.'[24]

Klossowski's own prose is an example of this latter 'science of stereotypes'. By his own admission, it is written in a '"conventionally" classical syntax' that makes systematic use of the literary tenses and conjunctions of the French language, giving it a decidedly erudite and even 'bourgeois' tone. At the same time, however, it is also sprinkled with minor grammatical improprieties and solecisms; certain of Klossowski's phrasings turn out to be fragments that are linked together through a profuse utilization of colons, semi-colons, and dashes, which often run the length of an entire paragraph. While we have tried to follow Klossowski's syntax as closely as possible, it has been impossible to reproduce many of his stylistic devices, and we have often elected to choose intelligible English renderings, perhaps at the cost of sacrificing some of his stylistic effects. Klossowski often makes use of the *présent historique* tense in the French, which we have generally translated by the past tense in the English.

(6) We have translated the unusual but important term *suppôt* as 'agent'. The word is derived from the Latin *suppositum*, 'that which is placed under'. In contemporary usage, it refers to a subordinate who acts on behalf of someone else, such as a 'secret agent', and usually implies that the subordinate is carrying out the designs of a wicked superior (*suppôt de Satan* is a current French locution for a 'hellhound' or evil person; the *suppôts de la tyrannie* refer to the 'henchmen' of a tyrant or a tyrannical regime). But Klossowski's use of the term also refers back to a more distant and technical philosophical history. In scholastic philosophy, the Latin *suppositum* was closely linked to the terms *substantia* ('substance') or *subjectum* ('subject'). In particular, it referred to a complete and individual subject that has its own existence, integrating heterogenous elements into a unique whole.[25] In sixteenth- and seventeenth-century philosophy, the French *suppôt* retained an analogous meaning, though it was applied to new philosophical problems.[26] Klossowski in turn has retrieved the term from the scholastic tradition, and applied it to a specifically Nietzschean problematic. The *suppôt* is itself a phantasm, a complex and fragile entity that bestows a psychic and organic unity upon the moving chaos of the impulses, primarily through the grammatical

fiction of the 'I', which interprets the impulses in terms of a hierarchy of gregarious needs (both material and moral), and dissimulates itself through a network of concepts (substance, cause, identity, self, world, God) that reduces the combat of the impulses to silence.[27] Unfortunately, there is no obvious translation for the term *suppôt*: the English word 'suppost' survived through the nineteenth century, but is now archaic. The term 'agent', while it does not adequately render all these nuances, nonetheless has the advantage of connoting both the colloquial and philosophical senses of *suppôt*. The three instances, in Chapter 3, where Klossowski uses the French term *agent* ('the agent of meaning') are indicated clearly in the text.

Moi has generally been translated as 'self'; however, it is also the French translation of the Freudian 'ego', and we have adopted this translation in contexts (such as Chapter 9) where Klossowski makes explicit reference to Freud.

This translation would not have been completed without the support of a Chateaubriand Fellowship from the French government, and a doctoral fellowship from the Chicago Humanities Institute at the University of Chicago. Their generosity is gratefully acknowledged. Elisabeth Beauregard, Peter Canning, Christoph Cox, Michael Greco, Eleanor Kaufman, Tracy McNulty, Graham Parkes and Alan Schrift provided welcome advice on various aspects of the translation. I consulted an earlier translation of Chapter 3 by Allen S. Weiss, which appeared in *The New Nietzsche: Contemporary Styles of Interpretation*, ed. David B. Allison (New York: Delta, 1977), pp. 107–20.

Introduction

This is a book that will exhibit an unusual ignorance. How can we speak solely of 'Nietzsche's thought' without taking into account everything that has subsequently been said about it? Will we not thereby run the risk of following paths that have already been travelled more than once, blazing trails that have been marked out many times – imprudently asking questions that have long ago been left behind? And will we not in this way reveal a negligence, a total lack of scruples with regard to the meticulous exegeses that recently have been written – in order to interpret, as so many signals, the flashes of summer lightning that a destiny continues to send our way from the horizon of our century?

What then is our aim – if indeed we have one? Let us say that we have written a *false* study. Because we are reading Nietzsche's texts directly, because we are listening to him speak, can we perhaps make him speak to 'us'? Can we ourselves make use of the whisperings, the breathings, the bursts of anger and laughter in what may be the most ingratiating – and also the most irritating – prose yet written in the German language? For those who can hear it, the word of Nietzsche gains a power that is all the more explosive insofar as contemporary history, current events, and the universe are beginning to answer, in a more or less circuitous manner, the questions Nietzsche was asking some eighty years ago. Nietzsche was interrogating the near and distant future, a future that has now become our everyday reality – and he predicted that this future would be convulsive, to the point where our own convulsions are caricatures of his thought. We will try to comprehend how and in what sense Nietzsche's interrogation describes what we are now living through.

We must not overlook two essential points that have hitherto remained veiled, if not passed over in silence, in the study of his thought. The first is that, as Nietzsche's thought unfolded, it abandoned the strictly speculative realm in order to adopt, if not simulate, the preliminary elements of a conspiracy. It thereby made our own era the object of a tacit accusation. The indictment had been handed down by the Marxist exegesis, which had at least exposed the *intention* of the conspiracy, since every individual thought of bourgeois origin necessarily reveals its complicity in a class 'conspiracy'. But there is a Nietzschean conspiracy which is not that of a class but that of an isolated individual (like Sade), who uses the means of this class not only against his own class, but also against the existing forms of the human species as a whole.

The second point is closely related to the first. Because Nietzsche's thought meditated on a lived experience to the point where it became inverted into a systematic pre-meditation, prey to an interpretative delirium that seemed to diminish the 'responsibility of the thinker', there is a tendency to grant it, as it were, 'extenuating circumstances' – which is worse than the Marxist indictment. For what do we want to extenuate? *The fact that his thought revolved around delirium as its axis.* Now early on, Nietzsche was apprehensive about this propensity in himself, and his every effort was directed toward fighting the irresistible attraction that Chaos (or, more precisely, the 'chasm') exerted on him – a *hiatus* which, starting in his childhood, he strove to fill in and cross over through his autobiography. The more he *probed the phenomenon of thought* and the different *behaviours* that result from it, and the more he studied the individual

reactions provoked by the structures of the modern world
(and always in relation to his conception of the *ancient world*),
the closer he drew to this chasm.

Lucid thought, delirium and the conspiracy form an
indissoluble whole in Nietzsche – an indissolubility that
would become the criterion for discerning what is of
consequence or not. This does not mean that, since it
involved delirium, Nietzsche's thought was 'pathological';
rather, because his thought was lucid to the extreme, it
took on the appearance of a delirious interpretation – and
also required the entire experimental initiative of the modern
world. It is modernity that must now be charged with
determining whether this initiative has failed or succeeded.
But because the world is itself concerned with Nietzsche's
initiative, the more the modern world experiences the threat
of its own failures, the more Nietzsche's thought gains in
stature. Modern catastrophes are always confused – in the
more or less short term – with the 'good news' of a 'false
prophet'.

What then is *the act of thinking*? There was a suspicion lurking
silently in the writings of Nietzsche's youth, which came to
the fore in an increasingly virulent way in the unpublished
fragments contemporaneous with *Human, All too Human* and,
especially, *The Gay Science*. *What is lucid* and *what is unconscious*
in our thought and in our actions? – a subterranean question
that *disguised* itself outwardly in a critique of culture, and that
intentionally made itself explicit in a form that could still be
integrated into the speculative and historical discussions of
his time. Nietzsche's thought thus followed, in an absolutely
simultaneous manner, two divergent movements: the notion
of lucidity was valid only to the degree that total obscurity
continued to be envisioned, and thus affirmed:

> 'At every moment chaos is still pursuing its work in our
> mind: concepts, images, feelings are there juxtaposed
> *fortuitously*, thrown together pell-mell. In this way,

relations that *astonish* the mind are created: the mind recalls something similar, it feels a *flavor*, it retains and elaborates both according to its art and its knowledge. – Here is the last small fragment of the world where something new is produced, at least as far as the human eye is concerned. In sum, here again it is a matter of a new chemical combination, which as yet has no parallel in the becoming of the world.[28]

A thought only rises by falling, it progresses only by regressing – an inconceivable spiral, which to describe as 'useless' is so repugnant to us that we are wary even of admitting that successive generations follow the same movement – even if this means that we associate ourselves with the rise of a mind only as long as it seems to follow, in unison with culture, the ascent of history. As for the remainder, we leave the descending movement of this spiralling thought to those who specialize in the failures, the dregs, the waste products produced by the function of thinking and living – experts who, in accordance with this convenient division of labour, hardly need to concern themselves with this tension between lucidity and obscurity, except perhaps to note, on the day when *each* reaches a verdict on the *other*, that they had picked up the *accent of delirium*.

To want to detect this accent in Nietzsche's thought would from the outset require us to consult the very authorities that his thought called into question. Either Nietzsche was delirious from the outset in even wanting to *attack these authorities*; or else he was clear-sighted in attacking the very *notion* of lucidity directly. This is why, at every step, Nietzsche's thought found itself circumscribed:

on the inside:
by the *principle of identity* on which *language* (the code of everyday signs) depends, in accordance with the *reality principle*;

on the outside:
by competent institutional authorities (the historians of
philosophy), but *also and above all* by the psychiatrists, the
surveyors of the unconscious who, for this very reason,
control the more or less variable range of the reality
principle, to which the person who thinks or acts would
bear witness;
finally:
on both sides, by science and its experimentations, which
sometimes separates and sometimes brings the two together,
thus displacing the boundaries and 'adjusting' the demarca-
tions between the *inside* and the *outside*.

As long as Nietzsche respected these variously delimited
spheres from the viewpoint of *inquiry*, his understanding
seemed to comply with two principles: *the principle of reality*
(insofar as he simply described reality *historically*, he analysed
it in order to reconstruct it, and thus to communicate the
results of his research to others) and *the principle of identity*
(insofar as he defined himself as a *teacher* in relation to what
he was teaching).

But once the demonstration (required by institutional
language for the teaching of reality) was turned into *the
movement of a declarative mood*, and the contagious mood or
tonality of the soul supplanted the demonstration, Nietzsche
reached the limit of the principles of identity and reality,
which were *answerable to the very authorities* his own discourse
was presumably based upon. Nietzsche introduced into
teaching what no authority responsible for the transmission of
knowledge (philosophy) had ever been advised to teach. But
Nietzsche introduced it surreptitiously, his language on the
contrary having pushed to an extreme severity the application
of the laws required for communication. The tonality of the
soul, in making itself thought, was pursuing its own inquiry,
to the point where the terms of the latter were *reconstituted as
a muteness*: this thought spoke to itself of an *obstacle* that the
intention to teach would stumble over at the outset.

This obstacle, whose muteness was experienced as intensity and resistance, put the aim of teaching itself in question. Now the resistance of the mute obstacle was nothing other than the virtual reaction *exerted by the authorities of identity and reality*. Muteness on the inside was merely *speech* on the outside. The assent (*assentiment*) of thought to this speech on the outside was merely the *resentment* (*ressentiment*) *of the mood or the mute tonality*. Nietzsche's *declarations* transferred the muteness of the *mood* onto thought, insofar as the mood came up against the resistance of *culture* from without (that is, the *speech* of universities, scientists, authorities, political parties, priests, doctors).

In *identifying himself with this mute obstacle* of the mood in order to *think* it, 'Professor Nietzsche' destroyed not only his own identity but that of the *authorities of speech*. As a consequence, he suppressed *their presence within his own discourse*, and along with their presence, he suppressed the *reality principle* itself. His declarations were directed to *an outside* that he had *reduced to the silence* of his own moods.

Though they were reduced to silence in Nietzsche's declarations, however, the *speaking agencies* had never been anything other than the *configuration* of his moods. The mute intensity of the soul's tonality could be sustained only as long as a *resistance* from the outside was still speaking: culture.

Culture (the sum total of knowledge) – that is, the intention to teach and learn – is the obverse of the soul's tonality, its intensity, which can be neither taught nor learnt. The more culture accumulates, however, the more it becomes enslaved to itself – and the more its obverse, the *mute intensity* of the tonality of the soul, grows. The soul's tonality catches the teacher by surprise, and finally breaks with the intention to teach: the servitude of culture thus breaks forth at the moment it collides with the muteness of Nietzsche's discourse.

Since Professor Nietzsche's *ultima verba* turned into aphasia, it is easy for doctors to see this as a confirmation of their own *reality principle*: Nietzsche went beyond the limits, he lapsed into incoherence, he ceased to speak, he howled or remained silent.

No one sees that science itself is aphasic, and that if it admitted it had no foundation, no reality would subsist – from which it derives a power that induces it to calculate: it is this decision that invents reality. It calculates so as not to have to speak, for fear of falling back into nothingness.

1
The Combat against Culture

1. Is the 'philosopher' still possible today? Is the extent of what is known too great? Is it not unlikely that he will ever manage to embrace everything within his vision, all the less so the more scrupulous he is? Would it not happen *too late*, when his best time is past? Or at the very least, when he is damaged, degraded, degenerated, so that his value judgement no longer means anything? In the opposite case, he will become a *dilettante* with a thousand antennae, having lost the great pathos, his respect for himself – the good, subtle conscience. Enough – he no longer either directs or commands. If he wanted to, he would have to become a great actor, a kind of Cagliostro philosopher.

2. What does a philosophical existence mean for us today? Isn't it almost a way of withdrawing? A kind of evasion? And for someone who lives that way, apart and in complete simplicity, is it likely that he has indicated the best path to follow for his own knowledge? Would he not have had to experiment with a hundred different ways of living to be authorized to speak of the value of life? In short, we think it is necessary to have lived in a totally 'antiphilosophical' manner, according to hitherto received notions, and certainly not as a shy man of virtue – in order to judge the great problems from lived experiences. The man with the greatest experiences, who condenses them into general conclusions: would

he not have to be the most powerful man? – For a long time we have confused the Wise Man with the scientific man, and for an even longer time with the religiously exalted man.[29]

Only now has it dawned on humanity that music is a semiological language of affects: and later we will learn how to recognize clearly the impulsive system of a musician through his music. In truth, he did not intend to *betray himself in this manner*. Such is the innocence of this type of *confession*, as opposed to every written work.

Yet this innocence also exists in the great philosophers: they are not conscious that they are speaking of themselves – they claim it would be a question of 'the truth' – when at bottom it is only a question of themselves. Or rather: their most violent impulse is brought to light with all the impudence and innocence of a fundamental impulse: it wants to be sovereign and, if possible, the aim of every thing and every event! The philosopher is only a kind of occasion and chance through which *the impulse is finally able to speak*.

There are many more languages than we think: and man betrays himself more often than he desires. How things speak! – but there are very few listeners, so that man can only, as it were, chatter on in the void when he pours out his confessions: he squanders his 'truths', as the sun does its light. – Isn't it rather a pity that the void has no ears?

There are ways of seeing that make man feel: 'This alone is true and just, and truly human; whoever thinks otherwise is making an error' – ways of seeing we term religious and moral. It is clear that what is speaking here is the sovereign impulse, which is stronger than man. In each case, the impulse believes it holds *the truth and the supreme concept of 'man'*.

Undoubtedly there are many men in whom an

impulse *has not become sovereign*: they have no convictions. This then is the first characteristic: every coherent system of a philosopher demonstrates that *one* impulse directs it, that *there is a fixed hierarchy in it*. This is what is then called: 'truth'. – And the felt sensation [can be described] thus: with this truth I am at the height [of] 'man'; the other person is of *a lesser kind than myself*, at least in terms of knowledge.

In rough and naïve men, one conviction also predominates in their mores, and even in their tastes: they are *the best possible*. In cultured people there reigns a certain tolerance in this respect: but one holds *all the more rigorously* to one's own criterion of *Good and Evil*: according to which one wants to have not only the most *refined* taste but also *the only legitimate* one.

This is the commonly *reigning form of barbarism*: that one doesn't even realize that morality is *a matter of taste*.

For the rest, there is in this domain a maximum of *imposture* and *lying*. *Moralizing* and *religious* literature is the most full of lies. The dominant impulse, whichever it may be, resorts to *ruse and lying* to prevail over the other impulses.

Alongside religious wars there is always a *moral war* going on: that is, *one* impulse wants to subjugate humanity; and as religions gradually die out, this struggle will become all the more *bloody* and *visible*. We are only at the beginning![30]

What then does the behaviour of the philosopher amount to? Is he a mere spectator of events, at once lucid and impotent? Or, if all commentary is useless, will he have to intervene directly? But how can he make a direct intervention? Through analyses, declarations, warnings, or incentives? Does he have to win over people's consciences in order to provoke an 'event' (*breaking the history of humanity in two*)? Or rather, does not this event, which the philosopher apprehends (the consequences of the disappearance of a unique God, the guarantor of identities, and the return of multiple gods), first have to be *mimed*, in accordance with the gestural semiotic of the Soothsayers and Prophets?

We must break with the classic rule of morality, which – on the pretext of realizing a human potential – makes humanity dependent upon habits adopted *once and for all*. Instead, we must behave in accordance with the strict demands that follow from relentless reflection. If a demand of thought can arise in an unforeseeable manner, it is because it can arise from behaviour itself, thereby opening up that same behaviour to the disparagement of a contradictory attitude. Behavior can never be limited by its regular repetition, nor can it limit thinking itself. A mode of thought that would restrict behaviour, or a mode of behaviour that would restrict thought – both comply with an extremely useful automatism: they ensure *security*. In reality, any thought that experiences the uneasiness of this provisional state reveals its own lassitude. By contrast, any thought that allows itself to be called into question, whether by an internal or external event, reveals a certain capacity for starting over. Either it retreats from, or it goes beyond, the statements made in the interval. It is on the basis of this lassitude or this capacity, this retreating or this going beyond, that Nietzsche will judge previous philosophers.

Neither Descartes, nor Spinoza, nor Kant, nor Hegel would have been able to construct their systems if, by some chance, they had renounced a teachable coherence in order to speak of existence from their own lived experience. (Though Descartes came close to doing so and seems to have concealed this intention.) Nietzsche maintains that they have only complied with a secret concern to express the movements of their own moods: 'They claim it is a question of "the truth" – when at bottom it is only a question of themselves. Or rather: their most violent impulse is brought to light with all the impudence and innocence of a fundamental impulse: it makes itself sovereign and, if possible, the aim of every thing and every event. *The philosopher is only a kind of occasion*

and chance through which the impulse is finally able to speak.'[31]
What then did Spinoza or Kant do? Nothing but interpret
their dominant impulse. But it was only the *communicable*
part of their behaviour that could be translated into their
constructions.

What this means is that Nietzsche rejected, purely and
simply, the attitude of the philosopher-teacher. He made fun
of himself for not being a philosopher – if by that we mean a
thinker who thinks and teaches out of a *concern* for the human
condition. Nietzsche here acted ruthlessly, disruptively, and
wound up achieving, one might say, a 'smashing' success [*il
'casse la baraque'*].

Nietzsche rejected any thought that was integrated into *the
function of thinking* because it is the least efficacious. For what
are the thoughts and experiences of a philosopher worth if
they serve merely to *guarantee* the society from which he
comes? A society believes itself to be morally justified through
its scientists and artists. Yet the very fact that they exist – and
that their creations exist – is evidence of the disintegrating
malaise of the society; and it is by no means clear that they
will be the ones to reintegrate the society, at least if they take
their activity seriously.

Since Nietzsche was thinking and writing in a solidly
bourgeois society – some thirty to forty years before its
first fractures appeared – his manner of seeing still seemed
to conform to the initiatives undertaken by that same
society. It is only today that we are able to measure the
impact of his words and of his rejection. 'Bourgeois' society
no longer exists, but something much more complex has
been substituted for it: an industrialist organization which,
while maintaining the appearance of the bourgeois edifice,
reorganizes and multiplies the social classes in accordance
with the increase or decrease of ever more diversified needs,
and which, because of its automatism, disturbs the sensitivity
of individuals.

What Nietzsche meant to say through his own *rejection of
the system* was that if philosophy merely concerns itself with

a transmission of 'problems', it will never get beyond the general interpretation a particular social state gives of its own 'culture'. For Nietzsche, to make an assessment of Western culture always amounts to questioning it in the following manner: what *can still be created* from the acquisitions of our knowledge, our practices, our customs, our habits? To what degree am I the *beneficiary* or the *victim* or the *dupe* of these habits? With regard to his contemporaries, Nietzsche's own manner of living and writing – and of thinking – was the answer to these diverse questions.

For Nietzsche, the moral question of knowing what is *true or false*, *just or unjust* could now be posed in the following terms: What is *sick or healthy*? What is *gregarious* or *singular*?

> The first shoots of fecundity, insofar as they are a sign of health and promote vigour and resistance, initially have the character of *sickness*. This first explosion of force and will to self-determination is a sickness that can destroy humanity; and even more sickly are the first, strange, and wild attempts of the mind to adjust the world to itself, to its own authority.[32]

It seemed to Nietzsche – who was himself subject to valetudinary variations, and constantly feared that his own thought showed the effects of his depressive states – that it would be equally revelatory to examine the forms of thought put forward by previous thinkers from the viewpoint of their relation to life, to the living, that is, from the viewpoint of *the rises and falls of intensity* in all their various forms: aggressiveness, tolerance, intimidation, anguish, the need for solitude; or on the contrary the forgetting of oneself in the midst of the turmoil of an epoch.

Nietzsche therefore judged morality to be the principal '*metaphysical virus*' of thought and science: 'I see all philosophers, I see science kneeling before a reality that is the reverse of the struggle for existence as taught by Darwin's school – that is to say, I see on top and surviving everywhere those who compromise life and the value of life.'[33] The mediocre dominate those surplus natures whose overabundance of life is a threat to the security of the species. There are therefore two powers: the *levelling* power of gregarious thought and the *erectile* power of particular cases.

This allowed Nietzsche to identify those metaphysical systems commanded by moralities whose only aim is to perpetuate the reign of gregarious norms and instincts: any system that does not receive their approval cannot survive. But there also exist systems that are impracticable to the greatest number, and which are consecrated to a particular case (Heraclitus, Spinoza); and others that form a code reserved purely for a limited group (La Rochefoucauld). The metaphysics of a Kant, by contrast, harbours a behaviour that Nietzsche summarized in the image of *the fox who returns to his cage after having broken out of it.*

> To construct systems (in the very epoch where we see science beginning) is pure childishness. In return: we must make *long-term* decisions regarding methods, for centuries! – for one day *the direction of the future* will have to pass into our hands!
>
> – Methods, however, that themselves come from our instincts, in regulated habits that already exist; for example, *the exclusion of ends*.[34]

But in Nietzsche's mind, these *methods* amounted to a reproduction of the very conditions that have formed and favoured his vision of the world – and which therefore had given his type of feeling and thinking a chance of success.

One day, these isolated cases will come into possession of their own *methods* for 'directing' the future of humanity. Did Nietzsche believe in the efficacy of these methods? Or rather, did he simply want to *transmit the states of his own soul* in order to make sure others would have the *means* of reacting and acting under the worst conditions, thereby enabling them not only *to defend themselves* but also *to counter-attack*?

At the end of this first inquiry, Nietzsche posed a new question in a tone of voice that was completely foreign to all previous speculation: Who is the *adversary*, who is the *enemy* to be destroyed? For the more thought can circumscribe its adversary, the more it can concentrate its strength. In determining the enemy, thought is able to create its own space, to extend it, to breathe freely. The enemy was not only Christianity, nor was it morality in itself, but a complex amalgam of the two; 'philistinism' is too weak a term, nor does 'bourgeoisism' adequately describe the monstrous hydra, for it is made up of extraordinarily diverse tendencies and deceitful practices. It is in all things, and in each thing. And Nietzsche himself had to struggle to free himself from the enemy, to eradicate all its germs, which he bore in himself like a hereditary sin. That was his first task.

To explore the foundation of Western culture, and especially 'bourgeois' culture, under the pretext of going deeper into it and making it bearable, always amounts to legitimating it in 'human' terms. But any possible legitimation was undermined in advance once Nietzsche denounced a society founded on the *ideological disavowal of the external constraints* it necessarily exerts. The ideological disavowal of constraints is expressed through the concept of culture – and thus, through a *false interpretation of culture* in a concept. The fact that modern society has merely formed a concept of culture is the proof of the disappearance of a lived culture.

The conception of the Greek state formed by the young Nietzsche became a phantasm that was all the more obsessive in that it was incompatible with the concept of culture. '*That slavery belongs to the essence of a culture is a truth that leaves no doubt as to the absolute value of existence. For the Promethean instigator of culture, it is the vulture that gnaws at the liver.*'[35]

A *lived culture*, according to Nietzsche, can never have a gregarious foundation. It is the *fact* of the particular case – and thus, from the viewpoint of the bourgeois concept of culture, a monstrosity. Though himself dependent on this concept, Nietzsche would nonetheless destroy it. Now the concept of culture is like the concept of freedom: both tend to cover over a specifically modern fact — the fact of *experimentation*. We will see later how experimentation restores the *servitude* that the concept of culture conjures away. Nietzsche summarized this in the following manner: there are *forces* present at the heart of an individual, struggles and *externalizable constraints*; which of them will be made into masters, and which into slaves? *Experimentation* always involves an inventor, an experimental object, *failures, successes, victims,* and sacrificers.

In 1871, well before he had passed through all the phases of his thought and discovered his own way of conceiving the meaning of successive Western cultures, Nietzsche had seen in *the report of the burning of the Tuileries during the Commune* an untenable argument for a traditional culture. He had written to Gersdorff (21 June 1871):

> If we could discuss this together, we would agree that precisely in that phenomenon does our modern life, actually the whole of old Christian Europe and its state, but, above all, the 'Romanic' civilization which is now everywhere predominant, show the enormous degree to which our world has been damaged, and that, with all our past behind us, we all bear the *guilt* that such a terror could come to light, so that we must make sure we do not ascribe to those unfortunates alone the crime of a combat against culture. *I know what that means: the combat against culture* [emphasis added]. When I heard of the fires in Paris, I felt for several days annihilated and was overwhelmed by fears and doubts; the entire scholarly, scientific, philosophical, and artistic existence seemed an absurdity, if a single day could wipe out the most glorious works of art, even

whole periods of art; I clung with earnest conviction to the metaphysical value of art, which cannot exist for the sake of impoverished people, but
which has higher missions to fulfil. But even when
the pain was at its worst, I could not cast a stone
against those blasphemers, who were to me only carriers of the general guilt, which gives much food for
thought.[36]

The young professor of philology of the 1870s was still
reacting and expressing himself like an erudite 'bourgeois'.
Yet the cynicism of a phrase like the one in which he
announces that art 'cannot exist for the sake of impoverished
people' points to his own critical use of irony, and he
expresses his own condemnation in the beginning and
ending lines. If art cannot exist for 'impoverished people',
then the latter assume the *guilt* of its destruction; but
they are simply manifestations of our 'own' culture, our
universal culture, which dissimulates our own iniquity in
the guise of culture. *To assume the crime of the combat against
culture* was an underlying theme of the young Nietzsche's
still-Hellenizing thinking. But this assumption was merely
the obverse of a theme that would become more explicit
in the years to come: *to assume culture's 'crime' against existing
misery* – which will finally put culture itself in question: a
criminal culture.

At first sight, this seems to be a totally aberrant vision: the
communards never considered attacking art in the name of
social misery. The way Nietzsche poses the problem here,
after reading an erroneous news item, reveals exactly what
he is himself admitting: *a feeling of bourgeois guilt.* But it is
on the basis of this feeling that he poses the *true* problem.
*Am I guilty of enjoying the culture of which the impoverished class
is deprived, or not?*

What he means by *our guilt* (a guilt which, according
to him, was ascribed to the arsonists' gesture) is to have
allowed *Christian and post-Christian* morality to promote

confusion: namely, the illusion and hypocrisy of a culture that would have no social inequalities, whereas it is *inequality* alone which makes culture possible: inequality and struggle (between different groups of affects).

At the end of his short career, Nietzsche would side with the 'criminal' as an *irretrievable force*, virtually superior to an order of things that excludes it. His *refusal* to 'cast a stone' at the 'unfortunate' communards, at the *'carriers* of the *general guilt'*, pointed both to an instinctive (though still unavowed) solidarity and to a problem, unsolvable for the young Nietzsche in the terms thus posed: 'culture' – 'social misery' – 'crime' – 'combat against culture'.

> It was only very late that I was able to discover what, strictly speaking, I was absolutely lacking: namely, *justice*. 'What is justice? Is it possible? And if it were not possible, how would life be bearable?' – This is what I was constantly asking myself. And when I delved into myself, I was deeply distressed to find nothing but passions everywhere, perspectives from a determinate angle, the thoughtlessness [*irréflexion*] of everything that is deprived of the prior conditions of justice in advance: but where then was reflection? – Reflection from a vast perspicuity. The only thing I could attribute to myself was *courage* and a certain *durability*, the fruit of a long domination of myself.[37]

As long as culture implies slavery and is the product of (unavowed) slavery, the problem of *guilt* persists.

Does living in culture means that one wills slavery? What would happen to culture if slavery were suppressed? Would culture have to be extended to each and every person? Would we then have a culture of slaves? But this, it seems, is a false problem. Culture is the product of the Slave; and having produced culture, he is now its conscious Master – this is what Hegel demonstrated.* Nietzsche is the incorrigible beneficiary of this culture. But for Nietzsche, the slave who has become the master of culture is nothing other than – *Christian morality*. And because the latter will be prolonged in certain forms of 'communality' (first in the form of 'bourgeois culture', and then in the socializing form of industrialization) Nietzsche, out of his own *ignorance*,† will attack the Hegelian dialectic at its roots. In his analysis of the unhappy consciousness, Hegel distorts the 'initial Desire' (the will to power): the *autonomous consciousness* (of the Master) despairs of ever having its autonomy recognized by another autonomous being, since it is necessarily constituted by a *dependent consciousness* – that of the Slave.

In Nietzsche, there is no such need for *reciprocity* (this is his 'ignorance' of this passage of the Dialectic). On the contrary, given his own *idiosyncracy* – *the sovereignty of an incommunicable emotion* – the very idea of a '*consciousness for itself mediated by another consciousness*' remains foreign to Nietzsche.

Sovereignty lies in the arbitrary manner by which one feels existence, which can be enriched through hostile resistance, or increased through the emotion of an accomplice. The Slave renounces his emotion and opposes it to *labour*, which diverts him from the emotion and justifies him against the arbitrary. To the degree that he does not *renounce his idiosyncracy*, objectivation (the liberator of the emotion) is increased all the more in the one who does not seek an *equivalent* to his madness. The entire cultural, historical and

---

* We are here following, in broad outlines, Alexandre Kojève's remarkable exegesis of this passage from the *Phenomenology of Spirit*, in his *Introduction to the Reading of Hegel*, ed. Raymond Queneau and Allan Bloom, trans. James H. Nichols, Jr (New York: Basic Books, 1969).

† It was the intimidating genius of Georges Bataille (in *Inner Experience*, trans. Leslie Anne Boldt [Albany: State University of New York Press, 1988]) that emphasized this ignorance in the *Genealogy of Morals*. For the relationship between Nietzsche and Hegel, see Gilles Deleuze's magisterial study, *Nietzsche and Philosophy*, trans. Hugh Tomlinson (New York: Columbia University Press, 1983).

human world that the servile consciousness had begun to construct under the constraint of the *autonomous consciousness*, and through which the *servile consciousness* in turn becomes *autonomous* and triumphs over the consciousness of the Master – in short, the world of *culture* – it was precisely against this world, against this culture, of which he was both the product and the beneficiary, that Nietzsche rebelled. Nietzsche led this *objectivation* of the servile consciousness in the cultural world back to its source.

Yet the *reproduction of the world of affects through art* has been possible only thanks to this historical and cultural world constructed by the servile consciousness. Is not art evidence of a consciousness that has become *autonomous*? But a *new servitude* now reigns over this fact. For the historical and human world has not managed to *silence* the *affects*: in order for this newly *autonomous consciousness* to triumph completely over the initial Desire (*represented by the idleness of the Master*), it was necessary for art to disappear (and we will see to what degree Nietzsche foresees its disappearance in the industrial plans of the future), and for the *affects* to be swallowed up entirely in the fabrication of exchangeable products. As long as these affects remain and presuppose *idleness* – do they necessarily require the servitude of a large number of people? But this is where the problem becomes displaced: for *the affects are themselves enslaved by other affects* – and not (at least not initially) by the affects of other individuals, but by those within the *same* individual. And for Nietzsche, *gregarious* means *servile*. Nietzsche will remain within this perspective of a *guilty culture* up to the time he puts *consciousness and its categories* in question – in the name of the world of affects. Until then, there will always be '*carriers* of the *general* guilt' of a culture that masks the antinomies of bourgeois morality: in his phantasm, Nietzsche saw the *marvels of the Louvre in flames*. What was important were not the marvels, but the emotions that lay at their origin. For these emotions make *inequality* prevail: and if inequality makes life unbearable, then 'courage and endurance' are required to bear it.

To give men back the courage of their natural drives –

To check their *self-underestimation* (not that of man as an individual but that of man as *nature* –) –

To *remove antitheses* from things *after comprehending* that we have projected them there –

To remove the *idiosyncrasies of society* from existence (guilt, punishment, justice, honesty, freedom, love, etc.)[38]

Thus Nietzsche in turn undertook his own *combat against culture* – in the name of a culture of the affects – which would be built on the ruins of the hypostases of consciousness and its antinomies, insofar as they are born from the *guilt* of consciousness *toward itself*, which will propel it toward the totality of *Spirit*. This culture of *affects* will be possible only after a progressive dislocation of the *substructures* that are elaborated in language. Toward the middle of the years 1880-8, Nietzsche retraced the stages of his own moral itinerary in a concise manner:

How long have I already sought to prove to myself the perfect innocence of becoming! How many singular paths has this already taken me down! At first, it seemed to me that the just solution was simply to decree: 'Existence, as something similar to art, does not fall under the jurisdiction of morality; furthermore, morality itself belongs to the domain of phenomena.' Next, I said to myself: 'Every concept of guilt is objectively devoid of value, but subjectively, every life is necessarily unjust and alogical.' Finally, the third time, I took on myself the negation of any aim, from the fact of experiencing the unknowability of any causal chain. And why all this? Was it not in order to procure for myself the feeling of total irresponsibility? – to situate myself outside of all praise and all blame, completely independent of yesterday and today, in order to pursue my own aim in my own manner?[39]

2

The Valetudinary States at the Origin of a Semiotic of Impulses

The euphoria that gripped Nietzsche after each of his crises, from 1877 to 1881, led him to scrutinize ever more carefully the forces that had been revealed through the disturbances of his organism. He gave them free rein, during which time he returned to his notebooks and submitted them to his vocabulary. A series was thereby formed, a group of reflections on certain aspects of history, on certain arguments of scientists or thinkers or artists, on certain gestures of politicians – all of which, depending on the diverse level they represented, seemed to bear witness, actively or passively, to the *same* forces that had just given Nietzsche's brain, his organism, a short respite. The anger, tenderness, impatience, or calm he experienced, in the context of certain motives and circumstances, were already sanctioned by received terms. Yet the afflux or reflux of these forces, their tension or relaxation, could find an apparent outlet only by being translated into words, images, reasonings, or refutations. For a moment arrived when they would again become muddled, intermingling and obscuring each other. They had been diverted, they had deviated far from an *aim*, and neither history, nor science, nor investigation, nor even the forms of art converged upon this aim. The writing stopped, the words were effaced, and a new and terrifying aggression exerted itself on Nietzsche's brain.

It may seem absurd to read Nietzsche's successive texts as so many 'migraines' inverted in words. Given the way Nietzsche was compelled to describe the various phases of his conscious states, however, he was unable to avoid the mechanism of such an inversion.

For a long period of time, and well before the positivist critique of *Human, All-Too-Human*, Nietzsche had dismissed the *intelligible-in-itself*, yet he could neither attack it in consciousness nor speak in the name of the *unspoken*. This is why he remained dependent for so long on the problems of culture posed by his vision of *Greek tragedy*. *The Birth of Tragedy* (out of *the spirit of music*) had served merely to make explicit, in a prestigious manner, the *Hellenizing* aspect of his secret phantasm: the search for a 'culture' that would accord with the forces of the unspoken. He would use this phantasm to protect himself from the forces of inertia as much as he would use it to influence other minds, with all the ambiguity such a project implies.

Within the circle of his acquaintances, Nietzsche's vision of the 'Hellenic state' had appalled Wagner, and Rohde as well. It was his encounter with Rée, a disabused spirit, that encouraged a demystifying tendency in him. But the furious assaults of his illness would soon throw him back into a period of isolation, which further encouraged his contemplative states and an ever greater abandonment to the tonalities of his soul. It was during one such moment, in the month of August 1881, at Sils-Maria, that the ecstasy of the Eternal Return would surprise him.

CORRESPONDENCE

To Gast

Saint-Moritz, 11 September 1879
I am at the end of my thirty-fifth year – 'the middle of life', as people for a millennium and a half have said of this age. It was at this age that Dante had his vision, and in the opening lines of his poem he mentions the

fact. Now I am in the middle of life and so 'encircled by death' that at any minute it can lay hold of me. From the nature of my sufferings I must reckon upon a sudden death through convulsions (although I should prefer a hundred times a slow, lucid death, before which I should be able to converse with my friends, even if it were more painful). In this way I feel like the oldest of men, even from the standpoint of having completed my life-task. I have poured a salutary drop of oil; this I know, and I shall not be forgotten for it. At bottom I have already undergone the test of my own view of life: many more will have to do it after me. Up to the present my spirit has not been depressed by the unremitting suffering that my ailments have caused me; at times I even feel more cheerful and more benevolent than I ever felt in my life before; to what do I owe this invigorating and ameliorating effect? Certainly not to my fellow men; for, with but few exceptions, they have all during the last few years shown themselves 'offended' by me; nor have they shrunk from letting me know it. Just read this last manuscript through, my dear friend, and ask yourself whether there are any traces of suffering or depression to be found in it. I don't believe there are, and this very belief is a sign that there must be powers concealed in these views, and not the proofs of impotence and lassitude after which my enemies will seek. . . .

I shall not come to you myself – however urgently the Overbecks and my sister may press me to do so; there are states in which it seems to me more fitting to return to the neighbourhood of one's mother, one's home, and the memories of one's childhood. But do not take all this as final and irrevocable. According as his hopes rise or fall, an invalid should be allowed to make or unmake his plans. My programme for the summer is complete: three weeks at a moderate altitude (in Weisen), three months in the Engadine, and the last month in taking the real St Moritz drink-cure, the best effect of which is not supposed to be felt before the winter. This working out of a programme was a pleasure to me, but it was not easy! Self-denial in everything (I had no friends, no company; I could read no books; all art was far removed from me; a small bedroom with a bed, the food of an ascetic – which by the way suited me excellently, for I have had no indigestion the whole of the summer) – this self-denial was complete except for one point – I gave myself up to my thoughts – what else could I do! Of course, this was the very worst thing for my head, but I still do not see how I could have avoided it. But enough; this winter my programme will be to recover from myself, to rest myself away from my thoughts – for years I have not had this experience.[40]

To Gast

5 October 1879

You would not believe with what fidelity I have carried out the programme of thoughtlessness so far; I have reasons for fidelity here, for 'behind thought stands the devil' of a tormenting attack of pain. The manuscript which you received from St Moritz was written at such a high and hard price that perhaps nobody would have written it if he could possibly have avoided doing so. Often I shudder to read it, especially the longer parts, because of the ugly memories it brings. All of it – except for a few lines – was thought out on walks, and it was sketched out in pencil in six small notebooks; the fair copy made me ill almost every time I set about writing it. I had to omit about twenty longish thought sequences, unfortunately quite essential ones, because I could not find the time to extract them from my frightful pencil scribblings; the same was true last summer. In the interim the connections between the thoughts escape my memory; I have to steal the minutes and quarter-hours of 'brain-energy', as you call it, steal them away from a suffering brain. Sometimes I think that I shall never do it again. I am reading the copy you made, and find it difficult to understand myself – my head is that tired.[41]

To Malwida von Meysenbug

14 January 1880

Although writing is for me one of the most forbidden fruits, yet I must write a letter to you, whom I love and respect like an elder sister – and it will probably be the last. For my life's terrible and almost unremitting martyrdom makes me thirst for the end, and there have been some signs which allow me to hope that the stroke which will liberate me is not too distant. As regards torment and self-denial, my life during these past years can match that of any ascetic of any time; nevertheless, I have wrung from these years much in the way of purification and burnishing of the soul – and I no longer need religion or art as a means to that end. (You will notice that I am proud of this; in fact, complete isolation alone enabled me to discover my own resources of self-help.) I think that I have done my life's work, though of course like a person who had no time. But I know that I have poured out a drop of good oil for many, and that I have given to many an indication of how to rise above themselves, how to attain equanimity and a right mind. I write this as an afterthought; really it should only be said on the completion of my 'humanity'. No pain has been, or should be, able to make me bear false witness about life *as I know it to be*.[42]

To Doctor O. Eiser

Early January 1880

To dare write a letter, I have to wait four weeks for a tolerable moment   after which I still have to pay for it! . . .

My existence is a *dreadful burden*: I would have rejected it long ago, had I not been making the most instructive experiments in the intellectual and moral domain in just this condition of suffering and almost complete renunciation – this joyous mood, avid for knowledge, raised me to heights where I triumphed over every torture and all despair. On the whole, I am happier now than I have ever been in my life. And yet, continual pain; for many hours of the day, a sensation closely akin to seasickness, a semi-paralysis that makes it difficult to speak, alternating with furious attacks (the last one made me vomit for three days and three nights, I longed for death!). I can't read, rarely write, visit no one, can't listen to music! I keep to myself and take walks in the rarified air, a diet of eggs and milk. No pain-relieving remedies work. The cold is harmful to me.

In the coming weeks I will go south to begin my existence as a walker.

My only consolation is my thoughts and perspectives. In the course of my wanderings I now and then scribble something on a piece of paper; I write nothing at my work-table, friends decipher my scribblings. My last product (which my friends wound up completing) will follow: accept it gladly, even if it does not conform to your own way of thinking. (I do not seek 'disciples' – believe me! – I enjoy my freedom and wish this joy to all those who have the right to spiritual freedom.) . . .

I have already lost consciousness several times. During the spring of last year, at Basel, they had given up all hope for me. My sight has visibly worsened since my last consultation.[43]

To Overbeck

Genoa, November 1880

Now my whole endeavour is to realize an ideal attic dweller's solitude, which will do justice to all those necessary and most elementary demands of my nature, as many, many torments have taught me to know them. And perhaps I shall succeed. The daily struggle against my head trouble and the laughable complexity of my distresses demand so much attention that I am in danger of becoming petty in this regard – well, that is the counterweight to very general, very lofty impulses which have such control over me that without the counterweight I would make a fool of myself. I have just come round from a very gruelling attack, and, having hardly shaken off the distress of the past two days, I find my foolery already pursuing quite incredible things, from the moment I wake up, and I think that no other attic dweller can have had the dawn shine upon more lovely and more desirable things.[44]

To His Mother

Sils–Maria, mid-July 1881

My nervous system is splendid in view of the immense work it has to do; it is quite sensitive but very strong, a source of astonishment to me. Even the long and severe maladies, an occupation which did not suit me, and a dead wrong treatment have not harmed it basically. Indeed, within the past year it has become stronger and owing to it I have produced one of the most daring, the sublimest and deepest of books ever spawned by a human brain and heart. Even had I committed suicide in Recoaro, a man would have died who was the most indomitable, and absolutely superior, not one who had given up in despair. With respect to the scientific material I require, I am in a better position than any and all physicians. More yet, my scientific pride is offended when you are suggesting that I should submit to new treatments and even express the opinion that I 'did not do anything for my sickness'. You should have a little more confidence in these matters! Up to now I have been under my own governance for only two years, and if I did make any mistakes it was always owing to the fact that I ultimately yielded to the earnest entreaties of others and submitted to experimentation. In this category belong my stays in Maumberg, in Marienbad, etc. Moreover, every competent physician has prognosticated my recovery but not before a number of years has elapsed. Above all, I must try and get rid of the grave aftereffects of all those wrong methods by which I have been treated for such a long time. I implore you, don't be angry with me if I seem to reject your love and sympathy in this matter. I fully intend to continue henceforth as my own physician. Moreover, people shall say after I am dead that I was a good physician – and not only in my behalf. – Be that as it may, I shall still have to look forward to many, many periods of illness. Do not become impatient the while, I beg of you with all my heart! This makes me more irritable than the sickness itself, because it demonstrates to me that my nearest relatives display so little faith in me.

Whoever could secretly look on me as I am practising combining my concern for my own recovery with promoting my great tasks, would pay me no mean compliment.[45]

Whatever the origin of Nietzsche's migraines (hereditary as he himself sometimes seemed to believe, or accidentally syphilitic, as the various cross-checkings of later witnesses tried to establish – and from which Jaspers concluded that Nietzsche's delirium was characterized by a general paralysis), the fact remains that, from the outset, the illness periodically struck Nietzsche in the cerebral organ.

Nietzsche often took long walks on foot. His thoughts came to him step by step, and then he would return home and work on the notes he had written in pencil outdoors. The migraines then appeared, sometimes affecting his vision. At times, he was unable to reread his notes and would leave the task to his friends: Peter Gast in this way learned how to decipher his illegible handwriting. Nietzsche was often forced to give up all reading, all writing, all reflection. He followed a treatment, a diet. He changed climate. Moreover, he distrusted therapeutics; little by little, he managed to invent a therapy of his own derived from his own observations. Once he recovered his faculties, he tried to describe this suspension of thought, to reflect on the cerebral functioning in relation to other organic functions – and he began to distrust his own brain.

The act of thinking became identical with suffering, and suffering with thinking. From this fact, Nietzsche posited the coincidence of thought with suffering, and asked what a thought would be that was deprived of suffering. Thinking suffering, reflecting on past suffering – as *the impossibility of thinking* – then came to be experienced by Nietzsche as the highest joy. But does thought really have the power to *actualize itself* without itself suffering, without reconstituting its own suffering? Does thought itself suffer from its own inability to actualize itself? What then is doing the suffering or enjoying? The brain? Can the cerebral organ enjoy the suffering of the body of which it is a function? Can the body rejoice in the suffering of its supreme organ?

★   ★   ★

It was when he felt most healthy and most robust, in complete control of his creative powers, that he came closest to his illness: and it was the forced rest and idleness that would again allow him to recover and to keep the catastrophe in suspense. (Lou A. Salomé)[46]

★   ★   ★

If the body concerns our most immediate forces as those which, in terms of their origin, are *the most distant*, then everything the body *says* – its well-being as well as its diseases – gives us the best information about our destiny. Nietzsche therefore wanted to go back toward what, in himself, was most distant in order to comprehend the most immediate.

Before describing 'how one becomes what one is', Nietzsche first put in question what one is. He never hesitated to say that certain of his books were written while his health was at such-and-such a point – for example, at the moment he felt it to be at its lowest point.

The agonizing migraines, which Nietzsche experienced periodically as *an aggression that suspended his thought*, were not an external aggression; the root of the evil was in himself, in his own organism: his own physical self was *attacking* in order to *defend* itself against a dissolution. But *what* was being threatened with dissolution? Nietzsche's own brain. Whenever his migraines subsided, Nietzsche would put his state of respite in the service of this dissolution. For the dissolution was judged to be such only by the brain, for whom the physical self and the moral self apparently coincide. But the body provided Nietzsche with a completely different perspective, namely, the perspective of *active forces* which (as organic and therefore subordinate functions) expressed a will to break with this servitude. But they could do so only if this will passed *through the brain*. The brain, on the other hand, could experience this will only as its own subordination to these dissolving forces: it was threatened with the impossibility of *thinking*.

Nietzsche experienced this dissolving confrontation between somatic and spiritual forces for a long time, and he observed it passionately. The more he listened to his body, the more he came to distrust *the person the body supports*. His obsessive fear of suicide, born out of the despair that his atrocious migraines would never be cured, amounted to a condemnation of the body in the name of the person being diminished by it. But the thought that he had not yet finished his life's work gave him the fortitude to side *with* the body. If the body is presently in pain, if the brain is sending nothing but distress signals, it is because a *language* is trying to make itself heard at the price of reason. A suspicion, a hatred, a rage against his own conscious and reasonable person was born. This person – fashioned by a particular epoch, in a familial milieu he increasingly abhorred – is not what he wanted to conserve. He would destroy the person out of a love for the *nervous system* he knew he had been gifted with, and in which he took a certain *pride*. By studying the reactions of his nervous system, he would come to conceive of himself in a *different manner* than he had previously known – and indeed, in a manner that will perhaps never again be known. Consequently, he developed a mode of intelligence which he wanted to submit to exclusively physical criteria. He not only *interpreted* suffering as energy, but *willed* it to be so. Physical suffering would be livable only insofar as it was closely connected to joy, insofar as it developed a voluptuous lucidity: either it would extinguish all possible thought, or it would reach the delirium of thought.

But he sensed yet another trap in serenity. Is a thought freed from all physical oppression something real? No, for other impulses are in the process of taking delight in it. And more often than not, such a delight is merely a *report* of the absence of such *sufferings* – which have apparently been *overcome* – and hence their representation! Serenity is merely a kind of armistice between irreconcilable impulses.

There seems to be a strict correlation between the phenomenon of pain, which is experienced by the organism as the aggression of an invading external power, and the biological process that leads to the formation of the brain.* The brain, which concentrates all the reflexes on fighting the aggression, is able to represent the *inflicted* pain as degrees of excitations oscillating between pain and pleasure. The brain can have representations only if it meticulously spiritualizes the elementary excitations into the *danger* of pain or the *good fortune* of pleasure – a discharge that may or may not result in further excitations. But the painful excitation can form a

---

* In the domain of animal biology, the formation of the brain presupposes an *exploratory progression* of which the brain is the *instrument*: in Nietzsche, there is a tendency to liberate the *exploration* in relation to the *instrument*, inasmuch as the latter would subordinate what is acquired in the exploration to its limited functional ends. This is why he aspires to a decentralization (and thus to a *ubiquity*). Whence also his rejection of a 'system of thought'.

satisfaction that is itself experienced as pain to the degree that
it upsets an equilibrium that had been momentarily attained
by the organism – an equilibrium that, in a prior state, it
was able to experience as a joy. This prior satisfaction of
the excitation leaves a trace of intensity in the brain, which
can then reactualize it as a joy (of re-excitation) by the act
of representing it to itself. But Nietzsche supposes that this
excitation is then being exercised on *another* 'self' [*moi*].

The body wants to make itself understood through the
intermediary of a language of signs that is fallaciously deciphered by consciousness. Consciousness itself *constitutes this
code of signs* that inverts, falsifies and filters what is expressed
through the body.

Consciousness is itself nothing other than a deciphering of
the messages transmitted by the impulses. The deciphering is
in itself an inversion of the message, which is now attributed
to the individual. Since everything leads to the 'head' (the
upright position), the message is deciphered in a way that
will maintain this 'vertical' position; *there would be no message
as such* if this position were not habitual and specific. *Meaning*
is formed in the upright position, and in accordance with its
own criteria: *high, low, before, after*.

Nietzsche did not speak on behalf of a 'hygiene' of the
body, established by reason. He spoke on behalf of corporeal
states as the authentic data that consciousness must conjure
away in order to be an individual. This viewpoint far surpasses
a purely 'physiological' conception of life. *The body is a
product of chance*; it is nothing but the *locus* where a group of
individuated impulses confront each other so as to produce
this interval that constitutes a *human life*, impulses *whose sole
ambition is to de-individuate themselves*. What is born from this
chance association of impulses is not only the individual
they constitute at the whims of circumstance, but also the
eminently deceptive principle of a cerebral activity that progressively disengages itself from sleep. Consciousness seems
to oscillate continually between somnolence and insomnia,
and what we call the *waking state* is merely the comparison

of the two, their reciprocal reflection, like a play of mirrors. But there is no mirror without a tain, and it is this tain that forms the ground of 'reason'. Forgetfulness is possible only because of the opacity of the impulses. There is no consciousness without forgetfulness. But once it 'scratches' the tain, consciousness itself, in its very transparency, merges with the flux and reflux of the impulses.

The body, insofar as it is grasped by consciousness, *dissociates itself* from the impulses that flow through it, and which, having come together fortuitously, continue to sustain the body in an equally fortuitous manner. The organ that these impulses have developed at the 'highest' extremity of the body considers this fortuitous yet obvious sustenance to be necessary for its conservation. Its 'cerebral' activity therefore selects only those forces that preserve this activity, or, rather, those that can be *assimilated* to it. And the body adopts only those *reflexes* that allow it to *maintain* itself *for* this cerebral activity, just as the latter henceforth *adopts the body as its own product*.

To understand Nietzsche, it is important to see this *reversal* brought about by the organism: *the most fragile organ it has developed comes to dominate the body, one might say, because of its very fragility.*

The cerebral activity, thanks to which the human body adopts the upright position, winds up reducing the body's presence to an automatism. The body as body is no longer synonymous with itself; strictly speaking, as an *instrument* of consciousness, it becomes the homonym of the 'person'. As soon as the cerebral activity diminishes, the body alone remains present, but in reality it no longer belongs to a *person*. Although it retains all the reflexes from which *one and the same* person could be reconstructed, the 'person' is absent from it. The more these purely corporeal manifestations assert themselves, the more the return of the 'person' seems to be delayed. The latter sleeps, dreams, laughs, or trembles, but these states are revealed in the body alone. The *person* can represent to itself the fact that it is laughing, trembling, enjoying, or suffering through an evocation of motives, but these are only an interpretation of corporeal sensations.

The 'person' that *claims these symptoms as its own*, when communicating with itself or with another person, can do so only before or after they have been produced. It can *deny* that it has been their subject *consciously*, and it can consent to retain them as its *own* only if they seem to conform to what it takes to be its normal state – namely, to anything compatible with the *upright position* of the body, or any other position that would depend on its '*decisions*' or *representations*. The person can *decide* to laugh, or to abandon itself to the reflex of laughter, or to the reflex of pain or fatigue. But in every such case, the decisions are only the result of an excited or excitable state; they are thus subsequent to the excitation rather than prior to it. In the intensity of pain or pleasure, and especially in voluptuousness, the 'person' disappears for a moment, and what remains of consciousness at that point is strictly limited to the corporeal symptom that its very structure inverts. The notion of the *unconscious* is here nothing more than an *image of forgetfulness – the forgetfulness of everything that owes its origin* to the *upright* position.

Every human being can lie down, but it lies down because it is certain that it will always remain the same, and that it will be able to get back up or change position. It always believes itself to be in *its own body*. But its own body is only the *fortuitous encounter* of contradictory impulses, temporarily reconciled.

I am sick in a body that does not belong to me. *My* suffering is only an interpretation of the struggle between certain functions or impulses that have been subjugated by the organism, and are now rivals: those which depend on me and those which escape my control. Conversely, the physical agent of my self [*le suppôt physique de moi-même*] seems to reject any thoughts I have that no longer ensure its own cohesion, thoughts that proceed from a state that is *foreign* or *contrary* to that required by the physical agent, which is nonetheless identical to myself.

But what then is the *identity* of the self? It seems to depend on the *irreversible history* of the body, a linkage of causes and effects. But this linkage is pure appearance. The body is constantly being modified so as to form one and the same physiognomy; and it is only when the resources for the body's rejuvenation are impoverished that the person becomes fixed, and its '*character*' hardens.

But the different ages of the body are all so many different states, each giving birth to the next. The body is the *same* body only insofar as a single *self* is able to and wills to be merged with it, with all its vicissitudes. The cohesion of the body is that of the self; the body produces this self, and hence its own cohesion. But for itself, this body *dies* and is *reborn* numerous times – deaths and rebirths that the self pretends to survive in its illusory cohesion. In reality, the ages of the body are simply the *impulsive movements* that form and deform it, and finally tend to abandon it. But just as these impulses are resources for the body, they are also threats to its cohesion. The purely functional cohesion of the body, in the service of the self's identity, is in this sense irreversible. The *ages* of the self are those of the body's cohesion, which means that the more this self begins to age in and with the body, and the more it aspires to cohesion, the more it also seeks to return to its starting-point – and thus to *recapitulate* itself. The dread of physical dissolution requires a retrospective vision of its own cohesion. Thus, because the *self*, as a product of the body, attributes this body to itself as its *own*, and is *unable* to create another, the self too has its own *irreversible* history.

The identity of the self, along with that of its 'own body', is inseparable from a direction or meaning [*sens*] formed by the *irreversible* course of a human life. It experiences this direction or meaning as its own accomplishment – whence *the eternity of meaning once and for all*.

There is, in Nietzsche, an initial conception of fatality that implies this irreversible course, insofar as the self cannot escape from it. At first sight, this love for the *fatum*, and hence for the irreversible, seemed to have been Nietzsche's primary imperative.

But beginning with the experience of the *Eternal Return*, which announced a break with this *irreversible once and for all*, Nietzsche also developed a new version of fatality – that of the *Vicious Circle*, which suppresses every goal and meaning, since the beginning and the end always merge with each other.

From this point on, Nietzsche would no longer be concerned with the body as a *property of the self*, but with the body as the locus of impulses, the locus of their confrontation. Since it is a product of the impulses, the body becomes *fortuitous*; it is neither irreversible nor reversible, because its only history is that of the impulses. These impulses *come and go*, and the circular movement they describe is made manifest as much in moods as in thought, as much in the tonalities of the soul as in corporeal depressions – which are *moral* only insofar as the declarations and judgements of the self re-create in language a property that is in itself inconsistent, and hence empty.

But despite all this, Nietzsche would not forgo *cohesion*. He struggled at one and the same time with the to-and-fro movement of the impulses, and for a *new cohesion* between his thought and the body as a *corporealizing* thought. To do this, he followed what he called, in several places, *the guiding thread of the body*. By examining the alternations in his own valetudinary states, he sought to follow this Ariadne's thread through the labyrinth of the impulses.

Convalescence was the signal of a new offensive of the 'body' – this rethought body – against the '*thinking Nietzsche self*'. This in turn paved the way for a new relapse. For Nietzsche, each of these relapses, up until the final relapse, heralded a new inquiry and a new investment in the world of the impulses, and in each case he paid the price of an ever-worsening illness. In each case the body liberated itself a little more from its own agent, and in each case *this agent* was weakened a little more. Little by little, the *brain* was forced to approach the *boundaries* that separated it from these somatic forces, in that the reawakening of the self in the brain was brought about *ever more slowly*. And even when it occurred, it was these same forces that seized hold of the functional mechanism. The self was broken down into a *lucidity that was more vast but more brief*. The equilibrium of the functions was reversed: *the self lay dormant* in words, in the fixity of signs; and *the forces were awakened* all the more in that they still remained silent; and memory, finally, was detached from the cerebral self, a memory that could no longer *designate* itself except in accordance with *its most distant* motifs.

How can the body subtract the cerebral activity from what we call the self? And first of all: how is the self re-established by the brain? There is no other way than by passing through the *limit* that is constantly redrawn in and by *the waking state*. But the waking state *never lasts more than a few seconds*. At every instant, the brain is flooded by excitations of greater or lesser intensity, excitations whose *overwhelming reception* must constantly be filtered. The new excitations are filtered through the traces of prior excitations, which have already been absorbed. But the new excitations can be co-ordinated with prior ones only through assimilation, namely, by comparing what is 'habitual' with what is foreign. As a result, the *limit* cannot help but be effaced; after a few seconds, a large part of the brain is already dormant. Any *decision* or resolution made to *not* think an action so as to be able to *execute it*, presumes that only the trace of prior excitations is admitted, which assures the permanence of the self's identity. *Thanks to the body's muteness, we appropriate the body for ourselves in order to remain upright.* We create for ourselves an image of a meaning or a goal that we pursue in our thoughts and actions, namely, to remain the *same* as what we believe ourselves to be.

To restore these 'corporealizing' forces (impulses) to thought amounts to an expropriation of the agent, of the self. Yet Nietzsche brought about this restoration and expropriation through *his brain*. He used his lucidity to penetrate the shadows. But how can one remain lucid if one destroys the locus of lucidity, namely, the self? What would this consciousness be without an agent? *How can memory subsist if it has to deal with things that no longer belong to the self? How can we remember as a being that can remember everything except itself?*

Nietzsche's researches in the biological and physiological sciences stemmed from a double preoccupation: first, to find a mode of behaviour, in the organic and inorganic world, that was analogous to his own valetudinary state; and second, based on this mode of behaviour, to find the arguments and resources that would allow him to re-create himself, beyond his own self. Physiology, as he understood it, would thus provide him with the premises of a liberatory conception of the forces that lay subjacent not only to his own condition, but also to the various situations he was living through in the context of his epoch. Nietzsche's investigations into science had the same aim as his investigations into art, or into contemporary and past political events. This is why he resorted to various terminologies, to which he gave increasingly equivocal turns of phrase. When borrowing from the various disciplines, he gave them his own emphases, and pursued a vision that escaped them – a vision which, because of its experimental character, lacked any 'objective' consideration.

Since the body is the *Self* [*Soi*],* the *Self* resides in the midst of the body and expresses itself through the body – for Nietzsche, this was already a fundamental position. Everything his brain had refused him lay hidden in his corporeal life, this intelligence that was larger than the *seat*

---

* The *Selbst*, for Nietzsche, has a double meaning: on the one hand, it is, morally speaking, the *Selbstsucht* (the greediness of the self, which is erroneously translated as 'egoism'), and on the other hand, it is force, unconscious to the cerebral consciousness, which obeys a hidden reason.

of the intelligence. All evil and suffering are the result of the quarrel between the body's multiplicity, with its millions of vague impulses, and the interpretive stubbornness of the meaning bestowed on it by the brain. It is from the body, from the *self*, that every creative force and every evaluation arises. And it is from their *cerebral inversion* that mortal spectres are born, starting with a voluntary ego, a mind *'deprived of itself'*. Likewise, the other person, the neighbour, is nothing but a projection of the *Self*, through the inversions of the mind: the *you* [*toi*] has no more reality than the *me* [*moi*], except as a pure modification of the *Self* [*Soi*]. The *Self*, finally, exists in the body only as a *prolonged* extremity of *Chaos* – impulses take on an organic and individualized form only when delegated by *Chaos*. It was this delegation that now became Nietzsche's interlocutor. From high in the cerebral citadel, besieged, it is called *madness*.

Once the body is recognized as the product of the impulses (subjected, organized, hierarchized), its cohesion with the self becomes fortuitous. The impulses *can be put to use by a new body*, and are presupposed in the search for new conditions. Starting from these impulses, Nietzsche suspected that beyond the (cerebral) intellect there lies an intellect that is infinitely more vast than the one that merges with our consciousness.

> Perhaps the entire evolution of the spirit is a question of the body; it is the *history* of the development of *a higher body* that emerges into our *sensibility*. The organic is rising to yet higher levels. Our lust for knowledge of nature is a means through which the body desires to perfect itself. Or rather: hundreds of thousands of experiments are made to change the nourishment, the mode of living and the dwelling of the body; consciousness and evaluations of the body, all kinds of pleasure and displeasure, are *signs of these changes and experiments. In the long*

run, it is not a question of man at all: he is to be overcome.[47]

Clear out the inner world! There are still many false beings in it! Sensation and thought are enough for me. The 'will' as a third reality is imaginary. Moreover, all the impulses, desire, repulsion, etc., are not 'unities', but *apparent* 'simple states'. Hunger: it is a feeling of discomfort and a knowledge of the means to suppress it. Similarly, without any knowledge, a series of movements can take place in the organism whose aim is to suppress hunger: the *stimulation* of this mechanism is *felt at the same time* as the hunger.[48]

Just as organs develop in multiple ways from a single organ, such as the brain and the nervous system from the epidermis, so it was necessary for all feeling, representing, and thinking to have been *one* at the beginning: sensation is thus an isolated *late* phenomenon. This *unity* must exist in the inorganic: for the organic begins by *separation*. The reciprocal action between the inorganic and the organic still needs to be studied – it is always a question of an *action at a distance* (in the long term), hence a 'knowing' is necessary prior to all acting: what is distant must be perceived. The tactile and muscular sense must have its analogue.[49]

Consciousness localized at the surface of the two hemispheres. Every 'experience' is a mechanical and chemical fact that cannot be stopped, but which *lives*: except that we *know* nothing of it![50]

Wherever there is life, we assume there is 'mind': but the mind as we know it is completely incapable of effectuating anything whatsoever. How miserable is every image of consciousness! No doubt it itself will merely be the *effect* of a modification, which then brings about another modification (action). Every action we 'will' is simply represented by us as the *appearance of the phenomenon* [*Schein der Erscheinung*]. All consciousness is nothing but a *marginal expression* of the intellect (!). What becomes conscious in us *cannot reveal the cause of anything*.

We should compare our *digestion* with our sensations of it![51]

Our intellect is completely incapable of grasping the diversity of an intelligent synthetic interaction, not to mention producing one, like the digestive process. It is the synthetic interaction of *several intellects*! Wherever I find life, I find this synthetic interaction! And there is also a sovereign in these numerous intellects! – But as soon as we seek to comprehend organic actions that would be executed with the assistance of several intellects, they become completely incomprehensible. We should rather conceive of the intellect itself as a final consequence of the organic.[52]

The essence of heredity is totally obscure to us. Why does an action become 'easier' the second time around? And 'who' experiences that it is made easier? And does this sensation have anything in common with the fact that the action is effectuated in the same manner the second time? Would the sensation of different *possible* actions then have to be *represented* before acting?[53]

The powerful organic principle seems essential to me because of the ease by which it incorporates inorganic substances. I do not see how this finality could be explained simply by *intensification*. I believe rather that there are eternally organic beings.[54]

Here is our way of being unequal: your mind is devoid of a self – whereas mine has a complete Self and is a mind only in word.

This is how I once spoke: meaning and the mind are tools and toys: behind them still lies the Self.

But when I looked for a Self behind these other minds, all I found were minds devoid of a Self![55]

Listen to me a moment, O Zarathustra – a disciple said to him one day – something is turning around in my head: or rather I would be prepared to believe that my head is turning around something, and thus that it describes a circle.

What then is our neighbour? Something within us, some modifications of ourselves that have become conscious: an image, this is what our neighbour is.

What are we ourselves? Are we not also nothing but an image? A something within us, modifications of ourselves that have become conscious?

Our Self of which we are conscious: is it not an image as well, something outside of us, something external, on the outside? We never touch anything but an image, and not ourselves, not our Self.

Are we not strangers to ourselves and also as close to ourselves as our neighbour?

In truth, we have an image of humanity – which we have made out of ourselves. And then we apply it to ourselves – in order to understand ourselves! Ah yes, to understand!

Our understanding of ourselves goes from bad to worse!

Our strongest feelings, inasmuch as they are feelings, are only something external, outside us, imagistic: similitudes, that's what they are.

And what we habitually call the inner world: alas, for the most part it is poor and deceptive and invented and hollow.[56]

Let us take at their word Nietzsche's physiological ideas concerning the relationships between thought and willing, and on the formation of meaning in a given declaration. Moreover, let us try to understand how, given his notion that conscious life is subordinated to fluctuations of intensities, he explains what we call an *intention* and a *goal at the level of consciousness*, and what this latter term signifies in relation to the term *unconsciousness*. What do these terms refer to in Nietzsche? Are they different from the terms *conscious* and *unconscious*, in Freud's sense of the 'iceberg'? For it would seem that neither *consciousness* nor *unconsciousness* – nor *willing* or *non-willing* – have ever existed. Within a system of designating fluctuations, there is only a discontinuity between *silence* and *declarations* in the agent. Inasmuch as exteriority is installed in the agent by the code of everyday signs, it is only on the basis of this code that the agent can make declarations or state opinions, think or not think, remain silent or break its silence. The agent thinks only as a product of this code. Now such a *thinking agent* exists only because of the greater or lesser *resistance* of the impulsive forces – which constitutes the agent as a (corporeal) *unity* with respect to the code of everyday signs. By what measure can we say that the agent is '*conscious*' of not speaking, of remaining silent, of acting or not acting, of deciding or remaining undecided? Only in terms of a more or less *unequal exchange* between the impulses and the signs of the everyday code. But is not the agent unconscious of what these impulses are willing for themselves? Hence the inequality of the exchange, and the fact that the impulses lose out in the transaction: an *intention* is formed through the signs – minus their impulsive intensity. The intensity oscillates while thought as such is being formed, but once the declaration is produced, it is reduced to the inertia of signs. Where then does the ebbing flow of the intensity go? It overflows the fixity of signs and continues on, as it were, in their intervals: each interval (thus each silence) belongs (outside the linkage of signs) to the fluctuations of an impulsive intensity. Is this the 'unconscious'? In itself, this term is merely a designation of the code of everyday signs that is applied afterward. What then is it that requires even the most lucid agent to remain unconscious of what is going on within itself? Nietzsche *knows*, for example, as he writes his notes on the impulses, that such impulses are acting in him, but that there is no accord between the *observations* he is transcribing and the impulses that have compelled him to write them. But if he is conscious of what he is writing, as the agent named Nietzsche, it is because he *knows* not only that he is ignorant of what has just occurred *in order* for him write, but also that he *must* be ignorant of it (if he wants to write and *think*). *At that very moment* he is *necessarily* ignorant of what he is about to call *the combat of the impulses among themselves*. Even if he stops writing, even if he tries *to stop thinking* – could we say that he is therefore abandoning himself to the *unconscious* (in the form of an extravagant reverie)?

This is one aspect of the phenomenon that would lead Nietzsche to try to specify the relationship between the 'conscious' agent and the so-called 'unconscious' activity of the impulses in relation to this agent – for it is the agent that is 'unconscious' of this 'subterranean' activity. His inquiry would be undertaken in the hope of demonstrating that morality, which lies at the origin of every investigation, will be arrested only when it destroys its own foundation. Nietzsche pursues his inquiry in order to make himself finally admit that there is neither subject, nor object, nor will, nor aim, nor meaning – not only at the origin, but for now and always.

The notions of *consciousness* and *unconsciousness*, which are derived from what is responsible or irresponsible, always presuppose the *unity* of the person of the ego, of the subject – a purely institutional distinction, which is why it plays such an important role in psychiatric considerations. From the outset, this unity appears as little more than a *flickering* memory, maintained exclusively by the designations of the everyday code – which intervene in accordance with *changing excitations*, upon which they impose their own linkages in order to conceal the total discontinuity of our state. What then is *forgetfulness*? It is the *occultation* of the signs we use to designate the groups of events that are being lived through or thought at a given moment, whether near or far. But what is it that occults this series of signs, if not the afflux of another excitation, at another moment, which absorbs all the *available designations* – while the rest of our 'general' apparatus is put into 'abeyance'? Either everything in us is unconscious, or *everything in us is conscious*. In the latter case, however, there would be a simultaneous activation of all the available signs, which would provoke a *generalized insomnia*. In the former case, only a minuscule portion of the signs would be active, and they would be *too weak* to have the slightest influence on what takes place in our depth. Our depth is governed by a completely different system of designations, for which there is neither outside nor inside. The fact remains that we are *possessed, abandoned, possessed again* and *surprised*: sometimes by the system of impulsive designations, and at other times by the system of everyday signs. It is the former that confronts us, invades us, and will remain long after we disappear. Outside of it, we are little, much, nothing – depending on whether we appeal to the everyday code or not. Within it, no one knows – nor would anyone know how to know – what is being designated within us. For even when we are alone, silent, speaking internally to ourselves, it is still the *outside* that is speaking to us – thanks to these signs from the exterior that invade and occupy us, and whose murmuring totally covers over our impulsive life. Even our innermost recesses, even our so-called *inner life*, is still the *residue* of signs instituted from the outside under the pretext of signifying us in an 'objective' and 'impartial' manner – a residue that no doubt takes on the *configuration* of the impulsive movement characteristic of each person, and follows the contours of our ways of reacting to this invasion of signs, which we have not invented ourselves. This then is our 'consciousness'. Where does that leave our 'unconscious'? We cannot even look for it in our dreams. For here again, if everything on *the other side* of the waking state were reconstructed, this would simply be *the same system of signs* of the everyday code being put to a different use. It is because of the difference between this use and the use that prevails in the waking state that we can more or less recall our dreams afterwards, and relate the strange words, or the words of a strange banality, that are offered there, through us or through other figures. Moreover, in the waking state we are capable of uttering things of the same type – whether in jest, or through fatigue, or through some other disturbance. When someone tells us that we are 'dreaming out loud', it means that something impulsive has shaken or upset the code of everyday signs: we have been *surprised* by our 'unconscious'. But this is nothing: *even for someone to say this to us*, the use of everyday signs is required – by the interlocutor, even if it is a psychiatrist. This implies that we are totally dependent on the everyday code, even when we let ourselves be surprised by our 'unconscious' – which, at the very least, will learn how to use the code in order to play with it and twist it around, as it pleases, even when we make fun of the psychiatrist and conceal our 'desire' to be 'cured'. This is why the strange behaviour that would result would be, in most cases, nothing but a ruse. But a ruse of what?

The ruse consists in making us believe in the coexistence of a *consciousness* and an *unconsciousness*; for if the latter survives in us, our consciousness would merely be a *capacity* to enter into an exchange with the exteriority of the code of everyday signs, and this capacity would amount to little more than receiving as much as possible while giving as little as possible. But we have no need to retain the greater part of this code – for the simple reason that we will never give up anything whatsoever of our own depth.

The more we hold our depth in reserve for use at the proper moment, the less we penetrate into our depth. A superfluous precaution: in effect, our depth is unexchangeable because *it does not signify anything*. Because of this unexchangability, we cover ourselves with the blanket we call understanding, culture, morality – all of which are based on the code of everyday signs. Beneath this cover, there would be only this *nothingness*, or this *depth*, or this

Chaos, or any other unnameable thing that Nietzsche might dare to utter.

Why then did Nietzsche so insist on the *unconscious* that he sought an *aim* and a meaning in it? And why, on the other hand, did he reduce consciousness to nothing more than a means to this end, to this 'unconscious' meaning? Once again, he did so in order to make use of language (the language of science and culture), to answer for what he had received, or thought he had received, as the last link in a long tradition. The suppression of the *true world* was also the suppression of the *apparent world* – and also entailed the suppression of the notions of *consciousness* and *unconsciousness* – the *outside* and the *inside*. We are only a succession of *discontinuous states* in relation to *the code of everyday signs*, and about which *the fixity of language* deceives us. As long as we depend on this code, we can conceive our continuity, even though we live discontinuously. But these discontinuous states merely concern the way we use, or do not use, the fixity of language: to be conscious is to make use of it. But how could we ever know what we are when we fall silent?

If we wished to postulate a goal adequate to life, it could not coincide with any category of conscious life; it would rather have to explain all of them as a means to itself –

The 'denial of life' as an aim of life, an aim of evolution! Existence as a great stupidity! Such a lunatic interpretation is only the product of measuring life by means of consciousness (pleasure and displeasure, good and evil). Here the means are made to stand against the end – the 'unholy', absurd, above all unpleasant means – : how can an end that employs such means be worth anything! But the mistake is that, instead of looking for a purpose that explains the *necessity* of such means, we presuppose in advance a goal that actually *excludes* such means; i.e. we take a desideratum in respect of certain means (namely pleasant, rational, and virtuous ones) as a norm, on the basis of which we posit what general purpose would be desirable –

The fundamental mistake is simply that, instead of understanding consciousness as a tool and particular aspect of the total life, we posit it as the standard and the condition of life that is of supreme value: it is the erroneous perspective of *a parte ad totum* – which is why all philosophers are instinctively trying to imagine a total consciousness, a consciousness involved in all life and will, in all that occurs, a 'spirit', 'God'. But one has to tell them that precisely this turns life into a monstrosity; that a 'God' and total sensorium would altogether be something on account of which life would have to be condemned – Precisely that we have *eliminated* the total consciousness that posited ends and means, is our great relief – with that we are no longer *compelled* to be pessimists – *Our* greatest *reproach* against existence was the *existence of God*.[57]

For Nietzsche, then, there would be an end (the unconscious life) because there would be a *means* (which would be consciousness) – this is the point we must emphasize here. Does this mean that it would be sufficient to treat consciousness as an tool that the unconscious uses in order to stop being insignificant? Or rather, was it not consciousness itself, which until Nietzsche had been posited erroneously as the supreme end, that had compelled Nietzsche toward the *unconscious* (and therefore bad) life, and compelled him to make *absurdity* the primary attribute of the authentic? This would mean: institutional language (the code of everyday signs) does not allow us to designate what is authentic otherwise than as something *insignificant*.

How then can we affirm the *authenticity* of life in an intelligible manner? When Nietzsche borrowed the terms *means* and *end* from language, he was paying tribute to *the valorization of language*. For although he knew that *meaning* and *goal* are mere fictions, as are the 'ego', 'identity', 'duration' and 'willing', it was nonetheless through these same designations that he agreed to speak in favour of an *end* – (neither Chaos nor the Eternal Return pursue any end other than themselves) – and of the *means* he was putting forward, which were capable of being *willed*.

Does this mean that Nietzsche thought of consciousness as the *means* to an end – an end that would lie in the so-called unconscious life? What was the point of denouncing consciousness as an *aim* that had hitherto been *erroneous*, inasmuch as it had usurped the authentic state of existence, making us 'pessimistic' toward it? It is a question here of a direct attack on the *necessity* of language: for even though language is the usurper, it never allows us to speak of our unintelligible depth except by ascribing to what is neither thought, nor said, nor willed – a meaning and an aim that we *think* according to language. And even if it were the *inverse* of a meaning or a thought-out aim, this inversion would still be, from the perspective of consciousness – a *play of language*.

Means and end still remain within the perspective of consciousness. To use conscious categories as a means to attain an end outside consciousness is still to remain subordinate to the 'false' perspective of consciousness. A consciousness that would be *conscious* of being an *instrument* of Chaos would no longer be capable of obeying the 'aim' of a chaos that would not even ask it to pursue such an aim. Chaos in turn would then be 'conscious' – and would no longer be Chaos. The terms *conscious* and *unconscious* are therefore applicable to nothing that is real. If Nietzsche made use of them, it was only as a 'psychological' convention, but he nonetheless let us hear what he did not say: namely, that the act of thinking corresponds to a passivity, and that this passivity is grounded in *the fixity of the signs of language* whose combinations simulate gestures and movements that reduce language to silence.

> – Every movement should be conceived as a gesture, a kind of language in which (impulsive) forces make themselves heard. In the *inorganic* world there is no

misunderstanding, communication seems to be perfect. *Error* begins in the *organic* world. 'Things',
'substances', 'qualities', 'activities' – we must guard
against their projection into the inorganic world!
These are errors of species, through which organisms live. The problem of the possibility of 'error'?
The contradiction is not between the 'false' and
the 'true' but between the 'abbreviations of signs'
and the 'signs' themselves. The essential point: the
creation of forms, which *represent* numerous movements, the invention of signs for all types of signs.

– *All movements are signs of an inner event; and every
inner movement is expressed by such modifications of forms.
Thought* is not yet the inner event itself, but only *a
semiotic corresponding to the compensation of the power of
the affects.*

– The humanization of nature – interpretation
according to we others.[58]

*From each of our fundamental impulses comes a perspectival
appreciation* of every event and of every lived experience.
Each of these impulses is hindered or favoured or
flattered by every other impulse, each with its own
formative law (its risings and fallings, its own rhythm,
etc.) – and one impulse dies when another one arises.[59]

Man as a plurality of 'wills to power': each with
a plurality of means and forms of expression. The
different so-called 'passions' (for example, man is
cruel) are only *fictive unities*, insofar as what enters
consciousness as *similar* from different fundamental impulses is synthetically imagined as a 'being',
an 'essence' or a 'faculty', a passion. Just as the
soul itself is an *expression* for all the phenomena
of consciousness: but we *interpret* it as the *cause*
of all these *phenomena* ('self-consciousness' is a fiction!).[60]

From this point of view, the first question we must ask concerns the function of the signs of language; or rather, in an even more rudimentary fashion: how and *where* are signs born?

'Every movement should be conceived as a gesture, a kind of language in which (impulsive) forces make themselves heard. In the inorganic world there is no *misunderstanding*, communication seems to be perfect. *Error* begins in the *organic* world.'[61]

In the inorganic world, communication seems perfect. Nietzsche means: there is *no possible disagreement* between what is strong and what is weak. 'Every power draws its ultimate consequence at every moment', he says elsewhere.[62] Persuasion is immediate.

In the organic world, by contrast, where exchange and assimilation are necessary, misunderstanding becomes possible, since exchange and assimilation take place only through interpretation: from trial and error to certainty – the certainty of the conditions of existence. The latter can be obtained only after a long experimentation with the similar and the dissimilar, and thus with identity. Only then can points of reference, repetition and comparison appear – and finally, comparable signs.

Now in a universe dominated by the inorganic, organic life is itself a fortuitous case – hence a possible *'error'* in the cosmic economy. It is within this economy that interpretation, *grounded in the fear of error*, becomes susceptible to *error*. Even if the origin of organic life lies in *purely random* combinations, it can no longer behave *randomly* once it comes into existence. It must believe in its *necessity*, and therefore it must maintain the conditions of its existence, and to do so it must avoid *chance* and not commit any *errors*. Hence the double aspect of *error* in Nietzsche: life depends on an illusion (its 'necessity') – whence the verdict: '*Truth is the kind of error without which a certain species of life could not live.*'[63]

Let us retain this complex in Nietzsche's thought formed by 'chance', 'error', and the 'interpretation of the conditions

of existence': the illusion of their necessity, as well as the
necessity of their illusion.

If interpretation is susceptible to error – whence the
possibility of *misunderstanding* – at the highest degree of
organic life, namely the human species – *for which truth is
an error without which it cannot live* – then a code must be
developed, the most evolved code of interpretation.

What is this code of signs? *An abbreviation of the (impulsive)
movements of gestures in signs*: no doubt the system of interpretation that offers the largest domain of error.

Nietzsche does not admit the existence of a power *that
would be unable to increase itself.* It is this incessant augmentation
that makes him say that it is not simply 'power', but *will* to
power. The term '*Wille ZUR Macht*', however, indicates an
intention – a tendency *towards* – something he has already
declared to be a fiction of language. A perpetual equivocity
ensues, despite all his efforts to distinguish his own use of the
term from the traditional concept of the will.

Nietzsche finds this 'will to power' – energy, in the
quantitative sense of physics – (as much in the inorganic
world as) in the organic world, where he then assimilates it
totally to what he himself calls an *impulse*. From the lowest
level of organic life to the human species, this impulse is
ramified and spiritualized, and persists both *beyond and before*
the organs the impulses have created. The same thing occurs
at the level of the human psyche, where the impulses are
subject, not only to a diversification, but to a total inversion
by the cerebral organ, which they have worked together to
form as their supreme obstacle.

On one side of the obstacle represented by the cerebral
function as intellect, the impulses are sometimes in league
with each other, and sometimes opposed to each other in
a perpetual combat; on the other side, they submit to a
deforming duplication by being *designated*. Now Nietzsche
insists on the fact that the combat of the impulses takes place
through a mutual interpretation of their respective intensities,
which implies their own 'code'.

The impulse reacts to *excitations*: this is all that remains of the impulse at the lowest level of organic life. However, chemical elements still intervene in these excitations, which in turn react on each other. An entire scale of interpretations is developed from the lowest level up to its extreme spiritualization. And in themselves, *impulse* and *repulsion* are already interpretive.

Every living being interprets according to a code of signs, responding to variations in *excited* or *excitable* states. Whence come *images*: representations of *what has taken place* or *what could have taken place* – thus a *phantasm*.

For the *impulse to become a will* at the level of consciousness, the latter must give the impulse an *exciting* state as an aim, and thus must elaborate the *signification* of what, for the impulse, is a phantasm: an anticipated excitation, and thus a possible excitation according to the schema determined by previously experienced excitations.

The attraction of the phantasm is produced from the relation between impulsive forces of varying intensity, which makes a discharge necessary. At the level of consciousness, this relation of forces is subject to modification by *contrary* impulses: impulsive *traces* that are equivalent to signs.

Thus, *conscious* or *unconscious* states exist only when already-existing signifying traces are (or are not) re-excited by a more or less variable afflux, this afflux itself being modified in the sense that other traces are then eliminated. The signs of language are entirely dependent on this excitation, and are produced whenever they coincide with re-excitable traces.

A phantasm, or several phantasms, can be formed in accordance with the relations among impulsive forces, some of which will be codified when these forces intensify this or that signifying trace. In this manner, something new and unfamiliar is misinterpreted as something *already known*, just as traces that have never been intensified previously suddenly *are* intensified: an old and uncodified circumstance appears as new.

'*The contradiction is not between the "true" and the "false" but between "abbreviations of signs" and the "signs" themselves.*'[64] What this means is that the impulses – which confront and interpret each other through their fluctuations of intensity and, at the level of organized beings, through *gestures* – create *forms* out of these movements and gestures, and cannot be distinguished from this invention of signs, which stabilizes them through *abbreviation*. For in abbreviating them, these signs reduce the impulses, apparently suspending their fluctuation *once and for all*. But in the intervals of the (fixed) signs of language, the intensity of the impulses can only be designated in an intermittent and arbitrary manner, in comparison with these abbreviations. Their movement is constituted as a *meaning* only if they take this designating abbreviation as their aim, and reach it through a combination of *unities*. The latter then form a declaration which sanctions *the fall of the intensity, once and for all*.

For consciousness, these *abbreviations of signs* (words) are in effect the *sole* vestiges of its continuity, that is to say, they are invented in a sphere where the 'true' and the 'false' necessitate the erroneous representation that something can *endure* or remain *identical* (and thus, that there can be an *agreement* between the *invented signs* and what they are supposed to designate). Moreover, this is why the impulses themselves must now signify a coherent 'unity', and their similarity or dissimilarity can be assessed only in relation to a *primary unity*. This unity will henceforth be the *soul* of the agent, or its *conscience*, or its *intellect*. In the final analysis, they are qualified as 'passions' insofar as they become an object of the agent's judgement, who considers them only insofar as they affect its unity or cohesion in the *absence* of such a judgement. They become the *passions* (or affections) of the 'subject', and just as the impulses are 'ignorant' of the agent, so the agent interprets the impulses as its *own* 'propensities', 'tendencies', or inclinations – terms that always concern the representation of an enduring *unity*, a fixity, a 'summit' that necessarily has '*slopes*'.

From this point of view, Nietzsche retains the word *affect* to indicate their autonomy in relation to the *forces* which, while *subordinate* to the fallacious 'unity' of the agent, constantly modify it, making it mobile and fragile. Itself a product of this 'abbreviation of signs', the agent nonetheless *'thinks' itself to be beyond the signs proper*, which are impulsive movements – and hence movements, according to Nietzsche, that function as interpretable gestures, including those executed by the agent, whether it speaks or remains silent.

But already, these gesticulations are no longer expressing the movements that were signifying each other mutually beneath the agent. If they feel the effects of each other's constraint and gesticulate as a consequence, the *system of 'signs' abbreviates* the gestures of the impulsive constraint, and lead it back to the coherent *unity* (of the agent), which forms the (grammatical) 'subject' in a series of propositions and declarations about everything that happens to it, whether from without or from within. Consequently, the *impulse* or *repulsion* (resistance or non-resistance), which originally served as a *model* for this *abbreviating system*, is now rendered insignificant by the agent. The intensities (impulse–repulsion) take on a signification only if they are first *reduced*, by the abbreviating system, to the *intentional* states of the agent. The agent now *thinks*, or *believes it is thinking*, depending on whether it feels its persistence to be *threatened* or *assured* – and notably the persistence of its intellect. The intellect is nothing more than a *repulsion* of anything that might destroy the cohesion between the agent and this abbreviating system (as when the adventure of the agent gives way to *fluctuations of intensity, devoid of any intention*); or, on the contrary, it is a pure and simple *impulse* (insofar as it abbreviates these fluctuations in the form of *thought*). Now how is thought itself possible – if not because the fluctuations of intensity are ceaselessly opposed to their own '*abbreviation*'? Nietzsche says that *we have no language to express what is in becoming*. Thought is always the result of a momentary relation of power between impulses, principally between those that dominate and those that resist. The fact that one thought succeeds another thought – the second *apparently engendered* by the first – *is the sign*, says Nietzsche, *of how the situation of power among the impulses is modified in the interval.* And he adds: '*the will*' – a fallacious reification. By which he means that all '*willing*' that starts with 'consciousness' is still merely a fiction, due to this *abbreviation of signs by the signs themselves.*

Now it is a condition of existence for the agent *to be ignorant of the combat* from which its thought is derived: it is not this living unity of the 'subject', but '*the combat of the impulses that wills to maintain itself*'.[65]

'*The combat that wills to maintain itself.*' This was the unintelligible and authentic depth out of which Nietzsche wanted to establish a *new cohesion,* beyond the agent, between the 'body' and 'Chaos' – a state of *tension* between the fortuitous cohesion of the agent and the incoherence of Chaos.

At the outset, a machinery appeared, which Nietzsche enjoyed studying but not without malice. Moreover, it was the forces themselves that implied a machinery, since they seemed to reduce the human being to the status of an automaton. Whence the liberatory sentiment: one can *reconstruct the living being* in conformity with these same forces, thereby restoring an impulsive spontaneity to it.

First, one must admit everything that is purely 'automatic': to dismantle an automaton is not to reconstruct a 'subject'. Since *perspectivism* is the characteristic illusion of this automaton, to provide it with the *knowledge* of this illusory perspective, the 'consciousness' of this 'unconscious', is to create the conditions of a new freedom, a creative freedom. The 'consciousness' of the 'unconscious' can consist only in a *simulation* of forces. It is not a matter of destroying what Nietzsche calls *the abbreviation (of signs) by signs themselves* – the encoding of movements – but of retranslating the '*conscious*' semiotic into the *semiotic of the impulses.* The 'conscious categories' that avoid, repudiate and betray these movements – and thus remain ignorant of the perpetual combat of forces – sustain the automatism under the apparent spontaneity of thought. To recover an *authentic spontaneity*, the producer of these 'categories', the intellectual organ, must in turn be treated as a simple automaton, a pure tool. By consequence, as a spectator of itself, the automaton finds its freedom only *in the spectacle* that moves from intensity to intention, and from the latter to intensity.

From time immemorial we have ascribed the value of an action, a character, an existence, to the intention, the purpose for the sake of which one has acted or lived: this age-old idiosyncrasy finally takes a dangerous turn – provided, that is, that the absence of intention and purpose in events comes more and more to the forefront of consciousness. Thus there seems to be in preparation a universal devaluation: '*Nothing has any meaning*' – this melancholy sentence means 'All meaning lies in intention, and if intention is altogether lacking, then meaning is altogether lacking, too'. In accordance with this valuation, one was constrained to transfer the value of life to a 'life after death', or to the progressive development of ideas or of mankind or of the people or beyond mankind; but with that one had arrived at a *progressus in infinitum* of purposes: one was at last constrained to make a place for oneself in the 'world process' (perhaps with the dysdaemonistic perspective that it was a process into nothingness).

In this regard, 'purpose' requires a more vigorous critique: one must understand that an action *is never caused by a purpose*; that *purpose* and *means* are *interpretations* whereby certain points in an event are emphasized and selected at the expense of other points, which, indeed, form the majority; that every single time something is done with a purpose in view, something fundamentally different and other occurs; that every purposive action is like the supposed purposiveness of the heat the sun gives off: the enormously greater part is squandered; a part hardly worth considering serves a 'purpose', has 'meaning'; that a 'purpose' and its 'means' provide an indescribably imprecise description, which can, indeed, issue commands as a prescription, as a 'will', but which presupposes a system of obedient and trained tools, which in place of indefinite entities posit nothing but fixed magnitudes (i.e., we imagine a system of shrewder but narrower intellects that posit purposes and means, in order to be able to ascribe to our only known 'purpose' the role of the 'cause of an action', to which procedure we really have no right: it would mean solving a problem by placing the solution in a world inaccessible to our observation −).

Finally: why could 'a purpose' not be an *epiphenomenon* in the series of changes in the activating forces that bring about the purposive action − a pale image sketched in consciousness beforehand that serves to orient us concerning events, even as a symptom of events, *not* as their cause? − But with this we have criticized *the will itself*: is it not an illusion to take for a cause that which rises to consciousness as an act of will? Are not all phenomena of consciousness merely terminal phenomena, final links in a chain, but apparently conditioning one another in their succession on one level of consciousness? This could be an illusion −[66]

Thus, there is no *intention* apart from the code of signs established by consciousness, insofar as the intention aspires to an *end* which is assigned to the 'will' by 'consciousness'. An *aim* is merely an image provoked by active forces, which are experienced and codified as an *intention*. Between the level of consciousness and that of active forces, there is what we call *a fit of ill-humour*, by which we mean something suffered at the hands of active forces, and which cannot be envisioned at the conscious level, except afterwards.

At the end of such a 'physiological' inquiry, there would remain no authority that human behaviour could appeal to, if not, on the one hand, the *exteriority* of institutional language, with all the consequences this entails for the individual, and on the other hand, an uncontrollable *interiority*, whose *unpredictability* has no limits other than those implied by institutional language. The *exteriority* that language represents (within the one who uses it), through which the individual tries to make itself understood, forces the individual to maintain these *entities* (destroyed by Nietzsche), and to make its own gestures and reflections conform to these entities. What would happen to human behaviour if it were grounded in a certain degree of lucidity (that is, once again, in the 'physiological' consciousness of oneself and others)? If at every moment individuals *understood each other* by the fact that they were not 'willing' *this* when they were nonetheless designating it? If in return they always experienced a '*that*' which each person would always have to infer in the other (which would be laughable from the point of view of 'good sense')? Indeed, it is obvious that, in varying degrees, if not this 'consciousness', then at least the veiled apprehension of a similar distrust, whether conventional or not, has always existed and arisen suddenly within 'good sense' itself.

Now Nietzsche clearly foresaw that such a lucidity (the *new consciousness* of the more or less subtle '*conditioning*' that underlies every mode of behaving, thinking, feeling, and willing), if it ever managed to prevail, would institute such a new conformity that he finally turned away from it in derision.

This, however, is the content of his 'invention' of the Eternal Return. For if such a lucidity is impossible, what the doctrine of the vicious Circle tends to demonstrate is that 'belief' in the Return, adherence to the non-sense of life, in itself implies an otherwise impracticable lucidity. We cannot renounce language, nor our intentions, nor our willing; but we could evaluate this willing and these intentions in a *different* manner than we have hitherto evaluated them – namely, as subject to the 'law' of the vicious Circle.

Moreover, the doctrine of the vicious Circle, which is a sign of forgetfulness, is grounded in the *forgetfulness* of what we have been and will be, not only for innumerable times, but for all time and always. We are other than what we are now: *others* that are not elsewhere, but *always* in this *same life*. Now for Nietzsche, is not lucidity (which means *the thought of a total discordance* between the hidden reality and the one that is claimed or admitted) the opposite of life? Is it not the inertia of power? Is it not precisely the non-true, the *error* that permits the human species to survive? Does not the *unconsciousness* of this '*physiological conditioning*' correspond to certain indispensable conditions of existence for this animal species? Is this not what Nietzsche has been ceaselessly affirming? However, had he not stated with equal force that *the only way we can overcome our servitude is by knowing that we are not free*? That as pure mechanisms, pure automatons, we gain in spontaneity by *knowing* this?

On the one hand, *forgetfulness* and *unconsciousness* are necessary to life; on the other hand, there is a 'will to unconsciousness' which, precisely because it is *willed*, implies the consciousness of our conditioned state: an irresoluble antinomy.

Now 'life itself created this grave thought [of the Eternal Return]; life wants to overcome its supreme obstacle'.[67]

3

The Experience of the Eternal Return

CORRESPONDENCE

To Gast

Sils-Maria, 14 August 1881

The August sun is overhead, the year is slipping away, the mountains and forests are becoming more quiet and peaceful. On my horizon, thoughts have arisen such as I have never seen before – I will not speak of them, but will maintain my unshakeable calm. I suppose now I'll have to live a few years longer! Ah, my friend, sometimes the idea runs through my head that I am living an extremely dangerous life, for *I am one of those machines which can EXPLODE*. The intensity of my feelings makes me shudder and laugh. Several times I have been unable to leave my room, for the ridiculous reason that my eyes were inflamed – from what? On each occasion I had wept too much on my wanderings the day before – not sentimental tears, mind you, but tears of joy. I sang and talked nonsense, filled with *a glimpse of things which put me in advance of all other men*.

After all, if I were unable to derive my strength from myself, if I had to wait for encouragement, comfort, and good cheer from the outside, where would I be! What would I be! There have indeed been moments, and even whole periods in my life (for example, the year 1878) when I would have felt a word of encouragement, a friendly handshake, to be the last word in restoratives – and precisely then everyone left me in the lurch, everyone on whom I thought I could rely and who could have done me the favor. Now I no longer expect it, and feel only a certain dim and dreary astonishment when, for example, I think of the letters that reach me nowadays – they are all so insignificant. Nobody has come to experience anything because of me, nobody has had a thought about me – what people say is very decent and well-intentioned, but it is remote, remote, remote. Even our dear Jacob Burckhardt wrote such a meek and timid little letter.[68]

FORGETTING AND ANAMNESIS IN THE LIVED EXPERIENCE OF THE ETERNAL RETURN OF THE SAME

The thought of the Eternal Return of the Same came to Nietzsche as a *abrupt awakening* in the midst of a *Stimmung*, a certain tonality of the soul. Initially confused with this *Stimmung*, it gradually emerged as a thought; nonetheless, it preserved the character of a revelation – as *a sudden unveiling*.

(The ecstatic character of this experience must be distinguished from the notion of the *Universal Ring* that already haunted Nietzsche during the 'Hellenic period' of his youth.)

But what is the function of forgetting in this revelation? More specifically, is not forgetting the source as well as the indispensable condition not only for the revelation of the Eternal Return, but also for *the sudden transformation of the identity* of the person to whom it is revealed?

Forgetting thus conceals eternal becoming and the absorption of all identities in being.

Is there not an antinomy, implicit in Nietzsche's lived experience, between the revealed content and the teaching of this content (as an ethical doctrine) in the formula: 'act as though you had to relive your life innumerable times and will to relive it innumerable times – for in one way or another, you must recommence and relive it.'

The imperative proposition supplements the (necessary) forgetting by invoking the will (to power); the second proposition foresees the necessity concealed in this forgetting.

Anamnesis coincides with the revelation of the Return: how could the return not bring back forgetfulness? Not only do I learn that I (Nietzsche) have been brought back to the crucial moment in which the eternity of the circle culminates, the moment in which the truth of its necessary return is revealed to me; but at the same time I learn that I was *other* than I am *now* for having forgotten this truth, and thus that I have become another by learning it. Will I change again, and once more forget that I will necessarily change during an eternity – until I relearn this revelation anew?

The emphasis must be placed on the loss of a given identity. The 'death of God' (the God who guarantees the identity of the responsible self) opens up the soul to all its possible identities, already apprehended in the various *Stimmungen* of the Nietzschean soul. The revelation of the Eternal Return brings about, as necessity, the successive realizations of all possible identities: 'at bottom every name of history is I' – in the end, 'Dionysus and the Crucified'. In Nietzsche, the 'death of God' corresponds to a *Stimmung* in the same way as does the ecstatic moment of the Eternal Return.

Digression:

The Eternal Return is a necessity that must be willed: only he who I am now can will the necessity of my return and all the events that have led to what I am – insofar as the will here presupposes a subject. Now this subject is no longer able to will itself as it has been up to now, but wills *all* prior possibilities; for by embracing in a single glance the necessity of the Return as a universal law, I deactualize my present self in order to will myself in *all the other selves whose entire series must be passed through* so that, in accordance with the circular movement, I once again become what I am at the moment I discover the law of the Eternal Return.

At the moment the Eternal Return is revealed to me, I cease to be myself *hic et nunc* and am susceptible to becoming innumerable others, knowing that I shall forget this revelation once I am outside the memory of myself; this forgetting forms the object of my present willing; for such a forgetting would amount to a memory outside my own limits: and my present consciousness will be established only in the forgetting of my other possible identities.

What is this memory? It is the necessary circular movement to which I abandon myself, freeing myself from myself. If I now admit to this willing – and, by willing it necessarily, I will have re-willed it – I will simply have made my consciousness conform to this circular movement: Were I to identify myself with the Circle, I would never emerge from this representation as myself; in fact, already *I am no longer in the moment when the abrupt revelation of the Eternal Return reached me*; for this revelation to have a meaning, I would have to lose consciousness of myself, and the circular movement of the return would have to be merged with my unconscious, until the movement brings me back to the moment when the necessity of passing through the entire series of my possibilities was revealed to me. All that remains, then, is for me to re-will myself, no longer as the outcome of these prior possibilities, no longer as one realization among thousands, but as a fortuitous moment whose very fortuity implies the necessity of the integral return of the whole series.

But to re-will oneself as a fortuitous moment is to renounce being oneself *once and for all*; for it is not 'once and for all' that I had renounced being myself and had to will this renunciation; and I am not even this fortuitous moment *once and for all* so long as I have to re-will this moment . . . *one more time!* For nothing? For myself. Nothing here is the Circle *once and for all*. It is a sign for everything that has happened, for everything that is happening, and for everything that will ever happen in the world.

How can willing intervene without forgetting what must now be re-willed?

For in fact, this very moment, in which the necessity of the Circular movement was revealed to me, appears in my life as having never taken place beforehand! The *hohe Stimmung*, the high tonality of my soul, was required in order for me to know and feel the necessity that all things return. If I meditate on this high tonality in which the circle is suddenly reflected – and if I accept it, no longer as a personal obsession, but as the only valid apprehension of being, as the sole reality – I will see that it is impossible for it to have not already appeared to me innumerable times, perhaps in other forms. But I had forgotten it, because it is inscribed in the very essence of the circular movement, which I necessarily forget from one state to the next (so that I can reach another state and be thrown outside of myself, even at the risk of everything coming to a stop). And even when I will not have forgotten that I had been precipitated outside myself in this life, I nevertheless had forgotten that I was thrown outside myself in another life – one in no way different from this life!

At the risk of everything coming to a stop? Is this to say that the movement was stopped at the moment of the sudden revelation? Far from it. The movement was not stopped, for I myself, Nietzsche, was unable to escape it: this revelation did not come to me as a reminiscence – nor as an experience of *déjà vu*. Everything would stop *for me* if I *remembered* a previous identical revelation – even if I were continually to proclaim the necessity of the return – for it would serve to keep me within myself, and thus outside the truth that I am teaching. It was therefore necessary for me to forget this revelation in order for it *to be true*! Within the series that I suddenly glimpse – the series that I must live through in order to be brought back to the same point – the revelation of the Eternal Return of the Same implies that *the same revelation* could just as well have occurred at *any other moment* of the circular movement. Indeed it must be thus: for in order to receive this revelation, I am *nothing* except this capacity to receive this revelation at *all the other moments* of the circular movement: nowhere in particular for me alone, but always in the movement as a whole.

Nietzsche speaks of the Eternal Return of the Same as the supreme thought, but also as the supreme feeling, as the highest feeling.

Hence, in an unpublished note contemporaneous with *The Gay Science*, he writes: 'My doctrine teaches: live in such a way that you must desire to live again, this is your duty – you will live again in any case! He for whom striving procures the highest feeling, let him strive; he for whom repose procures the highest feeling, let him rest; he for whom belonging, following, and obeying procures the highest feeling, let him obey. Provided that he becomes aware of what procures the highest feeling, and that he shrinks back from nothing. Eternity depends upon it!'[69] And earlier he had noted that present humanity no longer knows how to *wait* – as natures endowed with an eternal soul, fit for an eternal becoming and a future amelioration, are able to do. Here, the emphasis is placed less on willing than on desire and necessity, and this desire and this necessity are themselves linked to eternity: whence the reference to the highest feeling, or, in Nietzschean terms, to the *hohe Stimmung* – the high tonality of the soul.

It was in such a high tonality of the soul, such a *Stimmung*, that Nietzsche experienced the moment when the Eternal Return was revealed to him.

How can a tonality of the soul, a *Stimmung*, become a thought, and how can the highest feeling – the *höchste Gefühl*, namely the Eternal Return – become the supreme thought?

1 The tonality of the soul is a fluctuation of intensity.
2 In order for it to be communicable, the intensity must take itself as an object, and thus turn back on itself.
3 In turning back on itself, the intensity interprets itself. But how can it interpret itself? By becoming a counterweight to itself; for this, the intensity must divide, separate from itself, and come back together. Now this is what happens

to the intensity in what could be called moments of rise and fall; however, it is always the same fluctuation, a wave [*Onde*] in the concrete sense (we might note, in passing, the importance of the spectacle of sea waves in Nietzsche's contemplations).

4 But does an interpretation presuppose the search for a 'signification'? Rise and fall: these are 'designations', and nothing else. Is there any signification beyond this observation of a rise and fall? Intensity never has any meaning other than that of being an intensity. In itself, the intensity seems to have no meaning. What is a meaning? And how can it be constituted? What is the agent [*agent*] of meaning?

5 The agent of meaning, and thus of signification, once again seems to be the intensity, depending on its various fluctuations. If intensity by itself has no meaning, other than that of being an intensity, how can it be the agent [*agent*] of signification, or be signified as this or that tonality of the soul? We asked above how it could interpret itself, and we answered that, in its risings and fallings, it had to act as a counterweight. But this was nothing more than a simple observation. How then does it acquire a meaning, and how is meaning constituted in the intensity? Precisely by turning back on itself, even in a new fluctuation! By turning back on itself, by repeating and, as it were, imitating itself, it becomes a sign.

6 But a sign is first of all the trace of a fluctuation of intensity. If a sign retains its meaning, it is because the degree of intensity coincides with it; it signifies only through a new afflux of intensity, which in a certain manner joins up with its first trace.

7 But a sign is not only the trace of a fluctuation. It can also mark an absence of intensity – and here too, a new afflux is necessary, if only to signify this absence!

Whether we name this afflux attention, will, or memory, and whether we name this reflux indifference, relaxation, or forgetting, it is always a question of the same intensity, no different from the moving waves of the incoming tide. '*You and I*', Nietzsche said to them, '*we are of the same origin! the same race!*'[70]

This flux and this reflux will intermingle, fluctuation within fluctuation. Like the figures that rise to the crest of a wave, leaving behind them only foamy froth – such are the designations through which the intensity signifies itself. And this is what we call thought. But if, in natures as apparently limited and closed as our own, there still exists something open enough to make Nietzsche invoke the movement of waves, it is because – notwithstanding the sign in which the fluctuation of intensity culminates – the signification, because it exists only through an afflux, *can never absolutely disengage itself* from the moving chasms it masks. Every signification remains a function of Chaos, out of which meaning is generated.

Intensity is subject to a moving chaos without beginning or end.
Thus in each person, apparently as their own possession, there moves an intensity, its flux and reflux forming significant or insignificant fluctuations of a thought that in fact belongs to no one, with neither beginning nor end.

But if, contrary to this undulating element, each of us forms a closed and apparently delimited whole, it is by virtue of these traces of signifying fluctuations: that is to say, a system of signs that I will here call the code of everyday signs. As to where our own fluctuations start or stop (so that the signs can permit us to signify, to speak to ourselves and others), we know nothing – except that there is *one* sign in this code that always corresponds to either the highest or lowest degree of intensity: namely, the *self*, the *I*, *the subject of all our propositions*. It is thanks to this sign, which nonetheless is nothing but an always-variable trace of a fluctuation, that we constitute ourselves as *thinking*, that a thought as such occurs to us – even though we are never quite sure if it is not others who are thinking and continue to think in us. But what is this other that forms the *outside* in relation to this *inside* we believe ourselves to be? Everything is led back to a single discourse, namely, to fluctuations of intensity that correspond to the thought of everyone and no one.

The sign of the *self* in the code of everyday communication – insofar as it corresponds to the strongest or weakest intensity, and establishes a correspondence between our own degrees of presence or absence, and the degrees of presence and absence of the outside – thus assures a variable state of coherence both within ourselves and with our surroundings. The thought of no one, this intensity in itself, without any determinable beginning or end, finds a necessity in the agent [*suppôt*] that appropriates it for itself, and is assigned a destiny within the vicissitudes of memory and the forgetting of itself or the world. Nothing could be more arbitrary – once we admit that everything is on a single circuit of intensity. For a designation to be produced, for a meaning to be constituted, *my will* must intervene – but again this is nothing more than this appropriated intensity.

Now in a *Stimmung*, in a tonality that I will designate as the highest feeling, and that I will aspire to *maintain* as the highest thought – what has happened? Have I not surpassed my own limits, and thereby depreciated the everyday code of signs – either because thought abandons me, or else because I can no longer discern the difference between fluctuations from without and those from within?

Up to now, in the everyday context, thought was always referred back to me in the designation 'myself'. But what becomes of my own coherence at that degree of intensity where thought ceases to refer back to me in the designation 'myself', and instead invents a sign by which it would designate its own coherence with itself? If this sign is no longer my own thought, does it not signify my exclusion from all possible coherence? If it is still mine, how could it conceivably designate an absence of intensity at the highest degree of intensity?

Let us now suppose that, during such a high tonality of the

soul, an image of the Circle is formed. Something happens to my thought in this sign, it regards itself as dead, as no longer my own: my thought enters into such a strict coherence with it that the invention of this sign, of the circle, takes on the power of all thought. Does this mean that the thinking subject would lose its own identity in a coherent thought that would itself exclude identity? There is nothing here to distinguish the designating intensity from the designated intensity, to re-establish the coherence between the self and the world, as constituted by everyday designations. A single circuit brings me back to the code of everyday signs, and then makes me depart, again leaving me at the mercy of the sign, as soon as I try to explain to myself the event it represents.

For if, in this ineffable moment, I hear myself say, 'You are returning to this moment – you have already returned to it – you will return to it innumerable times', no matter how coherent this proposition may seem to be in terms of the sign of the Circle from which it is derived (for it is itself this very proposition), as an actual self in the context of everyday signs, I myself fall into incoherence. And this is a double manner: in relation to the coherence of this thought itself, and in relation to the code of everyday signs. According to the latter, I can only *will myself once and for all*, and it is on this basis that all my designations and their communicable meaning are constituted. But *to re-will myself one more time* indicates that nothing ever succeeds in getting constituted in *a single meaning, once and for all*. The circle opens me to inanity, and encloses me in the following alternative: *either* everything returns because nothing has ever had any meaning whatsoever, *or else* nothing has ever had a meaning except through the return of all things, without beginning or end.

Here is a sign in which I myself am nothing, a sign to which I always return – for nothing. What is my part in this circular movement in relation to which I am incoherent, or in relation to this thought that is so perfectly coherent that it excludes me *at the very moment* I *think* it? What is this sign of the Circle that empties every designation of its content for the sake of this sign? The high tonality of the soul becomes *the highest thought* only by restoring the intensity to itself, by integrating the Chaos from which it emanates with the sign of the Circle which it has formed.

The Circle says nothing through itself, except that existence has meaning only in being existence, and that signification is nothing but an intensity. This is why the intensity is revealed in a high tonality of the soul. But how can intensity attack the actuality of the self – this self that is nonetheless elated by this high tonality? By liberating the fluctuations that were signifying it as a *self*, in such a manner that it is the past that rings out anew in its present. It is not the fact of *being there* that fascinates Nietzsche in this moment, but the fact of *returning* in what becomes: this necessity – which was lived and must be relived – defies the will and the creation of a meaning.

In the circle, the will dies by contemplating this returning within becoming, and is reborn only in the discordance outside the circle. Whence the constraint exercised by *the highest feeling*.

These high Nietzschean tonalities found their immediate expression in the aphoristic form: even there, the recourse to the code of everyday signs is presented as an exercise in continually maintaining oneself in a discontinuity with respect to everyday continuity. When these *Stimmungen* blossom into fabulous physiognomies, it seems as if the flux and reflux of contemplative intensity seek to create points of reference for its own discontinuity. So many high tonalities, so many gods – until the universe appears as a dance of the gods: *the universe being nothing but a perpetual flight from itself, and a perpetual re-finding of itself in multiple gods.* . . .

This dance of gods pursuing each other is still only an explication, in Zarathustra's mythic vision, of this movement of flux and reflux of the intensity of Nietzsche's *Stimmungen*, the highest of which came to him under the sign of the *Circulus vitiosus deus*.

The *Circulus vitiosus deus* is merely a name for this sign, which here takes on a divine physiognomy under the aspect of Dionysus: Nietzsche's thought breathes more freely in the air of a divine and fabulous physiognomy than when it struggles internally against itself, as if in a snare where his own truth is trapped. Does he not say that *the true essence of things is a fabulation* of being that represents things, and without which *being could not be represented at all?*

The high tonality of the soul in which Nietzsche experienced the vertigo of Eternal Return created the sign of the Vicious Circle. What was instantaneously actualized in this sign was both the highest intensity of thought, self-enclosed in its own coherence, and the absence of any corresponding intensity in the everyday designations; by the same token, the designation of the *self*, to which everything had heretofore led, was itself emptied.

For in effect, with the sign of the *Vicious Circle* as the definition of the *Eternal Return of the Same*, a sign befalls Nietzsche's thought as *an event that stands for everything that can ever happen*, for everything that has ever happened, for everything that could ever happen in the world – and indeed, in thought itself.

THE ELABORATION OF THE EXPERIENCE OF THE ETERNAL RETURN AS COMMUNICABLE THOUGHT

The very first version Nietzsche gives, in *The Gay Science* (aph. 341), of his Sils-Maria experience – like those presented later in *Zarathustra* – is essentially expressed as a hallucination: at that very moment, the moment itself seems to be reflected in a *flash* [*échappée*] of mirrors. It is the self, the *same* 'self', that awakens to an infinite multiplication of *itself* and its own life, while a kind of demon (like a genie in the *Thousand and One Nights*) reveals to it: You will have to live this life once more and innumerable times more. The reflection that follows declares: If this thought gained possession of you, it would make of you an other.

There is no doubt that Nietzsche is here speaking of a *return* of the *identical self*. This is the obscure point that was the stumbling-block both to his contemporaries and to posterity. From the outset, this thought was commonly considered to be an absurd phantasm.

Zarathustra considers the will as being enslaved to the irreversibility of time; this is the first reflective reaction to the obsessional *evidence*. Nietzsche therefore seeks to grasp the hallucination once more at the level of conscious willing through an 'analytic' cure of the will. What is the relationship of the will to three-dimensional time (past–present–future)? The will projects its powerlessness on time, and in this way gives time its *irreversible* character: the will cannot reverse *the flow of time* – the non-willed that time establishes as an accomplished fact. This produces, in the will, the spirit of *revenge* against the unchangeable, and a belief in the *punitive* aspect of existence.

Zarathustra's remedy is to re-will the *non-willed*, inasmuch as he desires to assume the accomplished fact himself, thereby rendering it *unaccomplished* by re-willing it *innumerable times*. Such a *ruse* removes the *'once and for all'* character from the event. This is the subterfuge that the experience of Sils-Maria (which is in itself unintelligible) first offers to reflection. This reflection consequently hinges on *willing*.

Such a ruse, however, is only one way of eluding the temptation inherent in the very reflection on the Eternal Return: *non-action*, which Zarathustra rejects as a fallacious *remedy*, nonetheless implies the same inversion of time. If all things return according to the law of the vicious circle, then *all voluntary action is equivalent to a real non-action, or all conscious non-action is equivalent to an illusory action*. At the level of conscious decision, not to act corresponds to the *inanity* of the individual will. It expresses the intensity of the high tonality of the soul as much as does the decision to pursue an action. How could the re-willing of the past be creative? To adhere to the Return is also to admit that *only forgetting* enabled us to undertake old creations as new creations, *ad infinitum*. Formulated at the level of *the conscious self, identical to itself*, the imperative of re-willing would remain a *tautology*:

for it seems that this imperative (even though it demands a decision for eternity) concerns the will's behaviour only during the interval of an individual life, and that the past (the non-willed, the riddle of dreadful chance) is what we live through every day.

Now this *tautology* is represented, both in the sign of the Circle and in Nietzsche's own thought, by the *return* of all things, including itself.

The *parable* of two opposed paths, coming together under the arch of a gateway on whose pediment is inscribed '*Moment*' (in *Zarathustra*), simply takes up the image of the aphorism in *The Gay Science*: the same moonlight, the same spider, will return.[71] The two opposed paths are ONE, but an eternity separates them: individuals, things, events, go up one path and come down the other, and return as the same under the *gateway* of the *Moment*, having made *a tour of eternity*. Whoever stops in this 'gateway' is *alone* capable of grasping the circular structure of eternal time. But here, as in the aphorism, it is still the individual self who leaves and returns *identical to itself*. Certainly there is a link between this parable and the will's *cure* through a re-willing of the past. Except that it does not carry any conviction.

Yet the aphorism declares: in re-willing, the self *changes*, it becomes *other*. This is where the solution to the riddle lies.

Zarathustra is seeking a change, not in the *individual*, but in its will: to re-will the non-willed past – this is what the 'will to power' would consist in.

But Nietzsche himself dreams of a completely different kind of change – a change in individual behaviour. The re-willing of the past, if it is only an *assumption of the non-willed* by the will, as a creative recuperation (in the sense that fragment and riddle and dreadful chance are reconstituted in a significant unity), nonetheless remains at the level of a 'voluntarist' fatalism.

The change in the individual's moral behaviour is not determined by the conscious will – but rather by the economy of the Eternal Return itself. Under the sign of the

Vicious Circle, it is the nature of existence itself (independent of the human will) – and hence individual actions as well – that is intrinsically modified. As Nietzsche says in a note as revealing as it is brief:

'*My consummation of fatalism*: 1. Through the Eternal Return and pre-existence. 2. Through the liquidation of the concept of "will".'[72]

A fragment from Sils-Maria, dated August 1881, states: '*The incessant metamorphosis: in a brief interval of time you must pass through several individual states. Incessant combat is the means.*'[73]

What is this brief interval? Not just any moment of our existence, but the eternity that separates one existence from another.

This indicates that the re-willing has as its object a *multiple alterity* inscribed within an individual. If this is the *incessant* metamorphosis, it explains why Nietzsche states that 'pre-existence' is a necessary condition for the *being-as-such* of an individual. The *incessant* combat would indicate that the adherent of the Vicious Circle must henceforth practise this multiple alterity. But this theme will be taken up later when Nietzsche envisions a *theory of the fortuitous case*.

These fragments introduce many new elements for developing the thought of the Vicious Circle. It is no longer simply the will confronting an irreversible Time, which, when cured of its representation of a punitive existence, breaks the chains of its captivity by re-willing the non-willed, and by recognizing itself in the reversibility of time as a will to power – and hence as a creative will.

For these fragments also suggest a transfiguration of existence which – because it has always been the Circle – wills its own reversibility, to the point where it relieves the individual from the weight of its own acts *once and for all*. What is at first sight the most burdensome pronouncement – namely, *the endless recommencement of the same acts and the same sufferings* – now appears as redemption itself, once the soul realizes that it has already lived through other individualities and experiences – and thus is destined to live through even more – which deepen and enrich the only life that it knows *hic et nunc*. Those that have prepared for the present life, and those that the latter is preparing for others, remain totally unsuspected by consciousness.

Re-willing is the pure adherence to the Vicious Circle: re-willing *the entire series one more time* – re-willing all experiences, and all one's acts, but not as *mine*: this *possessive* no longer has any meaning, nor does it represent a goal. Meaning and goal are liquidated by the Circle. Whence Zarathustra's silence, his interrupted message. Unless it is a burst of laughter that conveys all his own bitterness.

At this point, Nietzsche will become divided in his own interpretation of the Eternal Return. The 'overman' becomes the name of the subject of the will to power, both the *meaning* and the *goal* of the Eternal Return. The will to power is only a *humanized* term for the soul of the Vicious Circle, whereas the latter is a pure intensity *without intention*. On the other hand, the Vicious Circle, as Eternal Return, is presented as a chain of existences that forms the individuality of the doctrine's adherent, who knows that he has *pre-existed* otherwise than he now exists, and that he will yet exist differently, from one 'eternity to another'.

In this way, Nietzsche introduces a renewed version of metempsychosis.

The need for purification; and hence a culpability that must be expiated across successive existences before an initiate's soul can attain a pure state of innocence, and be admitted into an immutable eternity: such is the ancient schema that was transmitted to the Christian gnosis by the esoteric religions of India and Asia.

But there is nothing of all this in Nietzsche – neither 'expiation', nor 'purification', nor 'immutable purity'. Pre- and post-existence are always the surplus of the same present existence, according to the economy of the Vicious Circle. It presumes that an individuality's capacity could never exhaust the differentiated richness of single existence, that is to say, its affective potential. Metempsychosis represents the *avatars* of an immortal soul. Nietzsche himself says: '*If only we could bear our immortality – that would be the supreme thing.*'[74] Now for Nietzsche, this immortality is not specifically individual. The Eternal Return suppresses enduring identities. Nietzsche urges the adherent of the Vicious Circle to accept the *dissolution* of his fortuitous soul in order to receive another, equally fortuitous. In turn, having passed through the entire series, this dissolved soul must itself return, that is, it must *return to that degree of the soul's tonality in which the law of the Circle was revealed to it.*

If the metamorphosis of the individual is the law of the Vicious Circle, how can it be willed? Suddenly, the revelation of the Circle becomes conscious. To remain in this consciousness it is sufficient to live in conformity with the necessity of the circle: re-willing this same experience (the moment we become *the one* who is initiated into the secret of the Vicious Circle) presupposes that one has lived through *all livable experiences*. All the existences *prior* to this moment – which privileges one existence among millions – no less than all those existences that will follow, are necessary. To re-will all experiences, to *re-will* all possible acts, all possible joys and sufferings – this means that if such an act were accomplished now, if such an experience were now lived, it would have been necessary for one series to have preceded and for others to follow – not within the same individual, but in everything that belongs to the individual's own potential – so that one day it could find itself *one more time*.

THE DIFFERENCE BETWEEN THE ETERNAL RETURN AND
TRADITIONAL FATALISM

Nietzsche's thinking concerning fatalism culminates in the dimension of the Circle.

Fatalism in itself (the *fatum*) presupposes a chain of events, pre-established in a disposition, which is developed and realized in an irreversible manner: whatever I do and whatever I decide to do, my decision, contrary to what

I may think, obeys a *project* that escapes me and of which I am unaware.

The *Vicious Circle* reintegrates the play of Chance (with its million combinations as so many series forming a chain) into the experience of the Fatum – in the form of a movement without beginning or end: an image of destiny which, as a circle, can be *re-willed* only because it must be *re-commenced*.

Chance is but one thing at each of the moments (the individual, singular and hence fortuitous existences) of which it is composed. It is by 'chance' that the figure of the Circle is revealed to an individual. From that moment on, that individual will know how to re-will the entire series in order to re-will itself. Or, in other terms, as soon as the individual exists it cannot fail to re-will all the prior and subsequent series of its own existence.

The feeling of eternity and the eternalization of desire merge in a single moment: the representation of a *prior* life and an *after*-life no longer concerns a beyond, or an individual self that would reach this beyond, but rather the *same life* lived and experienced through its individual differences.

The Eternal Return is merely the mode of its deployment. The feeling of vertigo results from the *once and for all* in which the subject is surprised by the dance of *innumerable times*: the *once-and-for-all* disappears. The intensity emits a series of infinite vibrations of being, and it is these vibrations that project the individual self *outside of itself* as so many *dissonances*. Everything resounds until the consonance of this single moment is re-established, where the dissonances are once again resolved.

At the level of consciousness, meaning and goal are lost. They are *everywhere* and *nowhere* in the Vicious Circle, since there is no point on the Circle that cannot be *both the beginning and end*.

Finally, the Eternal Return, at its inception, was not a representation, nor was it, strictly speaking, a postulate; it was a *lived fact*, and as a thought, it was a *sudden* thought. Phantasm or not, the experience of Sils-Maria exercised its constraint as an ineluctable necessity. Alternating between dread and elation, Nietzsche's interpretations will be inspired by this moment, by this felt necessity.

HOW NIETZSCHEAN FATALISM CULMINATES IN THE ELIMINATION OF THE CONCEPT OF THE WILL

Nietzsche does not say that the thought of the Eternal Return, and the pre-existence it presupposes, can itself bring fatalism to an end. He says, in the second place, that it is because the *concept of the will* has been eliminated that his fatalism is complete. If the thought of the Eternal Return in its various extensions already abolishes the identity of the self along with the traditional concept of the will, then Nietzsche, under the second aspect of his fatalism, would seem to be alluding to his own physiology. According to the latter, there is no will that is not a will to *power*, and in this regard the will is nothing other than the primordial *impulse*. No moral interpretation by the intellect could ever suspend the innumerable metamorphoses this impulse lives through, the shapes it adopts, or the pretexts that provoke them – whether it be an invoked *goal*, or the *meaning* that this impulse, in its various metamorphoses, or even at the level of consciousness, claims to give itself. In this way, fatalism would be merged with the impulsive force that exceeds the agent's 'will' and *already modifies it*, thereby *threatening its stable identity*.

4

The Valetudinary States at the Origin of Four Criteria: Decadence, Vigour, Gregariousness, the Singular Case

What was happening in me, strictly speaking? I did not understand myself, but the impulse was like a commandment to me. It seems that we are at the mercy of a distant and remote fate: for a long time we experience nothing but riddles. The choice of events, the fact of grasping them, the sudden desire, the rejection of what is most agreeable, often the most venerated: this is what terrifies us, as if a fit of ill-humour, something arbitrary, insane, volcanic, arose here and there from deep within us. But this is only the higher reason and prudence of our task to come. *Should the long sentence of my life − I was asking myself − perhaps be read backwards?* Reading it forwards, and here there is no doubt, all I found were '*words devoid of meaning*'.

An ever greater disengagement, an arbitrary becoming-foreign, an 'uprootedness', a cooling off, a sobriety − this and this alone was my desire during these years.

I shot at the target everything that had hitherto been attached to my heart, I returned the best, the dearest things, I examined their opposite, I took an opposing view toward everything that the human art of calumny and defamation had exercised in the most subtle way. At that moment, I examined many things that had hitherto remained foreign to me, with an attentive and even loving curiosity. I learned to experience more equitably our epoch and everything that is 'modern'. A disturbing game, no doubt, wicked perhaps – I was often sick of it. . . . But my resolution remained firm: and though sick, I kept up a good face during my 'game', and avoided any conclusion in which sickness, or solitude, or fatigue from wandering *could* have played the slightest role. 'Onward!' I told myself. 'Tomorrow you will be cured: today it is enough to *simulate health.*' At this moment, I managed to master everything in me that had been 'pessimistic', the very will to be cured, the *histrionics* of *health* was my remedy.[75] [Sketch for a new preface to *Human, All-Too-Human*, written in 1886]

The observation of his own valetudinary states led Nietzsche to live in a growing perplexity concerning what, in his own experience, would be *valuable* or not – and always in terms of two notions that would come to preoccupy him more and more: *health* and *morbidity*.

The *symptoms* of *vigour* and *decadence*, of *degeneration* and *strength* could be detected only by means of a distinction which, if it were to be rigorous, could gain only in ambiguity. This distinction is what grounds the term 'value' – in itself so equivocal – and the term 'power', which is the source of every active or sterile value. Because of this mobile base, a kind of *fault line* ran through Nietzsche's entire mental effort: what if the *act of thinking*, in the end, were nothing but a symptom of total impotence? Whence his reversal of Parmenides' statement, '*What is thinkable is real and what is real is thinkable,*' into its opposite: *What is thinkable is unreal* – which destroys the very principle of a received reality.

Nietzsche thus established a reiterated *censure* on his own reflections. The symptoms of decadence he revealed in the contemporary social world, or in its apparent history, corresponded to his personal obsession with what he was feeling and observing, in himself, of his own impulsive life and his own behaviour. The voice of the censor, which he sometimes called the *tyrant*, was ceaselessly insinuating itself: *this is something attributable to your heredity – this is a morbid desire – this is a weakness, it reveals an incapacity for living.*

But along with the criteria of what is *healthy* and what is *morbid*, Nietzsche also appealed to criteria of a different order, which would be combined with the preceding criteria: what is *singular* and what is *gregarious*?

decadence	*vigour*
morbid	*healthy*
weak	powerful

singular	gregarious
degenerate type	successful type
unexchangeable	exchangeable
unintelligible	comprehensible
muteness	communication
non-language	language

How can the attributes of power, health and sovereignty be restored to the singular, to the unexchangeable, to muteness – since language, communication and exchange have attributed what is healthy, powerful and sovereign to *gregarious conformity*? For it is gregariousness that presupposes exchange, the communicable, language: *being equivalent to something else*, namely, to anything that contributes to the conservation of the species, to the endurance of the herd, but also to the endurance of the signs of the species in the individual.

Hence a first question: are things that are *healthy* and *powerful* necessarily a product of *gregariousness* (that is, of the instinct for the conservation of the species), as language seems to require? Are they a product of the categories required for speech (that is, for the communication through which individuals can understand, help and recognize each other), such as the principles of contradiction and identity? Are they a product of the categories of the intellect – in other words, of consciousness?

Is everything that is singular, incommunicable and unexchangeable (that is, everything that is excluded from what we call the *norm*) not only condemned to muteness, but also condemned to disappear, or at least to remain 'unconscious'?

Or on the contrary, is everything that conforms to this norm the result of a process that has weakened the singular, the result of a slow equalization of surplus forces – to the point where their diminution leads to a compromise that forms a representative type which, because it is average, is also mediocre?

A second question concerns what, in lived experience, refers to the *singular* and what, in the way it is lived, belongs to the order of gregarious propensities. Nietzsche sometimes feared that his depressive states revealed such propensities in himself. But this suspicion did not preclude his premonition that there existed some subterranean force that obscurely seeks to affirm itself from one generation to the next – in the sense that the gregarious propensities, under the pretext of incorporating them into the (strictly gregarious) level of communication, would be the vehicle for, or would preserve, certain experiences that belong only to this or that singular case. The way Nietzsche questioned Western culture, whose metaphysics and traditional morality he was combating, was merely one aspect of the way he interrogated himself, as in this fragment entitled:

The typical forms of self-formation. Or: the eight principal questions.
1. Whether one wants to be more multifarious or simpler?
2. Whether one wants to become happier or more indifferent to happiness and unhappiness?

3. Whether one wants to become more contented with oneself or more exacting and inexorable?

4. Whether one wants to become softer, more yielding, more human, or more 'inhuman'?

5. Whether one wants to become more prudent or more ruthless?

6. Whether one wants to reach a goal or to avoid all goals (as, e.g., the philosopher does who smells a boundary, a nook, a prison, a stupidity in every goal)?

7. Whether one wants to become more respected or more feared? Or more despised?

8. Whether one wants to become tyrant or seducer or shepherd or herd animal?[76]

Another more explicit fragment is developed in the same interrogative form:

Points of view for *my* values: whether out of abundance or out of want? – whether one looks on or lends a hand – or looks away and walks off? – whether out of stored-up energy, 'spontaneously', or merely stimulated *reactively*, and provoked? whether *simple* out of a paucity of elements, *or* out of overwhelming mastery over many, so they are pressed into service when they are needed? – whether one is a *problem* or a *solution?* – whether *perfect* with a small task or *imperfect* with an extraordinary goal? whether one is *genuine* or merely an *actor*, whether one is genuine as an actor or merely the copy of an actor, whether one is a 'representative' or that which is represented? whether a 'personality' or merely a rendezvous of personalities – whether *sick* from sickness or excessive health? whether one goes on ahead as a shepherd or as an 'exception' (third species: as a fugitive)? whether one needs *dignity*, or to be a 'buffoon'? whether one seeks resistance or avoids it? whether one is imperfect through being 'too early' or 'too late'? whether one by nature says Yes or

No or is a peacock's tail of many colours? whether
one is sufficiently proud not to be ashamed even of
one's vanity? whether one is still capable of a bite of
conscience? (– this species is becoming rare: formerly
the conscience had too much to chew: now it seems
to have lost its teeth)? whether one is still capable of
a 'duty'? (– there are those who would lose their
whole joy in living if their duty were taken from them
– especially the womanly, the born subjects.)[77]

We must retain the specifically Nietzschean tone of these
alternatives: 'too early' or 'too late'; 'shepherd' or 'exception'
or 'fugitive'; 'dignified' or a 'buffoon'. The admirable image
of the 'peacock's tail', with its hundred eyes, would be
appropriate to define how Nietzsche felt, within himself,
what is in itself Western culture, our culture: omni-science
is the equivalent of these 'many colours', these thousand
nuances of knowledge that lead to a total apathy toward
the complete vision of what is now possible; so much so
that consciousness, in its deductive vigilance, disappears into
the unconscious and becomes opaque. Modern consciousness
is 'toothless' (unable to chew again), and is unashamed of its
own vacuity. But fate would interrupt these Nietzschean
alternatives: in the final scene, the 'buffoon' will have the
last word, and the philosopher will founder.
     The schema that sets morbid and healthy symptoms in
opposition to each other has its source in the schema that
sets the signs of *gregariousness* and *singularity* in opposition.
In Nietzsche's reflections, these two schemata were interchangeable and convertible. Every personal declaration is first
of all of a phylogenetic order – by consequence, *the species
is present* in the terms used to designate that which excludes
the species in the experience characteristic of the singular
state, or that which excludes from the species the subject
who singularizes this experience. In order to valorize the
declaration of the singular, language will have to circumscribe
the *singular muteness*, and what it contains that is *un*intelligible

to the species, with respect to the intelligibility required by gregarious institutions. But this is not to say that what forms the unintelligible depth of the singular case has always been so for the whole of the species.

From this point of view, the singular case represents a *forgetting* of previous experiences, which are either assimilated to the gregarious impulses by being relegated to the unconscious, and thus reprimanded by the reigning censure; or on the contrary, are rejected as being unassimilable to the conditions required for the existence of both the species and the individual within the species. For Nietzsche, the singular case rediscovers, in an 'anachronistic' manner, an ancient way of existing – whose reawakening in itself presupposes that *present* conditions do not correspond to the impulsive state which is in some manner being affirmed through it. Depending on the strength of its intensity, however, this singular state, though anachronistic in relation to the institutional level of gregariousness, can bring about a de-actualization of that institution itself and denounce it in turn as anachronistic. That every reality as such comes to be de-actualized in relation to the singular case, that the resulting emotion seizes the subject's behaviour and forces it into action – this is an adventure that can modify the course of events, following a circuit of chance that Nietzsche will make the dimension of his thought. To the extent that he isolates its periodicity in history, the plan for a conspiracy appears under the sign of the vicious Circle.

If we consider the experience that had just affected Nietzsche at Sils-Maria, which had appeared as a sudden thought, and followed who knows what emotional upheaval, we might ask what relationship this thought had with Nietzsche's investigation into the symptoms of health and morbidity, which was becoming increasingly obsessive. *Life invented this thought,* he said. If it was the most profound impulse, which emerged by signifying itself as the *vicious Circle,* would it suspend this search for points of reference concerning what is healthy and morbid? How could Nietzsche consider himself privileged for having had this experience of the Return? Between what was deteriorating in and around him, and what was exhilarating him, there passed the breath of a catastrophe.

In a posthumous fragment, dated Spring 1888, Nietzsche is still trying to demonstrate to himself that the supreme values of philosophy and traditional morality are merely morbid symptoms of impotence and non-resistance, and therefore that they are of the same order as representations of mental debility. But since he is also questioning himself, it may be (this is the underlying motif) that everything that he manages to think – and to think against the hitherto supreme values – is the result of a morbid state. This is why he introduces this fragment with a statement of principle:

> What is inherited is not the sickness but *sickliness*: the lack of strength to resist the danger of infections, etc., the broken resistance; *morally* speaking, resignation and meekness in the face of the enemy.
>
> I have asked myself if all the supreme values of previous philosophy, morality, and religion could not be compared to the values of the weakened, the *mentally ill*, and *neurasthenics*: in a milder form, they represent the same ills. –
>
> It is the value of all morbid states that they show us under a magnifying glass certain states that are normal – but not easily visible when normal. –
>
> Health and sickness are not essentially different, as the ancient physicians and some practitioners even today suppose. One must not make of them distinct principles or entities that fight over the living organism and turn it into their arena. That is silly nonsense and chatter that is no good any longer. In fact, there are only differences in degree between these two kinds of existence: the exaggeration, the disproportion, the nonharmony of

the normal phenomena constitute the pathological state (Claude Bernard).

Just as '*evil*' can be considered as exaggeration, disharmony, disproportion, '*the good*' may be a *protective diet* against the danger of exaggeration, disharmony, and disproportion.

Hereditary weakness as the *dominant* feeling: cause of the supreme values.

N.B. One *wants* weakness: why? Usually because one is *necessarily* weak.

– *Weakness* as a *task*: weakening the desires, the feelings of pleasure and displeasure, the will to power, to a sense of pride, to want to have and have more; weakening as meekness; weakening as faith; weakening as aversion and shame in the face of everything natural, as negation of life, as sickness and habitual weakness – weakening as the renunciation of revenge, of resistance, or enmity and wrath.

The error in treatment: one does not want to fight weakness with a *système fortifiant*, but rather with a kind of justification and *moralization*; i.e., with an *interpretation*. –

– Two totally different states confounded: e.g., the *calm of strength*, which is essentially forbearance from reaction (type of the gods whom nothing moves) – and the *calm of exhaustion*, rigidity to the point of anesthesia. All philosophic-ascetic procedures aim at the second, but really intend the former – for they attribute predicates to the attained state as if a divine state had been attained.[78]

What is inherited is not the sickness itself but the *morbid state*, which manifests itself in the *moral values* of *resignation and humility*. This is what Nietzsche states in the first two paragraphs. But this raises the question of whether or not what have hitherto been the *supreme values* are not merely pathological travesties.

If, after reading the last paragraphs of the fragment, we then return to the first, it seems that the fragment includes two contradictory propositions.

The first moves in the same direction as traditional morality: *it is an 'evil' for the agent to be unable to resist its impulses* (to resist harmful invasions).

The second proposition qualifies this lack of resistance (the strength of a broken resistance) as *resignation* and *humility*. From what point of view?

From Nietzsche's point of view (as well as that of pagan morality), *humility* and *resignation before the enemy* (hostile invading forces) are synonymous with *weakness*.

Humility and *resignation* – these are the values of traditional morality; more particularly, they are the *Christian virtues*.

But how can what is *humiliating* become a criterion of virtue, or resignation, a criterion of wisdom?

What we have here are two reactions which are *evaluated differently*. For if Nietzsche merely means to say that *the 'good' of the agent is measured in terms of its resistance to harmful invasions*, which thereby affirms the strength of its will, he would be in complete agreement with traditional morality. But what Nietzsche wants to demonstrate is precisely that the latter is a *weakness*. What then are these harmful invasions? The impulses? But is not the will to power the supreme impulse? How, and since when, could it be harmful for Nietzsche?

No doubt he means that the absence, or cessation, of the strength necessary to resist what is harmful to existence – this strength (and hence the instinct for conservation) having just disappeared in the individual – provoked a censure that became more severe as the non-resistance became more common or more frequent. (We will see below that he again takes up and develops this motif of 'invasions' and the morality it provokes.)

But here again, Nietzsche's reflections become more ambiguous in the last paragraphs (see the *Nota bene*), where he imputes to morality, as a task it imposes, the weakening of *desires*, the desires of the will to power.

And since *desire* and *the will* to power are obviously *positive for Nietzsche*, it seems that *one point of view is substituted for another point of view* in the same fragment: the first was that strength consisted in resisting harmful invasions; the second, that *weakness had to give way to the will to power* manifest in the desire. Thus the criteria of *health* and *morbidity* have varied not only because there are 'differences in degree' between one state of existence and another – this aspect of the fragment is more straightforward and clear – but also because Nietzsche himself, in wanting to prove that *traditional morality* is the *negation* of life, continues to hesitate on the question of what *constitutes* the *power* and *impotence* of living – thus he is unable to decide for himself what exactly is harmful.

It is *excess* that makes manifest that which exists: power cannot *not* be produced in order to prove that it exists.

But if excess is merely an exaggerated state, a magnification of a normal state, then what is a normal state? If the terms *morbid* and *healthy* are simply defined as differences in degree between one state and another, as so many nuances made manifest in the fact of existing, where can we situate ourselves in order to avoid making completely arbitrary decisions about whether something is *strong* or *weak*?

In another fragment dating from the same period, Nietzsche again returns to the same theme in order to establish a more precise distinction between what is *morbid* or *healthy* – this time, in terms of the *real or false symptoms* of power, and hence in terms of the impotence that exists beneath the appearance of strength. It is an exact demonstration *a contrario* in relation to the previous fragment. But as in the latter, the digression begins with what is haunting Nietzsche himself – his own heredity. Above, he had already declared that what is *hereditary* is the *morbid state*, and not *sickness*.

Certainly, no matter how laden he may be with a harmful heredity, Nietzsche by no means interprets this as a '*heredity weakness as the cause of the supreme values*'. But does this mean that this weakness would clothe itself in the forms and explosions of a fallacious power? What he fears is that he will wind up as a type of human open to *the most dangerous misunderstanding*. This is what the other fragment is entitled:

The most dangerous misunderstanding. – One concept apparently permits no confusion or ambiguity: that of *exhaustion*. Exhaustion can be acquired or inherited – in any case it changes the aspect of things, the *value of things.* –

As opposed to those who, from the fullness they represent and feel, involuntarily *give* to things and see them fuller, more powerful, and pregnant with the future – who at least are able to bestow something – the exhausted diminish and botch all they see – they impoverish the value: they are harmful. –

About this no mistake seems possible: yet history contains the gruesome fact that the exhausted have always been mistaken for the fullest – and the fullest for the most harmful.

Those poor in life, the weak, impoverish life; those rich in life, the strong, enrich it. The first are parasites of life; the second give presents to it. – How is it possible to confound these two?

When the exhausted appeared with the gesture of the highest activity and energy (when degeneration effected an excess of spiritual and nervous discharge), they were mistaken for the rich. They excited fear. – The cult of the *fool* is always the cult of those rich in life, the powerful. The fanatic, the possessed, the religious epileptic, all eccentricities have been experiences as the highest types of power: as divine.

This kind of strength that excites *fear* was considered preeminently divine: here was the origin of authority; here one interpreted, heard, sought wisdom. – This led to the development, almost everywhere, of a *will* to 'deify', i.e., a will to the typical degeneration of spirit, body, and nerves: an attempt to find the way to this higher level of being. To make oneself sick, mad, to provoke the symptoms of derangement and ruin – that was taken for becoming stronger, more superhuman, more terrible, wiser. One thought that in this way one became so rich in power that one could give from one's fullness. Wherever one adored one sought one who could give.

Here the experience of intoxication proved misleading. This increases the feeling of power in the highest degree – therefore, naively judged, power itself. On the highest rung of power one places the most intoxicated, the ecstatic. (– There are two sources of intoxication: the over-great fullness of life and a state of pathological nourishment of the brain.).[79]

Nietzsche thus foresaw, with a rare premonition, the *conclusions* that posterity would draw from his own demise. He would be counted among those who, through exhaustion, adopt a *fallacious attitude of power*, who seek to inspire fear through a 'degenerate' pathos: who make themselves sick, mad, who provoke the symptoms of their own ruin – all in order to attain the supreme degree of the superhuman.

Now he will put himself forward as the object of the *cult* one renders to the *fool*. – Later, in *Ecce Homo*, he fears he will one day be canonized by the very people who commit this 'dangerous misunderstanding' of confusing the *exhausted* type with the *rich* type. And it is there that he calls himself a *marionette*, and later, the *buffoon of eternities*.

Between this fragment on '*the most dangerous misunderstanding*', which dates from the spring of 1888, and the writing of *Ecce Homo* in the winter of the same year, the lucidity that inspires this guardedness in him apparently waned. Indeed, it seems that, after the period of this fragment, Nietzsche reserved for himself alone at least one of the *modes of expression* that figure in his multiple registers. Whether or not the form of ecstasy produced by epileptic behaviour can be imputed to degeneration; whether or not the *interpretation* it traditionally elicits is due to the misleading experience of intoxication or delirium, which would then be confused with a high degree of power – it is nonetheless true, on the one hand, that it is open to *interpretation* and, on the other hand, that we cannot rule out the possibility that a delirious intoxication flows from an *excess of life*.

The last sentence of the fragment presents an alternative: *intoxication* can result from an exuberance of strength as much as from a morbid nourishment of the brain.

During the spring of 1888, the last 'lucid' spring that would be granted to Nietzsche, was it not his own *Dionysianism* that was placed in doubt by Nietzsche himself? – A perplexity that attested to his constant effort to keep one step ahead of the final due date. But how could this due date be postponed by the decision that would resolve his dilemma? Had he not already chosen it at the moment of his experience of the Return? And what was this censorship exercised on the tonalities of his own soul, if not his own will to the *authentic*, his adhesion to that which is in becoming? But this will to the authentic passed through his *hatred* of anything in himself that might betray the slightest complaisance *toward hatred*, toward *ressentiment*. Nietzsche feared he might be a *conditioned* being, as he thought he had been in his relationship with Wagner. What he extolled as divine impassibility – refraining from reacting – as an authentic force – was still a remnant of his *Apollinism*, and stood opposed to his association, and ultimate identification, with Dionysus. The *integrity* that assumed this divine name would never be able to admit such an *impassibility* for an instant. Thus, *strength itself is not impassible either.*

But the opposition in which Nietzsche situated the symptoms of exhaustion and richness once again obscured this distinction between the *strength of resistance* and the *necessity of yielding.*

Power is the strength of resistance: and thus also the capacity *to hold one's ground* against the impulses as if against external attacks. To react means to yield a certain amount of one's strength to a provocation. To act is to take the initiative, to rely on one's own intact strength.

How is the asceticism that Nietzsche advocates elsewhere a force of resistance? How can one claim that it is *exhaustion* that requires asceticism? Or that asceticism renounces hostility? How can one reproach it for *renouncing the anger* that Nietzsche, moreover, considers to be a *waste of energy*?

At times, the dangerous power is domesticated; at other times, it reaches a state of equilibrium with itself. *But what is the equilibrium* of power? The equilibrium will be upset every time power increases, and power cannot *not* increase. The richness that constitutes power is not first of all the result of a will; it lies in the very *nature* of that which wants *more than it has*. This richness is thus always insufficient insofar as one wills its mutiplication, its overcoming. If this richness produces an *excess* which must in turn produce a new excess in order to subsist – it then becomes increasingly difficult to distinguish it from the excess to which *exhaustion* refers.

Power *resists everything*, except that it cannot *resist itself*. It must act – as long as it is not reacting, it must provoke in order not to be provoked. This is why there is 'will' to power: power wills itself as power, and cannot *not* will itself. Now there is a *degree* beyond which the *will* disappears *in power*.

The *will* merely concerns the *agent*. Power, which belongs to life, to the cosmos – which represents a degree of accumulated and accumulating force – produces the agent, in accordance with its *rises and falls*. Thus wherever there would be a will to power, the agent would be sick or healthy: if it is sick, it succumbs to the impulse; if it is healthy, it succumbs to its *over-fullness*, but all the same it succumbs to the movement of a *power* that it confuses with its own will. One's resistance to the invading and uncontrolled forces is only a question of interpretation – and is always the result of an *arbitrary* decision.

Among Nietzsche's unpublished notes, there exist two other fragments in which this same antinomy reappears, and for which the solution is sought in analytic declarations.

In the first, Nietzsche discusses the ability to resist from the point of view of the *passions*, and, more particularly, the privileged conditions under which the passions can be experienced positively. In the second, from the same point of view, Nietzsche insists on their *decadent* and thus hereditary character, an example of which is furnished by the *Parisian erotism* of the period. The first is entitled:

Morality as Decadence, 'senses', 'passions'. Fear of the senses, of the desires, of the passions, when it goes so far as to counsel us against them, is already a symptom of weakness: extreme measures always indicate abnormal conditions. What is lacking, or crumbling, here is the strength to restrain an impulse: if one's instinct is to have to succumb, i.e., to *have* to react, then one does well to avoid the opportunities ('seductions') for it.

A 'stimulation of the senses' is a seduction only for those whose system is too easily moved and influenced: in the opposite case, that of a system of great slowness and severity, strong stimuli are needed to get the functions going.

Excess is a reproach only against those who have no right to it; and almost all the passions have been brought into ill repute on account of those who were not sufficiently strong to employ them –

One must understand that the same objections can be made to the passions as are made to sickness: nonetheless – we cannot do without sickness, and even less without the passions. We *need* the abnormal, we give life a tremendous *choc* by these great sicknesses.

In detail, the following must be distinguished:

1. *the dominating passion*, which even brings with it the supremest form of health; here the co-ordination of the inner systems and their operation in the service of one end is best achieved – but this is almost the definition of health!

2. the antagonism of the passions; two, three, a

multiplicity of 'souls in one breast': very unhealthy, inner ruin, disintegration, betraying and increasing and inner conflict and anarchism – unless one passion at last becomes master. *Return to health* –

3. juxtaposition without antagonism or collaboration: often periodic, and then, as soon as an order has been established, also unhealthy. The most interesting men, the chameleons, belong here; they are not in contradiction with themselves, they are happy and secure, but they do not develop – their differing states lie juxtaposed, even if they are separated sevenfold. They change, they do not *become*.[80]

The first half of this fragment takes up more clearly the theme of non-resistance to harmful invasions – which, in the first of the previously cited fragments, Nietzsche had formulated in a manner that was both obscure and contradictory. In the earlier fragment, it was a question of demonstrating the unhealthy ground [*fond*] of traditional morality; but here, in a certain manner, he insists more on the 'constructive' utilization of one's 'personal' life, and explains moral concepts in terms of the frequent failure of this utilization. The line of thought that guides him here is much closer to Goethe than to himself. As for Nietzsche's own point of view, it becomes increasingly pragmatic, notwithstanding its own antinomies, precisely because of his plan to try to elaborate a doctrine of the will to power.

Here again, the overriding idea is that the meaning of the affects lies in their hierarchical unity. Whatever one's *dominant passion* may be, the essential point is that it ensures the strength of one's nature. What Nietzsche applauds in this movement toward cohesion is its *efficacy*, which he classifies as health. *What he fears most is exactly what he sees deep in himself: a mutual antagonism* of the passions, a multiplicity of souls in one breast, which points to an internal ruin. At the moment he experienced the *Return*, however, what he was praising as a principle of plurality, and indeed of metamorphosis, was the *necessity of passing through a series of different individuals*. But now, in the third paragraph, he is opposing this to what he defines as the *juxtaposition of different passionel states*. If he here distinguishes between *changing* and *becoming*, it is because, for Nietzsche, only *the intensity of a all-consuming passion* metamorphoses into a 'unity' – whereas 'chameleons', rather than bearing witness to a contradictory tension, merely offer a simulacrum of it. Once again, this is what had preoccupied Nietzsche ever since the failure of his adventure with Lou: to maintain his cohesion at any price; and with all the more urgency insofar as he has a foreboding of what he calls his 'internal ruin'.

Another fragment again concerns the inability to resist under the term of exhaustion – but here it is an acquired, and not a hereditary, exhaustion. He takes erotic *precociousness* as an example:

> Erotic precociousness: the curse in particular of French youth, above all in Paris, who emerge into the world from their *lycées* botched and soiled and never free themselves again from the chain of contemptible inclinations, ironical and disdainful toward themselves – galley slaves with all refinements (incidentally, in most cases already a symptom of the decadence of race and family, like all hypersensitivity; also the contagion of the milieu – to let oneself be determined by one's environment is *decadent*).[81]

The criterion of 'continence', which is presupposed by this denunciation of an unhealthy precociousness – even if it is a purely pragmatic criterion that implies an economy of impulses – nonetheless makes this one of the most betrayingly revelatory of Nietzsche's fragments: he too has known the slavery of galley slaves.

The libidinal forces, which played such a deadly trick on Nietzsche, nourished his own aggressiveness and turned them against himself. The other face of this aggressiveness remained masked for a long time. His entire debate about what is *healthy* and *unhealthy*, what is *exhausted* and *rich*, found its root here. Wagner's *Parsifal* was necessary for these forces to be identified as his own – the detour through an adversary was required. Their final explosion, the emergence of a Dionysian *satyr*, the divine animality, then provoked the 'collapse' of the *censor*.

Harmful invasions, like those of *power*, always go beyond the agent, that is, the individual. Thus, they are harmful to the purely defensive and gregarious impulses, which are elaborated by traditional morality as repressive phantasms.

5

Attempt at a Scientific Explanation of the Eternal Return

A double preoccupation seemed to agitate Nietzsche after the experience of Sils-Maria.

The verification of the lived fact by science would reassure him of his own lucidity, and at the same time it would provide him with a formulation that would be intelligible and compelling to others as much as to himself.

Now since it was a question of a high tonality of the soul, Nietzsche maintained that its thought attested to his own singularity: the unintelligible depth remained the criterion of the unexchangeable.

In his letters to Gast and Overbeck, written shortly after the event, Nietzsche, without betraying the thought of thoughts, was already speaking of the *effect* its disclosure would produce. Once disclosed, how would the content of a high tonality of the soul – namely, its depth of intensity – act upon human destiny apart from his own? Would it change the course of history? Had he not said, during this period, that its disclosure would *break the history of humanity in two*?

The ecstasy of the Eternal Return involved both an *evident fact* and, through its *content*, a possible explication (the suppression of individual identity, and the series of individualities to be passed through). As a thought, then, it implied the *hypothesis* of a *metamorphosis* based on pre-existence.

This hypothesis allowed for the following argument, which Nietzsche would develop later.

A single individual, as the product of an entire evolution, could never *reactualize* all the conditions and random events that led to his own consciousness. It is only in admitting his own *fortuitousness* that an individual will be open to the *totality of fortuitous cases*, and thus will conceive of his past as the future: the necessity of returning in the Circle, in which he will relive the series of cases and chance events that have led to the revelatory moment.

But as a hypothesis, this thought was *suspect*: it borrowed the means for developing the *evidence* – in itself *undemonstrable* – of the revelatory ecstasy from the schema of metamorphosis and pre-existence, which are both implicit in the condition of the return. In this form, which requires belief, the return would be an instance of what Lou called religious prophetism. And Nietzsche himself had said to Overbeck: '*if it is true or only believed to be true*' – a truthfulness that merely concerned the consequences of its repercussion as a doctrine. But in Nietzsche's mind, it had not yet achieved a doctrinal form – the secret experience remained an experience whose only evidence lay in its *intensity*.

At first sight, Nietzsche did not succeed in explaining his thought in a manner that would be totally free from what he termed *passive nihilism* – that is, the propensity toward the *non-sense* of life. In order for this propensity toward *non-sense* to mature into *the affirmation of life itself*, fatalism had to be pushed to the *extreme* point of *active* nihilism. But how could adherence to the Eternal Return not be *active* in itself?

Another motif seemed to have intervened in Nietzsche's hesitation. Did not the very experience of the Eternal Return bear witness, in Nietzsche, *to what he himself had denounced* as *exhaustion*? Was he or was he not a victim of what he called *the most dangerous misunderstanding* – namely, that the *symptoms* of exhaustion would be confused with those of an excess or overabundance of life? And did not this distinction, at once equivocal and lucid, confirm Nietzsche in his description of *decadence* and *vigour* – terms that had led him to distinguish, at the human level, his own level, between what was morbid and what was healthy, and thus between states of power or the lack of power, that is to say, between non-resistance and the strength to resist? Was it necessary to attribute to power the positing of a goal or the interpretation of a meaning? Or on the contrary, was not the very fact of believing in a goal or a meaning a manifestation of pure impotence? *Did not the greatest strength lie in living absurdly, in affirming the value of life apart from any signification and goal?* Why had the *Eternal Return*, which was experienced *in a moment* where all such questions disappeared, not *subsisted* as such in his thought – as *the thought of thoughts*? Why, if not because the *will to power*, according to this equivocal distinction between sickness and health, thus according to this equivocal distinction for itself, required *a goal* and *a meaning*, whereas *meaninglessness* was in itself the supreme violence. In keeping with this violence, it was necessary to choose between an *absolute muteness* (the muteness of the lived fact and the past) – or *speech* – and thus to re-establish the identity of the ego and, through that, the goal and the meaning.

IS THE THOUGHT OF THE ETERNAL RETURN IN NIETZSCHE RELATED TO THE PREMONITORY FEELING OF MADNESS?
Lou A. Salomé described the manner in which Nietzsche confided his secret to her as follows:

> Unforgettable for me are those hours in which he first confided to me his secret, whose inevitable fulfillment and validation he anticipated with shudders. Only with a quiet voice and with all the signs of deepest horror did he speak about this secret. Life, in fact, produced such suffering in him that the certainty of an eternal return of life had to mean something horrifying to him.

The quintessence of the teaching of eternal recurrence, later constructed by Nietzsche as a shining apotheosis to life, formed such a deep contrast to his own painful feelings about life that it gives us intimations of being an uncanny mask. Nietzsche was to become the harbinger of teachings that could only be endured by way of a love that outweighs life and would only be effective at the point where the thought of man soars up to a deification of life. In truth, all this must have been in contradiction to his innermost perceptions – a contradiction that finally destroyed him. Everything that Nietzsche thought, felt and experienced after the origination of his eternal recurrence concept arises from his inner split. Everything then moved between two poles: 'to curse, with gritted teeth, the demon of eternal life' and the awaiting of that 'tremendous moment' which lends power to the words, '*you [demon] are a god and I never heard anything more divine!*'

At that time, the recurrence idea had not as yet become a conviction in Nietzsche's mind, but only a suspicion. He had the intention of heralding it when and if it could be founded scientifically. We exchanged a series of letters about this matter, and Nietzsche constantly expressed the mistaken opinion that it would be possible to win for it an indisputable basis through physics experiments. It was he who decided at that time to devote ten years of exclusive study to the natural sciences at the University of Vienna or Paris. Then, after ten years of absolute silence, he would – in the event that his own surmise were to be substantiated, as he feared – step among people again as the teacher of the doctrine of eternal recurrence.[82]

Lou thus saw a contradiction between the revelation of 'the secret of the Eternal Return' and the suffering Nietzsche had experienced in his life. This suffering was compounded by the fact that he was, if not convinced, at least haunted by the possibility that the return of life (as such) would be a universal and thus necessary law.

The contradiction that Lou saw here merely concerned Nietzsche's painful life, his agonized experience of life. This was a strictly rational point of view. How can one re-will suffering? How can one tolerate the thought of reliving it millions and millions of times? Moreover, these were considerations that Nietzsche himself had developed with regard to the selective power of his doctrine's disclosure.

What was the meaning of this search for a *scientific foundation* — which Lou correctly designated as an error — and the fact that Nietzsche *was afraid of finding one*? Nietzsche hoped to rid himself of the horror and fear that his own idea inspired in him; when confiding to Lou (or to Overbeck), his fear was made manifest in *the tone of his voice*. But for this idea to be both horrible *and exhilarating*, there was also a second factor: *the very fact of having had this very idea*, of having received it as a revelation. For who was capable of receiving such an idea? Only a delirious intelligence. Nietzsche no doubt believed he had gone mad since he had received this thought. To prove the contrary to himself, he wanted to appeal to science, he expected from science a proof that he was not the victim of a pure phantasm. The vertigo of the *Eternal Return* concerned not only the universe and humanity — but Nietzsche himself, the power of his own thought, his own lucidity. Is it conceivable that, in himself, Nietzsche understood the thought of the Return as his own madness, and thus as *the loss of his lucidity*? Lou touched on this question when she suggested that there was something personally contradictory about the notion of the Return: *a disquieting mask* — and thus a means of concealing behind an ontological problem a completely different problem of a psychological nature. Nietzsche could not accept anything he could not will — something compelled him to contradict himself. Now it may be true that Nietzsche, under the pretext of being terrorized by the thought of the Return, had simply wanted to suggest or express in veiled terms his fear of his own madness: how would others react if he put forward such an idea? This is why he wanted it to be kept secret – it enveloped his apprehension about losing his reason under the supposed scruple of disclosing a doctrine whose diffusion, he believed, would result in the waste of a great number of people.

Lou's presumption that Nietzsche suffered *even more* from life to the degree that he was terrified by the infinite repetition of suffering in his conception of the Eternal Return was an 'all-too-human' argument for Nietzsche's own thought. Moreover, it was hardly any more *convincing* than Nietzsche's own idea about the selective force of the doctrine, whose pretext was that the greater part of humanity could not tolerate the thought. On the contrary, he himself had insisted too much on the intensive and thus 'vital' character of suffering not to see in the Return the strength of the desire that is affirmed in it.

Finally, Lou seemed to neglect completely the crucial point of the revelation of the *Return*. What was preoccupying Nietzsche at the same time, and what he presented almost as a corollary to his doctrine, was the *necessity for the individual to live again in a series of different individualities*. Hence the richness of the Return: to will to be *other* than you are in order to become what you are. To be lucid, an individuality is necessary. Only the experience of identity itself can blossom into a lucidity capable of conceiving the overcoming of identity, and hence its loss. Everything Nietzsche expressed through the heroic nostalgia of his own decline – the will to disappear – stemmed from this lucidity. Nonetheless, this nostalgia was inseparable from his anguish over the loss of a lucid identity. This is why the thought of the Return both exhilarated and terrified him: not the idea of reliving the same sufferings sempiternally, as Lou interpreted it, but rather the loss of reason under the sign of the Vicious Circle.

In the days after his painful adventure with Lou, which followed the experience of Sils-Maria, Nietzsche tried to snap out of a *state of passivity* and pure emotional receptivity. What he had just lived through, between 1881 and 1882 – including the great richness implied in the very *suffering* of this period – would remain a dupery if, at least in his thought, the lived fact did not make him capable of a decision. His own valetudinary states led him back to the notion of the will to power, which he began to elaborate anew without renouncing the *thought of thoughts*. The moment of extreme passivity, presupposed in the ecstasy of Sils-Maria, was surmounted by becoming a thought. But the thought was only a residue of the experience; it had to become the starting-point for an *action*; and this action would depend on the *magnum opus* that would set out the programme for this action. The demonstration of the law of the Return had displaced the content of the experience, and henceforth had to serve as the reference point for a kind of determinate *action*.

The search for a scientific argument did not affect Nietzsche's own mode of expression, which would now diverge in two directions that were foreign to each other. First, there was the pure poetic creation, the parabolic expression of his experience, through the *character* of *Zarathustra* – a creation in which Lou no doubt played a decisive role by trying to dissuade him from an explanation based on the discoveries of science. But this poem, with its dithyrambic style, was essentially a book of *sentences* whose bombastic movement alternates with riddles and their resolution in images: a *mise-en-scène* of the *thought* in wordplays and similitudes. It would later become apparent that Zarathustra is a buffoon in the guise of a false prophet, an imposter proclaiming the simulacrum of a doctrine.

Having produced this character, Nietzsche, under the cover of a creation unique in its genre, would again give himself over to the aporias of his own thought. He did so because *Zarathustra* had by no means relieved him of his obsession with the terrible distress Lou's flight had caused in him, and whose effects were still evident. *Zarathustra* was composed on a different level. The fact that he maintained himself through it all seemed to him to have been a miracle.

During this period, Nietzsche was overwhelmed by the obsession to produce a *magnum opus*. Certainly, the sentences and songs of Zarathustra would now serve as his points of reference; nothing exists elsewhere, he says, that has not already been inscribed in this prophetic work. The need to provide a 'systematic' commentary to his prophecy became even more imperative. The unintelligible evidence of the Sils-Maria ecstasy, the implicit intensity of the vertigo of the Return – in a word, the *high tonality of the soul* – was no longer Nietzsche's alone, but would be *mimed* by Zarathustra's *bombastic gesticulations*. But if Zarathustra was the prelude to the *breaking in two* of humanity, not only did the book's creation not bring about this rupture (since it still remained in the sphere of the unintelligible), but what is more, Zarathustra's miming of the *high tonality* seemed to ridicule Nietzsche's distress and make a mockery of it.

CORRESPONDENCE

To Overbeck

Nice, early March 1884

Heavens! Who knows what is wrong with me and what force I need to sustain myself! I don't exactly know how I have come to this – but it is possible that for the *first time* a thought has come to me that will break the history of humanity in two.

This *Zarathustra* is only the prologue, the preamble, the vestibule – I had to encourage myself, since only discouragement came to me from all sides: to encourage myself to *bear* this thought! for I am still far from being able to utter it and represent it. IF IT IS TRUE or rather if it is BELIEVED TO BE TRUE – then all things would be modified and would return, and all values hitherto will be devalued.[83]

In his debate concerning *exhaustion* and *overabundance* and their *symptoms* – relative to the notions of decadence and vigour – Nietzsche had evoked the force of the impulses as power and as 'will' to power, notably in the sense of a resistance or non-resistance to the invasion of dissolving forces.

In examining the mechanistic conception (newly the order of the day), Nietzsche found in it all the difficulties raised by the structure of the universe – in particular that of the equilibrium or non-equilibrium of energy, and its loss or conservation. But when, in speaking of non-equilibrium – the proof of eternal movement – he emphasized the condition of *a new distribution of forces*; or when, in criticizing the mechanistic conception as inevitably anthropomorphic, he pointed to the analogy between the behaviour of the atom and the 'subject' – what was important to him was the fact that *every power draws its ultimate consequence at every moment*; that a quantum of power is defined by the action it exerts and by that which it resists; that this *quantum* is essentially *a will to do violence* and to defend itself against all violence, and *not self-preservation*; and that every atom affects the whole of being, which would be thought away if we did not conceive of this radiation of the *will to power*.

[My theory would be: –] that *the will to power is the primitive form of affect*, that *all other affects* are only developments of it;

that it is notably enlightening to posit power in place of individual 'happiness' (after which every living thing is supposed to be striving): 'there is a striving for power, for *an increase of power*'; – pleasure is only a symptom of the feeling of power attained, a consciousness of a difference (– there is no striving for pleasure: but pleasure supervenes when that which is being striven for is attained: pleasure is an accompaniment, pleasure is not the motive –);

that all driving force is will to power, that there is no other physical, dynamic or psychic force except this.

In our science, where the concept of cause and effect
is reduced to the relationship of equivalence, with the
object of proving that the same quantum of force is
present on both sides, the driving force is lacking: we
observe only results, and we consider them equivalent
in content and force –

It is simply a matter of experience that change *never
ceases*: we have not the slightest inherent reason for
assuming that one change must follow upon another.
On the contrary: a condition once achieved would
seem to be obliged to preserve itself if there were
not in it a capacity for desiring *not* to preserve itself –
Spinoza's law of 'self-preservation' ought really to put a
stop to change: but this law is false, the opposite is true.
It can be shown most clearly that every living thing does
everything it can not to preserve itself but to become
more – [84]

Is 'will to power' a kind of 'will' or identical with
the concept 'will'? Is it the same thing as desiring? or
commanding? Is it that 'will' of which Schopenhauer said
it was the 'in-itself of things'?

My proposition is: that the will of psychology
hitherto is an unjustified generalization, that this will
does not exist at all, that instead of grasping the idea of the
development of one *definite will* into many forms, one
has eliminated the character of the will by subtracting
from it its content, its *'whither?'* – this is in the highest
degree the case with Schopenhauer: what he calls 'will'
is a mere empty word. It is even less a question of a *'will
to live'*; for life is merely a special case of the will to
power; – it is quite arbitrary to assert that everything
strives to enter into *this form* of the will to power.

There is neither 'mind', nor reason, nor thought, nor
consciousness, nor soul, nor will, nor truth: so many
useless fictions. It is not a matter of 'subject' or 'object',

but of a certain animal species who thrives because of a *justice*, and above all *regularity relative* to its perceptions (so that it can capitalize on its own experience).[85]

As a primordial impulse – this is what must be emphasized – the will to power is the term that expresses *force itself*. If the will to power appears in the human species and the phenomenon of animality – that is to say, in the phenomenon of the 'living being' – as a 'special' case, and thus as an 'accident' of its essence, it *will not be conserved* in the species or the individual it acts upon, but by its very nature will disrupt the conservation of an attained level, since by necessity it will always exceed this level through its own increase. Thus, for everything that might want to preserve itself at a certain degree, whether a society or an individual, *the will to power appears essentially as a principle of disequilibrium*. And insofar as knowledge accompanies power and increases in proportion to acquired power, knowledge (and thus culture as well) must in turn disrupt the equilibrium of a determined state; however, says Nietzsche, knowledge will never be anything more than an instrument of conservation – for there will always be a *discordance* between the excess of (the will to) power and the feeling of security that knowledge procures.

In all this, Nietzsche was at first sight putting forward nothing that would contradict his 'notion' of the Eternal Return. Even better, the definition of the will to power as the primordial impulse would still confirm the revelation of the Vicious Circle. For if '*life invented this thought in order to surmount its own obstacle*'; and if this 'power', which inspires in the individual a 'will' that exceeds the individual, revealed itself in the sign of the Vicious Circle as an incessant movement – it would also be readying the individual *to will its own annihilation* as an individual by teaching the individual to exceed itself by re-willing itself, and to re-will itself only in the name of this *insatiable* power.

The *Eternal Return* would here form the counterpart to knowledge, which, if it increases in proportion to power, nonetheless has the *conservation* of the species as its major preoccupation.

Now the *Eternal Return* (as the expression of a *becoming* with neither goal nor purpose) makes knowledge 'impossible', at least with regard to ends, and always keeps knowledge at the level of *means*: the means of conserving itself. This in turn is what determines the reality principle, which therefore is always a variable principle. But not only does the Eternal Return not determine reality, it suspends the very principle of reality, and in a certain manner leaves it to the discretion of the more or less felt degree of power – or better, to its intensity.

The Eternal Return lies *at the origin of the rises and falls of intensity* to which it reduces intention. Once it is conceived of as the *return of power* – that is to say, as a *series* of *disruptions of equilibrium* – the question then arises of knowing whether, in Nietzsche's thought, the Return is simply a pure *metaphor* for the *will to power*.

FOUR FRAGMENTS

The first fragment no doubt presents one of the most wide-ranging projects in which Nietzsche tried to integrate his own experience of the Return into a universal and historical system. The schematic indications of the preamble,* in which he reverses the traditional perspectives and moves of philosophy and science, define his position on almost every fundamental point. The most characteristic one is his proposal to substitute for *sociology* his notion of *formations of sovereignty*. This fragment – and in particular, his idea that the supreme degree of *spiritualization* would correspond to the high point of energy (God) or the lowest point of disorganization –

---

* 'Fundamental innovations' – according to Schlechta's reading. In fact, according to the final reading established by Colin and Montinari, the five paragraphs form a separate fragment. But this fragment figures in the same series as the one that begins with 'God as moment of culmination'. This latter fragment, nonetheless, is preceded by the fragment that begins 'Excess force . . .'.

will serve as our point of reference as we follow Nietzsche through his various attempts to develop his doctrine.

The second fragment, which is presented as a variant of the first, again takes up the term *God* and uses it as *an expression equivalent to the maximum of energy* – within the historical framework of an *epoch*.

The third and fourth fragments establish an equivalence between the behaviour of *energy* and the will to power. They contain the most precise reference to the intensity of the soul's tonality in the experience of the Return. But at the same time, they again pose certain difficulties with regard to the coherence of the doctrine Nietzsche wants to develop, once they return to the level of human societies (formations of sovereignty), and once Nietzsche introduces a notion of *will* to power as manifested in organic life. For in the latter case, the will to a goal and a *meaning*, which is necessary to the power of sovereign formations, finds itself in a discordant relationship with *the absence of a goal and of a meaning* that characterizes the behaviour of quantitative energy and, more particularly, the very 'sign' of the vicious Circle as Eternal Return. In effect, if the will to power lies at the origin of every manifestation of existence, and is subjacent to any and every aspiration, we can no longer speak of either a goal or a meaning in itself: an action due to a relation of forces suppresses the very notion of *cause and effect*. 'There are only the consequences of something unforeseen, and because something can be calculated afterwards does not mean that it is necessary. In this case, a goal is reached only by a combination of random events.'[86]

This conception of the will to power that *does not seek to preserve its level* but *can only increase or decrease* is the analogue of *an energy that cannot tolerate the state of equilibrium*. What is the goal and meaning of this will? To always remain the strongest. Now if it increases, it must destroy its obstacle. If it *exceeds* its agent, it will destroy the agent, that is, the agent will no longer be able to bear it. This consideration is the result of the same remark: power *does not lie in self-preservation*.

This point is in agreement, on the other hand, with the lived intensity of the experience of the Eternal Return, which casts the agent that experiences it outside of itself. But the entire paradox of the will to power, inasmuch as it would depend on the circular movement of energy, manifests itself as soon as Nietzsche believes he has uncovered it in organic life – and more particularly, at the level of human societies.

First Fragment

Fundamental innovations: In place of '*moral values*', purely *naturalistic* values. *Naturalization* of morality.

In place of 'sociology', a theory of the *formations of sovereignty*.

In place of 'society', the *culture complex*, as *my* chief interest (as a whole relative to its parts).

In place of 'epistemology', a *perspective theory of affects* (to which belongs a hierarchy of the affects; the affects transfigured; their *superior order*, their '*spirituality*').

In place of 'metaphysics' and religion, the *doctrine of the Eternal Return* (this as a means of training and selection).[87]

'God' as the moment of culmination: existence an eternal deifying and un-deifying. But in that *not a culminating point of value*, but culminating points of power.

Absolute *exclusion* of *mechanism* and *matter*: both are only expressions of lesser degrees, the most despiritualized form of affect (of 'will to power').

Retreat from the *culminating point in becoming* (the highest spiritualization of power on the most slavish ground) to be represented as a *consequence* of this highest energy, which, *turning against itself* when it no longer has anything left to organize, expends its force *on disorganization* –

a. The ever-increasing *conquest* of societies and subjection of them by a smaller but more powerful number;

b. the ever-increasing conquest of the privileged and stronger and the consequent rise of democracy, and ultimately *anarchy* of the elements.[88]

Excess force in spirituality, setting itself new goals; but *by no means* merely commanding and leading on behalf of the lower world or the preservation of the organism, the 'individual'.

We are *more* than individuals: we are the whole chain as well, with the tasks of all the futures of that chain.[89]

Second Fragment

The sole way of maintaining a meaning for the concept 'God' would be: God *not* as the driving force, but God as a *maximal state*, as an *epoch* — a point in the evolution of the *will to power* by means of which further evolution just as much as previous evolution *'up to him'* could be explained.

Regarded mechanistically, the energy of the totality of becoming remains constant; regarded economically, it rises to a high point and sinks down again in an eternal circle. This *'will to power'* expresses itself in the *interpretation*, in the manner in which force is *used up*; transformation of energy into life, and 'life at its highest potency', thus appears as the goal. The same quantum of energy means different things at different stages of evolution.

That which constitutes vigour in life is an ever more thrifty and more far-seeing economy, which achieves more and more with less and less force — As an ideal, the principle of the smallest expenditure —

That the world is not *striving* toward a *stable condition* is *the only thing that has been proved*. Consequently one *must* conceive its climactic condition in such a way that it is not a condition of equilibrium —

The absolute necessity of similar events occurring in the course of one world, as in all others, is in eternity *not* a determinism ruling events, but merely the expression of the fact that the impossible is not possible; that a certain force cannot be anything other than this certain force; that it can react to a quantum of resisting force only according to the measure of its strength; – event and necessary event is a *tautology*.[90]

Third Fragment

Critique of the mechanistic theory. – Let us here dismiss the two popular concepts '*necessity*' and 'law': the former introduces a false constraint into the world, the latter a false freedom. 'Things' do not behave regularly, according to a rule: there are no things (– they are fictions invented by us); they behave just as little under the constraint of necessity. There is no obedience here: for that *something is as it is*, as strong or as weak, is not the consequence of an obedience or a rule or a compulsion –

The degree of resistance and the degree of superior power – this is the question in every event: if, for our day-to-day calculations, we know how to express this in formulas and 'laws', so much the better for us! But we have not introduced any 'morality' into the world by the fiction that it is obedient –.

There is no law: *every power draws its ultimate consequence at every moment*. Calculability exists precisely because things are unable to be other than they are.

A *quantum of power is designated by the effect it produces and that which it resists. The adiaphorous state* is missing, though it is thinkable. It is essentially *a will to violate and to defend oneself against violation. Not self-preservation: every atom affects the whole of being* – it is thought away if one thinks away this *radiation of power-will*. That is why I call it a quantum of 'will to power': it expresses the characteristic that cannot be thought out of the mechanistic order without thinking away this order itself.

A translation of this *world of effect* into a visible world

– a world for the eyes – is the conception 'motion'. This always carries the idea that something is *moved* – this always supposes, whether as the fiction of a little clump of atom or even as the abstraction of this, the dynamic atom, a thing that produces effects – i.e., we have not got away from thc habit into which our senses and language seduce us. Subject, object, a doer added to the doing, the doing separated from that which it does: let us not forget that this is mere semeiotics and nothing real. Mechanistic theory as a theory of *motion* is already *a translation* into *the sense language* of man.

We need 'unities' in order to be able to reckon: that does not mean we must suppose that such unities exist. We have borrowed the concept of unity from our 'ego' concept – our oldest article of faith. If we did not hold ourselves to be unities, we would never have formed the concept 'thing'. Now, somewhat late, we are firmly convinced that our conception of the ego does not guarantee any actual unity. In order to sustain the theory of a mechanistic world, therefore, we always have to stipulate to what extent we are employing two fictions: the concept of motion (taken from our sense language) and the concept of the atom (= unity, deriving from our psychical 'experience'): the mechanistic theory presupposes a *sense prejudice* and a *psychological prejudice*.[91]

Fourth Fragment

The fact that a state of equilibrium is never reached proves that it is not possible. But in an indefinite space it would have to have been reached. Likewise in a spherical space. The *shape of space* must be the *cause* of eternal *movement*, and ultimately of all 'imperfection'. That 'force' and 'rest', 'remaining the same', contradict one another. The measure of force (as magnitude) as fixed, but its essence in flux.

'Timelesses' to be rejected. *At any precise moment of a*

*force, the absolute conditionality of a new distribution of all its
forces is given: it cannot stand still. 'Change' belongs to the
essence, therefore also temporality: with this, however,
the necessity of change has only been posited once more
conceptually.*[92]

In these passages on energy, which concern the structure of
the world, there is no term that could not be immediately
applied to the psychic state, that is, to the world of the
impulses. Nor is there any term that, thus applied, could not
define the psychic state in its relationship with an 'external'
event. At a given moment of the accumulated force of the
emotions, there is also *the absolute condition of a new distribution*,
and hence *a disruption of equilibrium*. Nietzsche conceives of
a universal economy whose effects he experiences in his
own moods.

Will to Power and Causalism. – From a psychological
point of view the concept 'cause' is our feeling of power
resulting from the so-called act of will – our concept
'effect' the superstition that this feeling of power is the
motive power itself –

A condition that accompanies an event and is itself an
effect of the event is projected as the 'sufficient reason'
for the event; – the relation of tensions in our feeling of
power (pleasure as the feeling of power), of a resistance
overcome – are they illusions? –

If we translate the concept 'cause' back to the only
sphere known to us, from which we have derived it,
we cannot imagine any *change* that does not involve
a will to power. We do not know how to explain
a change except as the *encroachment of one power upon
another power*.

Mechanics shows us only the results, and then only
in images (motion is a figure of speech). Gravity itself
has no mechanistic cause, since it itself is the ground of
mechanistic results.

The will to *accumulate force* is special to the phenomena of life, to nourishment, procreation, inheritance – to society, state, custom, authority. Should we not be permitted to assume this will as a motive cause in chemistry, too? – and in the cosmic order?

Not merely conservation of energy, but maximal economy in use, so the only reality is *the will to grow stronger of every centre of force* – *not* self-preservation, but the will to appropriate, dominate, increase, grow stronger.

The possibility of science should be proved by a single *principle of causality*? 'From like cause like effects' – 'A permanent law governing things' – 'An invariable order'? – Because something is calculable, does that mean it is necessary?

If something happens thus and not otherwise, that does not imply a 'principle', 'law', 'order', [but the operation of] *quanta* of energy the essence of which consists in exercising power against other *quanta* of energy.

Can we assume a striving for power divorced from a sensation of pleasure and displeasure, i.e., divorced from the feeling of enhanced or diminished power? Is mechanism only a sign language for the internal factual world of struggling and conquering *quanta* of will? All the presuppositions of mechanistic theory – matter, atom, gravity, pressure, and stress – are not 'facts-in-themselves' but interpretations with the aid of *psychical fictions.*

Life, as the form of being most familiar to us, is specifically a will to the accumulation of force; all the processes of life depend on this: nothing wants to preserve itself, everything is to be added and accumulated.

Life as a special case (hypothesis based upon it applied to the total character of being –) strives after *a maximal feeling of power;* essentially a striving for more power; the basic and innermost thing is still this will. (Mechanics is merely the semiotics of the results.)[93]

No doubt *the intensity of the soul's tonality* and *the behaviour of energy* could each refer to the other: as a flux and afflux of power, they would signify each other through the Vicious Circle *without goal or meaning*. Neither energy nor intensity seeks *to endure*; there is only increase and decrease, rise and fall.

But the behaviour of organisms is completely different. For here again, if power increases, it ends in the pleasure of an accomplishment, as both a *meaning* and a *goal* realized in *the duration of a whole*. And even though what science discovered in the organic world was the convertibility of energy and a coexistence of forces of different orders, it is certain that what Nietzsche found in the latter, in accordance with the laws of increase and decline, was an image not only of power but of the *will* to power, subject here to a *goal* and a *meaning* whose very energy in itself remains destitute. And even though this 'will' is only an impulsive reaction to an excitation, or the discharge of a force accumulated by the organism, nevertheless the representation of this excitation or this discharge of force at the level of the organism is still interpreted as a *goal* and a *meaning*.

What Nietzsche sought from the experience of the *Return of all things* – namely, *to lead intention back to intensity* – was still confirmed in this notion of energy without goal or meaning.

Now since it was a question of willing more than of power; and since, in accordance with the imperative of the Return, it was a question of re-willing life in terms of intensity; then as soon as his examination of the theory of energy concurred with that of biology, namely, relative to *the growth and decline of organisms*, Nietzsche in turn applied them to the life of societies and individuals (the former to be decomposed in favour of the latter). Conforming to its own aspirations, Nietzsche demanded from both phenomena a contradictory demonstration of his own doctrine: if the same power, *devoid of any meaning or goal* as energy, was rediscovered in the life of organisms and at the historical level of human societies as a *will* (to power) pursuing *a goal* (which, in order to endure, is subject to the *meaning* these organisms give themselves), it was necessary for this *will* to have had *another object than this power* as energy devoid of any goal or meaning. *Energy cannot maintain a state of equilibrium*, it is forbidden to do so by the movement of the Circle that designates it; organic life seeks an equilibrium and struggles a long time to find it; and finally, the individual that results from the impatience of the first and the insecurity of the second winds up in a state of ill-being. Because of this ill-being, Nietzsche was determined to inscribe a goal and a meaning in the Vicious Circle, without for all that admitting that the *Circle* would itself be this *goal and this meaning*.

'Excess force in *spirituality* setting *itself* new goals . . .'[94]

Power must be given a goal, and thus must set free a meaning, in order to overcome the absurd movement of the Eternal Return, so that this absurdity will not give force a pretext to *disorganize* (nihilism).

Once the *will* to power is given a goal, once it requires a *meaning*, once *our futures* hold *new tasks* in store for us, the *thought of thoughts* (the Eternal Return) singularly changes nature. The very anthropomorphism he was fighting against, and which he criticized even in the most 'objective' theories of science, was now reintroduced by Nietzsche himself – he became an accomplice, certainly not in order to safeguard human feeling, but rather to 'overcome' it, as he said; in fact, to dehumanize thought.

The culminating point of universal energy – 'God' as an *epoch* – but as the '*spiritualization*' of power – *would this point coincide with the high tonality of the soul*, with the tonal intensity of the Sils-Maria ecstasy?

It seems that the opposite is the case. For at the moment the loss of universal energy reverberates in the moral sphere of the human as a 'despiritualization', namely, at the intellectual and social level through nihilism – thus through destruction, 'because there is *no longer anything to organize*' – it is awakened, in the isolated individual, as the ultimate *resonance* between the *culminating point* and the *lowest point*. But to interpret the *culminating* point as the *lowest point* is only a retrospective interpretation. It gives an account of the *willed* confusion between a universal economy of forces, in themselves *without intention,* and a state of the soul that would feel *their insignificance.* To the degree that the soul *signifies* this resonance, it experiences it as a vertigo before an abyss – or as an anguish provoked by the imminence of *Chaos* (*abyss* or *Chaos* here being the terms through which inconsistency is designated by delimited forms, or in relation to a solid foundation, and hence from the viewpoint of *consistency*).

If there is a *de-spiritualization* in this descending movement, in this regressive movement toward *the lowest point* (at which '*mechanism*' *reappears*), would it not lie in the fact that the intensity, in the high tonality of the soul – which is thrown *outside of itself* by the violence of this same intensity – designates itself by tracing the sign of the *Circle of the Return* at a *pole opposed* to any spiritualization, re-establishing itself as a *pure energy* devoid of any goal or meaning. It becomes its own meaning and goal, since it has none outside of itself (having thrown the soul outside of itself, outside of its identity).

Now if a *fluctuation of intensity* can take on a signification only in the *trace* it leaves – that is, in the *meaning* of a sign – then the sign of the *Circle* is at once the trace (in the mind), the meaning, and the intensity itself. In this sign (*circulus vitiosus Deus*), everything becomes merged with the movement itself, which by turns resuscitates and abandons the trace, empty, to itself.

Yet this *trace*, in order to signify the *Circle*, is experienced as full of intensity only at the *privileged* moment of an isolated case, at that degree where the sign of the *self* in its tonality is *devoid of intensity,* and where all significations of this self are emptied – at *the lowest point.*

For the *intensity* now to be conceived of as an *energy* limited in space, as a *quantitative power* – culminating in a high point where it would signify itself, and falling to the lowest point where it would have only insignificance (despiritualization –

disorganization) – must we say that the quantity of energy is no longer able to convert itself into quality – whereas, according to Nietzsche, it is *quality itself:* the *'will'* to do violence and to resist all violence? How, at this degree of *de-deification*, can existence *re-deify* itself? Is it not in the *moment itself* that it suddenly becomes divine? Had it ever ceased to be divine? Is there an absolute coincidence between the lowest point and the culminating point?

In the fragment entitled *Fundamental Innovations*, Nietzsche speaks of the inversion of the supreme spiritualization of power into its extreme *servitude.* Why *'servitude'*? It is here that power, at the level of societies, would manifest its will or the absence of its will to power in the *meaning* of history. In accordance with the criteria of the composition of societies, and *their decomposition by their individual members*, the *will* to power becomes the interpreter of the *Eternal Return.* The *vicious Circle*, argument of domination, historicizes energy in order to introduce the absurd automatism into history: sometimes the triumph of a small number of privileged over subservient societies, sometimes the triumph of the greatest number of disadvantaged over the privileged. The last paragraph touches on the content of the revelation of the Eternal Return: *'we are more than individuals: we are the whole chain as well, with the tasks of all the futures of that chain.'*[95]

The postulate derived from the experience of the Return is in this way reinscribed in this vision of ascending and descending movement: *to pass through the entire series of individualities implicit in the Circle.* Except for one notable difference: the *fortuitous* individual, to which Nietzsche will later return, here yields to a new preoccupation: *the tasks of all the futures* of the chain – hence the *fixing* of a goal.

But whereas a power is unable *not* to ceaselessly will *more power* – how and through what will it be able to will its *increased growth* if not by *giving itself a goal?* And if it transgresses this goal, another one will be required – to the point where *every conceivable goal has been attained.* But this equilibrium, Nietzsche claims, would then exist as *a final state of inertia*. The fact that no state of equilibrium can ever be maintained proves that no attained goal could ever represent the absorption of the total mass of energy. The *disproportion between the goal and the means to attain it* implies that there is always a constant *disrupting* of the state of equilibrium. Energy always surpasses the goal.

But if *energy always surpasses the goal*, it is because the latter is nothing other than *energy itself*. At the maximum level of accumulated power, all power can do is to *transform itself* into a meaning that is the *opposite* of what this maximum *signifies*. If energy goes beyond the attained goal, it is not only because energy is itself its own goal, but because the means prevail over the end – a fact that will assume an ever greater importance in Nietzsche's later elaborations. The means that are brought into play prevail over the *meaning* that consciousness gives to the pursued goal, the *unconscious* meaning of the goal prevails over the consciously fixed meaning. This is why the *consciousness of means* takes precedence over the consciousness of an end, *only the means are conscious: the fragment of consciousness is only one more means for the development and extension of life.*

But if energy goes beyond a maximum state of power, which would be its supreme state of spiritualization ('God'), it is because this very *designation* would be unsuitable for a power whose attribute is to signify its own *insignificance*. This is why the *circulus vitiosus* is a god whose essence is always to flee himself in order to meet up with himself. And a degree of spiritualization could not keep him from throwing himself into the final state of a purely quantitative force – thereby eluding any durable signification.

Whatever its total magnitude, this *energy* constantly remains equal to *itself*. Its means are its *limited number of combinations*, and its apparent ends are only *variations of its own end* – that of always remaining the same *quantity* of energy. Once all the combinations are exhausted, they must be reproduced anew, out of necessity – and this necessity is inscribed in its essence. Now this repetition is an eternal repetition, without beginning or end. Yet there are more profound differences between this structure of the universe (which defines existence as well as an economy) and the biological laws of growth and decline than there are between these same biological laws and the historical development of human societies – even if, with regard to the formation of individuals within societies, there would be a greater analogy between *gregarious impulses* and *particular cases*, and a greater affinity with this conception of the behaviour of energy.

This cyclical conception of history is not original with Nietzsche, and his mechanistic speculations on *quanta* do not add anything to his initial experience of the *Return*. Yet what results from this consultation is at least a principle according to which the absurdity of the Vicious Circle would coincide with the behaviour of power – even though the will is the interpreter that ascribes significance to power. *Power is insignificance*, and what is insignificant in itself exercises the greatest violence. The less violence there is, the more *interpretation* and signification there is. And in effect, if (as the preceding schema indicated) the *culminating moment* of 'spiritualization' is 'God', and thus the maximum of signification, then at that moment this signification is already in a *state of equilibrium* that *must be disrupted*. So it is only *at the last degree* – at the moment when energy *disorganizes* what it had created – that, in the absence of any possible signification, *the greatest possible violence* is *recovered*.

But if there is *insignificance* in uninterpretable *power*, what does it mean to say that the *will* to power interprets? A new equivocation. For the will to power is nothing but an impulse, and every impulse, in order to be produced, presupposes a meaning and a goal – a state of satisfaction to attain, a non-satisfaction to avoid, and thus an interpretable comparison between lived states.

On the other hand, Nietzsche thus refers to a description of forces without any goal or meaning in order to inquire into their 'absurd' behaviour as a *goal* in the organic creation of societies. For if the exercise of power is verified in this way, then *sovereign formations* would have no other purpose than *to mask the absence of any goal or meaning* in their sovereignty through the *organic* goal of their creation.

> This apparent conformity to a goal *is simply subsequent to this will to power unfolding in every event*; – the becoming-strongest brings with itself organizations that have a certain resemblance to a plan of finality: – the apparent goals are not intentional, but once the supremacy over a lesser power is attained, and the latter is made to work on behalf of the greatest, a hierarchical order of organization must take on the appearance of an order of means and ends.[96]

In this second schema, Nietzsche says: *the same quantum of energy signifies something different from the different degrees of evolution.* We might object that it is not the same type of energy in these different degrees! Specifically different forces *coexist* according to their own rhythm, and it is their interaction that produces what we call *organic life.* To presume that the same energy lies at the *origin* of this interaction amounts to a theology – that of the *God of the Vicious Circle* – or more specifically, Nietzsche's own *emotion.* It is precisely this emotion that had initiated him into a dimension that, for the moment, has been forgotten – the only dimension which corresponds to an *authenticity* that can be formulated without any reference points, without any necessary verification. It was this authenticity that *constrained* Nietzsche to wander among so many theories, which would always be revised, surpassed and contradicted in his effort to persuade.

The fundamental thought derived from the theory of quantitative energy is the *insignificance* of power – a power that is *uninterpretable* with regard to intentionality. But how can Nietzsche apply this to what he calls *Herrschaftesgebilde,* the formations of sovereignty? The *insignificance* of power, the *violence* it exercises through its own *absurdity*, can moreover find a reference point in these formations only in the *unadmitted* (and hence *unconscious*) goal that they were pursuing – in the guise of significations and *goals* that presided over their constitution. Inversely, these *formations of sovereignty* cannot claim to exercise *the absurd as violence* – if they do not assign themselves a meaning – a meaning in which servitude, the subjected forces, would participate – and this meaning can never be that of *pure absurdity*.

If such formations can be constituted only by assigning them a new goal, it will not be enough, in order for them to consciously conform to this principle, *to tell them that the only goal of power is to increase itself.* For these formations have become powerful precisely because they have conceived of *a meaning* – for if a signification responded to a state of power, reciprocally this state of power must lay claim to this signification in order to maintain itself.

Nietzsche's purpose becomes clearer once he calls upon *formations of sovereignty* to become conscious of the law of the disruption of *equilibrium*, which at present he is trying to describe in order to prescribe it as a *sine qua non* condition of their action. Every *sovereign formation* will thus have to *foresee* the required moment of its disintegration. It will have to reinvent a new signification through a new goal to be pursued, and to re-create new organs, thus admitting that, since *insignificance* is the *supreme violence*, the latter can be exercised only in the name of *a value* (a meaning) which makes life appear absurd as the *supreme overabundance*, and thereby converts absurdity into spirituality.

No *formation of sovereignty*, in order to crystallize, could ever endure this sting of conscience: for as soon as the formation becomes conscious of it in its individual members, *these same individuals decompose it.* Nietzsche is here challenging his own distinction between what is *gregarious* (the preservation of the species) and what is *singular* in the individual. *Sovereignty* participates in what excludes this singularity in gregariousness and in what excludes the latter in the individual. The *privileged*, in small numbers, are a group of singularities and thereby express a devaluation of what is gregarious. The *disadvantaged* (the mediocre), at the level of gregariousness, can tolerate the privileged only if they maintain a gregarious reason for their singular group. Now what this singular group exercises is violence – once the behaviour of this group affirms the *absurdity* of existence. Put differently, insignificant energy cannot serve as a goal. Hence the enslavement moves in the opposite direction: the *singular cases* are eliminated in favour of the gregariousness of the mediocre, the disadvantaged, who in turn exercise violence in the name of the *specific signification* of the species.

6

The Vicious Circle as a
Selective Doctrine

Political Version of the
Eternal Return

The Conspiracy of the
Vicious Circle

WHAT DO THE PROJECTS OF 'TRAINING AND SELECTION'
SIGNIFY IN NIETZSCHE'S PATHOLOGY?
'*As soon as we act practically*', he says, '*we have to follow the
prejudices of our sentiments.*'[97] This is exactly what Nietzsche
did with the intention of putting forward a new meaning
and goal.

Nietzsche now seemed to be struggling against the imminence of delirium, *and also struggling to find an equilibrium
between this threat and the 'reality principle'*. He was not
worried about the fate of the human species, nor was he
guided by the fear of suffering or the distress of humanity:
it was rather the necessity of acting externally, of *assimilating
other consciousnesses to himself* so as to *flee the destruction of his
own*. Whence his repeated efforts to develop the themes
announced in his various projects and outlines – which

alternated between two, three, or four principal definitions ('*The Philosophy of the Future*' or '*The Innocence of Becoming*' or '*The Eternal Return*' or '*The Will to Power*').

Nietzsche was fleeing, not the idea of suicide, which he flirted with more than once during his personal afflictions – but the incessant combat of his metamorphosis, which he fled as one flees the most seductive of *trials*; he was fleeing the trial of his own metamorphosis, he was postponing its demonstration, a final experiment he would undertake and survive with his *lucidity* intact – the hour having not yet come, or having already passed. . . . Such a trial, however, was already going on silently, unbeknownst to him, despite the fact that he had succeeded in postponing its due date. But if he could manage, on the contrary, to set in motion a *direct action* – or at least to prescribe one, to bring to light its *means*, to anticipate them – then perhaps this carefully deliberated trial could in turn be reabsorbed into what he was then calling his *magnum opus*. Still, he did nothing but string together titles and subdivisions, draw up tables of contents, and insert a brief commentary here and there. Nonetheless, his aphoristic production continued – from *Human, All-Too-Human*, *The Gay Science*, *Beyond Good and Evil* and *The Genealogy of Morals*, to the short works that formed his last expressions. *Zarathustra*, whose composition extended from 1884 to 1886, represented an obstacle to the conceptual development, in the sense that all its images, parabolic figures and ambiguities expressed the experience of the Eternal Return in an exclusive fashion. But the fact that Nietzsche did not continue with this form proved that it could not settle his later conflicts either.

'*Nature has no goal and realizes something. We others have a "goal" but obtain something other than this goal.*'[98]

We *interpret* our obscure impulses, in accordance with institutional language, as if they had a will, which presupposes a *cause exerting its effect*. A play of forces, of relations between forces, fallaciously interpreted.

How can lucidity ever be possible? The only conceivable

lucidity would be to admit our state of servitude. But even to sustain *this* level of *lucidity* requires a constant effort that *liberates us from ourselves as well as from nature.* This means: we are aware of our mechanism; we must dismantle it. But to dismantle it is also to make use of its parts in order to reconstruct it, and thus to lead 'nature' toward our own 'goal'. But whenever we reason in this manner, we are once again masking the impulse that is driving us: it is true that we obtain something we have *interpreted* as *willed*, but this is simply 'nature' which, without willing anything, has realized itself for other 'ends'.

> *If no goal resides in the whole history of human destinies,* then one must be inserted into it: assuming that a goal is *necessary* for us, and on the other hand, that the illusion of an immanent end has become transparent to us. A goal is necessary for us because a will is necessary for us – our dorsal spine. *The will as a compensation for belief,* for the representation of a divine will, which offers something to our intention.[99]

But to give a meaning and a goal to existence – what would this amount to? To nothing, insofar as existence (under the guise of human destinies) invents meanings and goals *by itself*, through individuals and societies.

Nietzsche himself was divided between two different perspectives, even though he attempted to present them as a unique and coherent decision:

on the one hand: the Eternal Return is the way in which the universe 'explicates' itself;

on the other hand: the nihilism that history has led to requires a 'revaluation of values', which will institute criteria for a new 'selection' of the species.

A series of alternatives follows from this:

Assuming that the law of the Eternal Return is the *modality* of existence and that *power* is its *essence*, we must believe that this law brings about a *selection* of beings without *any* intervention of the will – even if the will itself results from it.

But how can this be corroborated with Nietzsche's (anti-Darwinist) observation that 'natural selection' is favourable *to the weak* and not to the strong? To *think* the Return fully is to admit nothing more than an *alternation* between energy and exhaustion.

First alternative:
either the Return *selects* in and through itself, apart from any conscious or unconscious intervention,

or else the *Return was revealed to Nietzsche* so that *a conscious and voluntary selection* might *intervene.* Now according to this principle, the Return has been *revealed* innumerable times.

Hence, a *second alternative*:
if the Return has been revealed innumerable times, it may be that a conscious and voluntary selection has also been brought about, and brought about innumerable times! But this matters little! For it has now been *revealed anew, whereas no one had even dreamed it was possible before Nietzsche's fortuitous experience at Sils-Maria.* The question is therefore posed anew with urgency:

Third alternative:
either the selection depends on the *disclosure* of the Eternal Return (as a sign of the Vicious Circle: putting humanity to the test; the result: a new species, or rather, the attaining of a higher level through which every orientation, every decision, and all behaviour would be changed. A *scientific demonstration* of the Eternal Return becomes necessary.)

or else the selection will take place in *secret* (the *Vicious Circle*), that is, it will be undertaken *in the name of this secret* by certain experimenters (the Masters of the Earth). A purely experimental doctrine of selection will be put into practice as a 'political' philosophy.

In this latter case, the secret of the Vicious Circle can also be regarded as an *invented* simulacrum in accordance with one of Nietzsche's *phantasms*.

★ ★ ★

On the genesis of the nihilist. – It is only late that one musters the courage for what one really *knows*. That I had hitherto been a thorough-going nihilist, I have admitted to myself only recently: the energy and non-chalance* with which I advanced as a nihilist deceived me about this basic fact. *When one moves toward a goal it seems impossible that 'goal-lessness as such' is the principle of our faith* [Emphasis added].[100]

★ ★ ★

In certain plans for *The Revaluation of All Values*, the *Philosopher of the Future* – which Nietzsche himself prefigures – appears *here* as 'experimenter', *there* as 'imposter'.

In other plans, those of *training and selection*, it is a question of masters and slaves. We must here distinguish the master–slave relationship as it appears in past (traditional) hierarchies from what still remains of it in the existing order (democratic liberal Europe), and also, in our own mobile organization, from the *formations of sovereignty* that are the objects of Nietzsche's prophecies. But these past hierarchical orders (the slave-based Helleno-Roman state, aristocratic-feudalism), with the various physiognomies they have produced, serve as the starting-point for the

---

* Montinari deciphers *nonchalance* here where Schlecta reads *radicalism*.

philosopher's speculations, which will lead, in modern conditions, to various experimental projects ('training and selection').

Some of Nietzsche's notes make a rigorous distinction between the experimental philosopher and the 'future Master'; others merge the two together. Those who will initially oversee the 'training and selection' are not the Masters but the scientists and philosophers – those who, in the present state of generalized servitude (our modern industry), are the first to introduce new methods into it.

The experimenter is simply an elaboration of the figure of the 'Master' – the 'Master' being the fruit of experience. On the one hand, it is not a question of a Master who would exercise the prerogatives of his social standing, any more than it is a question of creating 'new' slaves for this master. The *Master* and the *slave* are *states* which, respectively, *are the result of a test*. And this test always remains the adherence to the *sign of the vicious circle*, or its rejection. The sign of the Vicious Circle – of the Eternal Return – thus remained the hinge and springboard for the projects termed *training and selection*. This already renders impossible any confusion with the regimes that some have tried to attribute to these projects.

Before entering into the details of these characters of the *Master* and the *slave* (to the degree permitted by the fragmentary nature of Nietzsche's notes), it will first be helpful to examine briefly those notes that describe or suggest the physiognomy of the philosopher (hence an aspect of Nietzsche's own thought). How does Nietzsche himself act in this role?

The various motifs that converged in Nietzsche's description of the tasks of 'political' or 'sociological' or simply 'concrete' philosophy, were derived from his personal reactions toward *culture* as a whole. Whether it was a question of history, or historiography, or natural science, or physiology, or, finally and most importantly, the creations of art – it was the latter that remained the fundamental point of view from which, and according to which, Nietzsche evaluated both history and science. This is why we must here emphasize the influence of historical *types* as *suggestions*, indeed *obsessions*, on Nietzsche's descriptions – *obsessions* that were inseparable at first from the idea of a 'creation' that Nietzsche wanted to undertake through the expedient of scientific experiments. Next, we will see how Nietzsche again seized hold of this same obsession and sought a formulation for it in his idea of the 'philosopher-imposter'.

The term '*Versucher*', which occasionally appears in Nietzsche's texts, has the double meaning of 'experimenter' and 'tempter'. Every creator is at once someone who tempts others and who *experiments on (tempts) himself and others* in order to create something that *does not yet exist*: a set of forces capable of *acting upon* and *modifying that which exists*.

Once the 'machinery' of behaviour has been taken apart piece by piece – whether in terms of the inner motives that act upon it, or of the external pressures that provoke it – the temptation that is thereby awakened is the following: under what conditions can it be made to act on behalf of a determined meaning and end? How can such a foreseeable condition be provoked? How can those who perpetuate themselves negatively be destroyed? If the whole of human nature is so fragile and so passive, what long-standing habits must be introduced into it in order to initiate a transition?

Whenever Nietzsche considered the chances of a human type capable of acting counter to (or to the detriment of) the modern conditions of contemporary humanity, he was seeking means that could *methodically re-establish the fortuitous conditions* of the past that have favoured some remarkable individuals. This project – which could not be more contradictory to the first interpretation of the Eternal Return – was derived from his 'physiological' vision of the human being and from the conclusions he had drawn with respect to the ends of 'applied physiology': nothing is more fecund, or more rich, or more malleable than this nature, once it is submitted to *constraints* and inoculated with them in the form of thoughts, obsessions, habits, customs, imperatives –

everything prudently measured out in doses. Through this kind of idiosyncratic Prometheanism, Nietzsche believed he could seize hold of and anticipate our own industrialized social apparatus: he had a premonition of it, but he feared it all the more in that he foresaw the methods of conditioning that would be able to be exploited by the social groupings that, in one way or another, would maintain power. Which groupings? Once again, gregariousness would win out over singular cases.

It was from this perspective of 'applied physiology' that Nietzsche's thought returned to its own criteria of *health* and *morbidity*, the *gregarious* and the *singular* – which were applied to examples from history and from the future that contemporary science promised to bring about. Thus, Nietzsche's struggle against Christian bourgeois morality – and its continuation in mercantile society, up to and including the humanistic social movement – attempted to construct from this post-Christian bourgeois morality and its own economic antinomies *the physiognomy of a single and unique* adversary – namely and always, the *gregariousness* that exists or is yet to come – even if it was this same gregariousness that would have to furnish the substance for his own creative ambitions.

Among the projects termed '*Training and Selection*', there are some that allude to the physiognomy of the future *Masters of the Earth* without having any *explicit* relation to the doctrine of the *Vicious Circle*.

These fragments explore the dispositions that will be required of the experimenter – dispositions that are pronounced in strong natures, such as '*criminals in the grand style*': the courage of an existence *outside the law*, as much with regard to one's reputation, state and origin as to one's conscience toward duty; a *total absence* of scruples in willing *these means* in order to attain *that end*. Whenever Nietzsche sketches the experimenter philosopher, he always casts a glance on the monstrous aspect of these characters. Such sketches do not say *what* these experiments would consist of; nor does the fact that they end in the sacrifice and waste of human lives, as certain fragments seem to suggest, explain the manner in which these experiments would be undertaken – if, on the one hand, we dismiss the hypothesis of physiological experiments and if, on the other hand, we do not retain the moral test of the *Vicious Circle* – when precisely this test is not mentioned in the fragments in question, such as the following:

> *The pessimism of those who have the strength to act*: the 'Why?' following a horrible struggle, a victory over oneself. That there is something a hundred times more valuable than knowing if we feel ourselves to be good or evil: the fundamental instinct of all strong natures, and consequently, more important than knowing if *others* feel themselves to be good or evil. In short, the fact that we have an aim, out of love for which we do not hesitate *to sacrifice human lives*, to take any risk, to take on oneself the worst of all evils: the great passion.[101]

If the meaning of all eminent creation is to break the gregarious habits that always direct existing beings toward ends that are useful *exclusively* to the oppressive regime of mediocrity – then in the experimental domain *to create* is to *do violence* to what exists, and thus to the integrity of beings. Every creation of a new type must provoke a state of *insecurity*: creation ceases to be a game at the margins of reality; henceforth, the creator will not re-produce, but will itself produce the *real*.

> The first problem is: to what degree does the 'will to truth' penetrate the depth of 'things'? – The fact that we measure the entire value of the unconscious in terms of the means of conservation of the living, as well as the value of simplifications *in general* and the value of regulative *fictions*, for example, those of logic;

and that we evaluate, above all, the value of *elaborated interpretations*, and the degree to which there thus subsists not a '*that is*' but a '*that signifies*' – leads to this solution: the 'will to truth' develops in the service of the 'will to power' – and considered rigorously, its task, strictly speaking, is *to ensure the triumph and endurance of a certain type of non-truth, to take a coherent set of falsifications as the basis of the conservation of a certain living species.*

Second problem: to what degree does the will to goodness reach the depth of things? We see exactly the opposite everywhere in plants and animals: indifference, or severity, or cruelty ('justice', 'punishment'). Solution: compassion exists only in social formations (to which the human body belongs, and for which living beings have a mutual sentiment), *following upon the fact that a greater totality wills to conserve itself against another totality,* and once again because in the economy of the world *happiness would be a superfluous principle.*

Third problem: to what degree of profundity does reason refer to the depth of things? *Critique of aims and means* (a point of factual relation, which is nothing but a relation projected by interpretation). *The characteristic of waste, of mental derangement is normal in the economy of the whole. 'Intelligence' appears as a particular form of unreason, almost as its most wicked caricature.* To what degree is a high rationality always the symptom of declining races, an impoverishment of life?

Fourth problem: How far does the will to the beautiful extend? *Unscrupulous development* of forms: *the most beautiful are merely the strongest*: being victorious, they stand firm and rejoice in their type: propagation. (Plato's belief that philosophy itself is a kind of sexual and procreative impulse.)

Hence, the things that until now we have hitherto appreciated as 'true', 'good', 'reasonable', 'beautiful', turn out to be, as isolated cases, inverted powers – I point out this perspectivist falsification in favour of which the human species affirms itself. This is its condition of life: that it takes pleasure in itself (the human being experiences joy in the means of its conservation: these means include the fact that human beings do not want to be deceived and that individuals are ready to help and support each other: on the whole, the successful types know how to live to the detriment of the lesser types). *The will to power is being expressed in all this, with its unscrupulous recourse to the means of deceit – and one can conceive the evil pleasure that a god experiences at the spectacle of a human being admiring itself.*

In short: the will to power.

Consequence: if this representation is *hostile* to us, why do we cede to it? . . . *The beautiful simulacra are ours! Let us be the deceivers and the embellishers of humanity!* – In fact, this is precisely what a *philosopher* is.[102]

THE SIMULACRUM OF THE IMPOSTER-PHILOSOPHER, THE PHANTASM AND THE REALITY PRINCIPLE

To be fair to Nietzsche, we must first of all emphasize the shocking nature of this proposition: *The simulacra are ours! Let us be the deceivers and the embellishers of humanity!* This is what all potentates worthy of the name are supposed to say. But Nietzsche now wants the savant to speak this kind of language. In this sense, he is taking up an *occult conception of political mystification* and making it pass into *the hands of the philosophers.* According to this esoteric tradition – which goes back to the sophists and, passing through Frederick II of Hohenstaufen, continues up through the Encyclopedists, Voltaire and Sade – *one demystifies only in order to mystify better.* Although this programme was initially tied to the exercise of power, it here becomes a rule of thought, a metaphysical conception, a judgement concerning the economy of being, and therefore human destiny and behaviour. It is not simply a matter of destroying the notions of the true and the false; it also concerns the entrance of obscure forces on to the stage through the *moral ruin* of the intellect.

What we see at work here is a positive notion of the false, which, as the basis of artistic creation, is now *extended to every problem raised by existence*. Mystification, according to Nietzsche, is not simply the way a potentate operates. It is the very ground of existence. Demystification had hitherto been the unadmitted task of the savant. But *demystifying in order to mystify better* (no longer simply to *exploit* but to *favour these obscure forces* as creative and fecund) now becomes the practice, no longer of the philosopher, but of the *psychologist* – and of Nietzsche, notably in his attempt to overcome the despair into which scientific demystification, by destroying values, would have thrown Western humanity. The remedy would thus be a *remystification* that would generate new conditions of life, that would validate the creative force of the impulses.

This, at first sight, seems to be the intention of this proposition. Yet the very terms 'demystification' and 'remystification' – if, rationally speaking, they seem to correspond to this project – serve only to make the project seem completely untenable. How can one demystify anew?

Nietzsche must therefore have had something in mind other than the promulgation of deception through the invention of a simulacrum.

If we affirm that '*the only being guaranteed to us is being that represents itself, and is therefore changing, non-identical to itself, completely relative*'[103] – in other words, that existence is sustained only through fabulation – then we are stating clearly that existence itself is a fabulation. Thus Nietzsche, who feared the spread of *Nirvanaism* in the West, was in fact simply dreaming of inverting this Nirvanaism into a praxis of the simulacrum: the attraction of nothingness can be overcome only by developing the very phantasms the Buddha tried to liquidate.

'*Nihilism (in the passive sense) manifests itself as soon as the ability to invent new fictions and interpret them is exhausted.*'[104] This is how the contemporary moral situation appeared to Nietzsche as he considered the role of the philosopher-imposter, the mind that knows how to derive conclusions from the processes of cultures and societies. The *moralities* that produce the *criteria* of knowledge as well as of behaviour (and these criteria in turn engender new moralities), depend exclusively on the interpretation of humanity at a determinate level of his psyche; the phantasms of the latter are externalized in simulacra. In the absence of new simulacra, while the existing simulacra lie dying, the intellect and the phantasm of the impulses find themselves in a desperate face-off. Because of their reciprocal incommunicability, Nietzsche can say that *the intellect is the caricature of unreason*. (Because it is not recognized as such, the intellect, in the absence of new simulacra, itself becomes a phantasm: scientific 'naturalism' and 'objectivity' are among its many forms.) The inability to invent simulacra is therefore merely a symptom of degeneration – a situation that defies a force of invention sustained by a determinate impulse, which not only produces its own phantasms, but still knows how to interpret them.

Nothing exists apart from *impulses* that are essentially *generative* of *phantasms*.

The simulacrum is not the product of a phantasm, but its skilful reproduction, by which humanity can *produce* itself, through forces that are thereby exorcized and dominated by the impulse.

In the hands of the 'imposter' philosopher, the *Trugbild* – the simulacrum – becomes the *willed* reproduction of non-willed phantasms, born from the life of the impulses.

In order to exercise its constraint, the simulacrum must correspond to the necessity of the phantasm. If the impulse already 'interprets' something for itself, the phantasm remains unintelligible, below the level of consciousness: it is merely the intellect's *ossified incomprehension* of a *state of life*. Because of this, the intellect once again represents the most malicious caricature of 'unreason', that is, a caricature of the life of the impulses; moreover, the intellect deforms what the phantasm wants to 'say'.

But as such, the phantasm cannot have any meaning

outside the time of the intellect, outside its dimensions: something monstrous that takes shape only through a delimitation of the non-comprehensible. What for the intellect is a function of continuity – from cause to effect – is for the phantasm something without any preconditions: a gesture, an action, an event of which the phantasm is the residue, having at the same time the value of a gesture, an action, an event already accomplished or yet to come. Now there is only one mediator that can say what a phantasm 'wills': through its conventional procedures, *art* essentially reconstitutes in its own figures the conditions that have constituted the phantasm, namely, the intensities of the impulses. The simulacrum, in relation to the intellect, is the licence that the latter concedes to art: a *ludic* suspension of the reality principle.

But here we see that, under the pretext of modifying human behaviour with regard to the real, the 'imposter' philosopher sets out to experiment with the licence of the simulacrum in every domain of thought and existence, using the methods of science. To abolish *the principle of (so-called) reality*, it is enough to draw the final consequences of 'physiology' – even if this means denouncing the mystifying monopoly of the intellect, whose censure still keeps the methods of science within the limits of this principle.

If phantasms arise as 'unintelligible' signs, it is not some kind of moral censure that is responsible for their sterile manifestation, but their coincidence with the *reality principle*. Art is itself an accomplice in this censoring, insofar as it acts only within its own limited sphere. Science, for its part, explores the universe and life without ever drawing the slightest consequence for human behaviour with regard to the reality principle. The fact that science is essentially an *institutional* principle dictated by reasons of security and for the (gregarious) continuity of existence – this is, once again, what forms the background-thought of this project of philosophical *imposture*.

To fix a goal, to give a meaning – not merely to orient living forces, but also to elicit *new centres of forces*: this is what the simulacrum does: a simulacrum of goal, a simulacrum of meaning – *which must be invented!* Invented from what? From the phantasms of the life of the drives – the impulse, as '*will to power*', already being the first interpreter.

It might be objected, however, that if the fluctuations of intensity in the impulses are necessarily inverted by the intellect, in accordance with a meaning and a goal (the guarantors of gregarious security), it goes without saying that the herd's 'will to power' would win out over all the other impulses. How can we fail to recognize that the *intellect* and its *categories* are the organic products of this primordial impulse (of the conservation of the species), and that if there is a *phantasm, here* as elsewhere, it is one that has managed to produce its own *simulacrum* – the most efficacious simulacrum of humanity – from which human behaviour has created for itself a whole set of diverse spheres, all of which are so many *aspects of the reality principle* – namely, the demarcation between acting and non-acting. Now knowledge itself – initially contemplative and theoretical, then increasingly experimental – is also an interpretive 'will to power' that in each case *reinvents the real* in terms of its own modes of apprehending its objects, and then of manipulating them. It is here that two wills to power collide: the gregarious will to power, and the will to power which, through individual initiative, breaks with gregariousness.

Now for this impulse to knowledge that tries to intervene and reinvent, where does the real begin, and where does it end? The more science explores, the more it becomes aware of its own *ignorance* through *what it knows*, the more the 'supposed' real *resists* it as an X.

For Nietzsche, however, it was the *gregarious impulse* which, in science, had resisted him as the reality principle – the limit-point at which knowledge *opens onto Chaos*, and where the species is destroyed. Did not Nietzsche repeat many times that the notion of this '*abyss*' as '*truth*' was unassimilable to the function of living, and that the term 'truth' was merely an *error* indispensable to the maintenance of a certain species of living beings? But what does the security of the species matter!

> At bottom, science seeks to establish the way the *human being* – and *not* the individual – feels in relation to all things and to itself; hence it seeks to *eliminate* the idiosyncrasy of isolated individuals and groups, and thus to establish the *persistent* relation. It is not the truth but the human being that is known in this manner, notably in all the epochs in which it existed. *Which is to say that a phantom is constructed* [Emphasis added], and that everyone is constantly contributing to it in order to find out *that which requires our unanimity*, because this would belong to the essence of humanity. In doing so, we have learned that innumerable things were not essential, as had long been believed, and that, in establishing the essential, we proved nothing concerning reality except that *the existence of the human being up to that point* had relied on the belief in this 'reality' (such as the body, duration, substance, etc.). *Thus, science does nothing other than seek the process that has constituted the essence of the species, which tends to render the belief in certain things endemic, and to eliminate the incredulous so as to let them perish.* The acquired *analogy* of sensibility (as to the species, the feeling of time, of what is large and small) becomes a condition of the existence of the species, but has nothing to do with the truth. The 'insane', the 'mentally deranged', the idiosyncratic do not prove the non-truth of a representation, but its anomaly; it does not allow the masses to *live*. It is also the instinct of the mass that reigns in the domain of knowledge; the mass constantly wants to have a better knowledge of its own conditions of existence in order to live longer and longer. The uniformity of feeling, formerly sought in society or religion, is now sought after by science: the *normal taste*

for all things is established; knowledge, which rests on the belief in persistence, is in the service of the *crudest forms* of persistence (the mass, the people, humanity) and it tends to eliminate and kill the more subtle forms, the idiosyncratic taste – it works against *individualization*, against any taste that is the condition of existence for a *single individual.* – The species is the cruder error, the individual the more subtle error, which comes *later.* The individual *fights* for its own existence, for its new taste, for its relatively *unique* position in relation to all things – he holds this position to be better than the general taste, which he distrusts. He wants to *dominate.* But then, he discovers that he is himself something that changes, that his taste is changeable; his subtlety leads him to unveil the secret that there is no individual, that at every moment he is different than at the preceding moment, and that his conditions of existence are those of innumerable individuals: *the infinitesimal moment* is the reality, the higher truth, a lightning–image springing out of the eternal flux. He thereby learns that all knowledge which *enjoys* knowing rests on the crudest error of the species, on the more subtle errors of the individual, and on the most subtle of all errors, that of the creative instant.[105]

Science can therefore be divided into two antagonistic impulses, both of which are expressed through it: on the one hand, *knowledge,* and on the other hand, the instinct to conserve the species. But is not knowledge, for Nietzsche, *the gregarious will to power that interprets the conditions of existence to conserve the species?* Are not its experiments always determined by the same reality principle? What then can be said of its way of determining what is *real?* The philosopher-imposter knows what he must hold on to in this crucial point – this limit-point – at which his own intention of producing simulacra from the phantasms of the impulses coincides with the activity of the scientist.

Since simulation is *the attribute of being itself,* it also becomes the very principle of knowledge. Like every impulse that interprets its phantasms as a 'condition of existence' (that is to say, as a means of dominating, of appropriating for itself a power over what resists it), science itself, when it comes into contact with a given phenomenon, is interpreting its own *phantasms.* It invents simulacra that conform to these phantasms (and always in terms of the same schemes of stable *unities* that constitute every semiotic) – simulacra through which the human mind does not so much *comprehend* as *mime* the behaviour of what is foreign to it by nature. It assimilates the latter only by *reconstituting the processes* that science examines at the level of *efficacy.* But the latter corresponds to the sempiternal anthropomorphic superstition, according to which the mind cannot tolerate that there be an absence of a reason, if not of intention, *at the origin of a phenomenon.* Now although science admits in principle that there is no *intention at the origin of a given process,* once it *reconstitutes* this process, it nonetheless introduces an *intention* into the process through the very act of reproducing it: the reconstituted process can be reconstituted only through the simulacra of *unities* (that is, through a *calculus* that verifies them). But it is through the simulacrum, calculating the process, that the intention of the knower intervenes, which is one of efficacy.

The simulacrum of the calculus wills the calculator to become the *simulated author* of the reconstituted process: the intellect, introduced as the consciousness of the (unconscious) phenomenon, simulates the intention, which was 'previously' absent from the phenomenon.

The application of the *'laws'* of the process of a phenomenon thus accounts for the *liberating* function of efficacy. Efficacy assumes that the human being, rather than merging with the processes it analyses, does not preserve them in itself as so many phantasms, but instead externalizes them under the pretext of utilizing them. It thereby creates a *sphere of extra-human objects,* not so much in order to exploit them for its own well-being and material security, but in order to verify its reason and guarantee its psychic and moral security.

Yet science in no way wishes to acknowledge that the species might itself be increasingly monopolized as an object by this initially extra-human sphere, to the detriment of its psychic and moral security. For a long time already, there has been an absolute discordance between the *reality principle*, of which science believes itself to be the guardian, and a completely different impulse that acts within science and attacks the very notion of security.

If the human being *mimes* the natural phenomena it analyses – by means of simulacra that allow it to reconstitute these phenomena – it is because, in the simulacrum, there is a force that refuses to tolerate the *durable fixity* of the species. Through the detour of science and art, humanity has already rebelled against this *fixity* many times, and thus is by no means simply concerned with its own specific conservation. And this capacity notwithstanding, the gregarious impulse has made this rupture fail in and through science. The day human beings learn how to behave as *phenomena devoid of intention* – for every intention at the level of the human being always implies its own conservation, its continued existence – on that day, a new creature would declare the integrity of existence.

When Nietzsche says that all we have of *being* is a certitude – that is to say, that being *is something that represents itself*, that *posits itself before itself* – this kind of *fabulation attributed to being* is taken up in the term *Chaos*. As long as its definition as a *rival force* does not intervene, chaos is a state prior to this *self-fabulation*. The *will to power* as a formulation is a *fabulating* formulation – not in the sense of a *subjectivism*, but of a behaviour that surpasses the human.

Chaos, it might be objected, is already a *phantasm* in Nietzsche, a *term that simulates the most distant of domains*, and therefore the *supreme authority* which *every phantasm born in the closest region, the most immediate domain* (i.e. that of the individual in relation to itself and others) *would appeal to*. For science, *Chaos* does not exist – any more, Nietzsche will say, than the *species* or the *individual* exists. *Laws* exist only because of our need to *calculate*. Only *quantities of force* exist. *Chaos*, then, is already nothing more than the term of a negative formulation that we establish on the basis of our own conditions of living. Chaos does not exist as an *intention*. And we cannot conceive of ourselves other than as intentional beings. Where does this impossibility come from? From the fact that the forces we improperly name 'Chaos' have *no* intention whatsoever. *Nietzsche's unavowable project is to act without intention*: the *impossible morality*. Now the total economy of this intentionless universe creates intentional beings. The species 'man' is a creation of this kind – *pure chance* – in which the intensity of forces is inverted into *intention*: the work of morality. The function of the simulacrum is *to lead human intention back to the intensity of forces*, which generate phantasms. This is not the function of science which, denying intention, *compensates* for it in a beneficial and *efficacious* activity.

> The metamorphosis of humanity requires thousands of years for the formation of a type, then generations; finally an individual during its life passes through *several* individuals.
>
> Why could we not suceed in doing with humanity what the Chinese have learned to do with a tree – making it bear roses on one side and pears on the other?
>
> These natural processes of *anthropo-culture*, for example, which until now have been practised with extreme slowness and clumsiness, could be taken in hand by humanity itself; and the old acts of cowardice of the races, the racial struggles, could then be reduced to brief periods of time – at least in an experimental fashion. – Entire continents henceforth consecrated to this *conscious experimentation!*[106]

Nietzsche denounces the absolute discordance between the development of science as a creator of methods (or of *means*) and the non-development of the norms of the moral conscience (as the *end* of humanity).

The non-development of moral norms inhibits the creative force of scientific methods, and diverts them from any initiative capable of destabilizing the specific fixity of humanity. The notion of scientific reality has always been reinterpreted merely in terms of the moral notion of the reality of self and others. The notion of the scientific real thus winds up corroborating the moral reality of the integrity of the person – and more generally *the specific fixity of the human species*. Science rests on this specific fixity and integrity, since the very fact of knowing – or even being able to know – depends on this integrity. . . . How could something whose primordial dignity consists in *knowledge* ever place itself in question through its own knowledge!

This is the kind of quarrel Nietzsche inspired in himself when, haunted by his phantasm of an 'anthropo-culture', he imputed to science the consolidation, rather than the destruction, of the (gregarious) principle of reality. From whence is derived a double censure, which Nietzsche's thought deliberately transgresses,

– by authorizing itself to remove every experimental limit, to the point of putting in question institutions and their code of designation (the suppression, along with the concepts of *conscious* and *unconscious*, of the principle of prophylactic psychiatry, since the experimental initiative will now be the prerogative of singular cases, whose pathos will constitute the sole criterion of behaviour) –

even if this means

(– incurring the wrath of every subsequent 'respectable' philosophy, and having to answer for the 'acts of racial cowardice' – as he himself puts it – that might be undertaken by the worst kind of gregarious cretinism, which would lack this phantasm of 'anthropo-culture' he was advocating – and for this reason) himself becoming

– an (experimental) object of science, namely, an object of psychiatric investigations, both contemporary and subsequent, and hence, under the pretext of enriching their repertory, furnishing numerous arguments in favour of the surveillance of particular cases – thus also perpetuating the subservience of his own thought to the (positive) concept of the conscious and to the (negative) concept of the unconscious.

Now given his depreciation of 'conscious categories', did Nietzsche ever assert that it was necessary to confide the safeguarding of the unconscious to 'pathological cases'? Did he not himself recommend, in his notes, that the most severe restrictions be imposed on the 'degenerate', namely, that they be *forbidden to reproduce themselves*? And did he not go so far as to feign an interest in public health by envisioning a rather tedious set of 'prenuptial examinations' – under the pretext of preventing a *calamitous propagation*? His own suspicion that he was the son of a degenerate family, or the victim of some accident of pleasure, here again comes to light. These are the more or less obscure pretexts that wound up nourishing his Malthusian rage – whose persistent motif remained Nietzsche's phobia toward all gregarious phenomena.

The dilemma, however, was inscribed in Nietzsche's position once it required the *invention of simulacra* through an interpretive *force*, and once the pathos of the singular case – even if it is that of a *metapsychologist* – was called upon to *institute* what is *valuable*, what is *real* and what is *not*.

The fact that the integrity of the human being would see itself offended, trampled and broken more than once, not only in the name of the worst racial and national 'acts of cowardice', but also in more subtle and underhanded ways, and always in the name of the *respect* and safeguarding of the specificity of the human species – all this was no doubt something that never escaped Nietzsche's eye – and whose prolongations we must here continue to pursue.

To press everything terrible into *service*, one by one, step by step, experimentally: this is what the task of culture demands; but until it is strong enough for this, it must oppose, moderate, veil, even curse all this.

Everywhere that culture *posits evil*, it gives expression to a relationship of *fear*, thus a *weakness*.

Thesis: everything good is the evil of former days made serviceable. *Standard*: the greater and more terrible the passions are that an age, a people, an individual can permit themselves, because they are capable of employing them as *means, the higher stands their culture* (the realm of evil becomes ever *smaller*).

The more mediocre, the weaker, the more submissive and cowardly a man is, the more he will posit as *evil*: it is with him that the realm of evil is most comprehensive. The basest man will see the realm of evil (i.e. of that which is forbidden and hostile to him) everywhere.[107]

In Summa: domination of the passions, *not* their weakening or extirpation! – The greater the dominating power of a will, the more freedom may the passions be allowed.

The 'great man' is great owing to the free play and scope of his desires and to the yet greater power that knows how to press these magnificent monsters into service.

The 'good man' is at every stage of civilization the *harmless* and the *useful* combined: a kind of *mean*; the expression of the general consciousness of the kind of man whom one has no reason to fear but whom one must nonetheless not despise.[108]

Education: essentially the means of ruining the exceptions for the good of the rule, a deviation, seduction, sicklying over.

Higher Education: essentially the means of directing

taste *against* the exceptions for the good of the mediocre.

That is hard but, considered economically, perfectly reasonable. At least for that long time.

Only when a culture has an excess of powers at its disposal can it also constitute a hothouse for the luxury cultivation of the exception, the experiment, of danger, of the nuance: this is the tendency of every aristocratic culture.[109]

The high points of culture and civilization do not coincide: one should not be deceived about the abysmal antagonism of culture and civilization.

The great moments of culture are always, morally speaking, times of corruption; and conversely, the periods when the taming of the human animal ('civilization') was desired and enforced were times of intolerance against the boldest and most spiritual natures. Civilization has aims different from those of culture – perhaps they are even opposite – [110]

The *reality principle* of science and the *reality principle* of morality (of a gregarious origin), which consciousness and institutional language confuse, are separated, opposed and finally liquidated by Nietzsche when he declares that the only valuable reality is the *force that compels the appreciation of a given state*. As soon as this force is lacking in individuals or societies, they once again begin to confuse the two principles of morality and science in the form of the reality principle of gregarious language.

Science – which is the first to place them in question – demonstrates by its own methods that the *means* it ceaselessly elaborates only reproduce, *externally*, a *play of forces* which themselves have *neither goal nor end*, but whose combinations obtain this or that *result*. Thanks to their *reproduction*, consciousness is made explicit outside of itself through a set of efficacious applications of knowledge, which have no common measure with the institutional explication of consciousness.

Now science in turn afflicts with sterility societies that are impervious to its principle; yet no science can ever develop apart from a socially constituted group. To prevent science from *putting social groups in question*, these groups take science into their own hands and, since it is 'non-productive', they must combine it with their own needs and their own conservation, thereby rendering it 'productive'.

Science is today completely integrated into an extraordinary diversity of industrial plans, and its own autonomy seems almost inconceivable.

How then can it ever recover its autonomy? It had never possessed it formerly except in certain individuals, who were persecuted for this fact, or at least suspected and placed under surveillance.

If some conspiracy, in accordance with Nietzsche's wish, were to use *science and art* to no less suspect ends, industrial society would seem to foil the conspiracy in advance by the kind of '*mise-en-scène*' it presents of science and art, for fear of being subjected *in fact* to what this conspiracy has in store for it: namely, the breakup of the institutional structures that mask the society in a plurality of experimental spheres that finally reveal the authentic face of modernity – the final phase toward which Nietzsche believed the evolution of societies was leading. From this perspective, art and science would emerge as *sovereign formations* which Nietzsche said constituted the object of his counter-'sociology' – art and science establishing themselves as *dominant powers*, on the ruins of institutions.

This presupposes that – in the midst of the legal and moral distortion of institutions brought about by the industrial conditions of production – these powers, as they take form, would take over these same means of production, that they would appropriate the means by which existing industrial society, in accordance with its own interests, *sterilizes* the *idiosyncratic phantasms* of the affects in order to stifle their expression.

Now since it is a question of *experimentation* (which, if its aim is to promote gregarious insecurity, requires the security of the experimenter's mind – namely, that he be *sheltered and isolated*, so that he can surrender himself, without witnesses, to the various phases of *failure* that his success requires), Nietzsche believes in the idiosyncrasy of the *inventor* – and above all, the *artist* – the *singular case* – even if this means imagining this conspiracy of philosopher-despots and artist-tyrants, of which he is, strictly speaking, the sole representative.

> From now on there will be more favourable preconditions for more comprehensive *formations of sovereignty*, whose like has never yet existed. And even this is not the most important thing; the possibility has been established for the formation of international genetic associations whose task will be to rear *a race of masters, the future 'Masters of the Earth'* – a new, tremendous aristocracy, based on the severest self-*legislation*, in which *the despotic will of philosophers and artist-tyrants* will be made to endure for millennia – a higher kind of man who, thanks to the superiority in will, knowledge, riches, and influence, employ *democratic Europe* as their *most pliant and supple instrument* for getting hold of *the destinies of the earth*, so as to work as artists *on 'man' himself*.
>
> Enough: the time is coming when politics will have a different meaning.[111]

Is this a fit of rage? A joke? Or both? Nietzsche here gives a *literal* version of *applied physiology*: moreover, the proceedings he institutes against *science* – *as the guardian of a reality principle* which is *surpassed* by *the very means it implements* – are clearly aimed at the *possibility* of modifying the species behaviour of humanity *physiologically*.

A science *emancipated* from its social foundations, and

placed in the exclusive hands of a small group of individuals who are not answerable to any institution or dependent on any industry for the resources their experiments require – such is, in Nietzsche, the fantastic portrayal of the concrete conditions presupposed by the projects for *The Revaluation of All Values*. With regard to science, the *Revaluation* is based on the idea that as knowledge makes greater use of *means*, it becomes less and less concerned with the goal or end. So many ends, so many *means*. A goal pursued and attained is merely a pretext for giving birth to new *means*: the act of *creation* inaugurates the triumph of the arbitrary idiosyncrasy, which is disconcerting to the gregarious habits of thinking and feeling.

These different aspects of science – its *continual development* of methods (without being concerned with a goal), its *experimental power*, its *subordination to ends* that inhibit its creativity, and finally its *implication in the economy* – all intervene as the motifs of Nietzsche's prophetic phantasms, as so many obstacles to the *creation-imperative* he wants to introduce into science. In the name of this imperative, the experimenter must seek out the physiological and psychic conditions favourable to the evolution of some rare individuals, the beginnings of a human type that will be the sole justification of the species, its sole *raison d'être*. This 'justifying type' would therefore be the arbitrary reproduction of a phantasm. This reproduction, however, seems arbitrary only in relation to the presently existing species: what motivates this creative initiative is the impulsive need to engender a being that surpasses our species. For what is this phantasm, if not *'a being that humanity presupposes, who does not yet exist but indicates the goal of his existence. This is the freedom of all willing – and thus of everything arbitrary! In this aim resides love, the accomplished vision, nostalgia!'*[112]

Thus formulated, the postulate of the 'overman', which is not an individual but a *state*, is the means by which Nietzsche – who does not believe existence has a goal – will nonetheless give existence both *a meaning* and *a goal to pursue.* In this way, Nietzsche winds up substituting the creative initiative of the individual for the million random events of existence. In doing so, however, he is suppressing the crucial point of his thought, namely, that these 'random events' were implicit in the Eternal Return, which alone makes them succeed in producing something, independently of the willing or non-willing of humans.

Though unable to *forget* his revelation, the only thing Nietzsche will retain from it – in order to *exploit* it – is its sign. Having passed beyond the 'reality principle', he immediately falls back *on this side* of the principle, re-establishing it through a *voluntary* reconstitution of the law of the Return by means of science:

> To be capable of sacrificing innumerable beings in order to attain something with humanity. We must study the effective means by which a great man could be realized. Until now, every ethic has been infinitely limited and local: and blind and lying about surplus in the face of real laws. It existed to prevent certain actions, not to clarify them; and it was certainly unable to engender them.
>
> Science is a dangerous affair, and before we are persecuted because of it, we should stop speaking of its 'dignity.'[113]

To better understand what Nietzsche meant by his prophetic phantasm of the '*Masters of the Earth*', we would first of all like to know who the 'slaves' of such masters would be.

Nietzsche himself seems to provide the answer to this question when he asks, '*Where are the masters for whom all these slaves are working?*' What this means is that it is impossible to conceive of our industrial society apart from a generalization of the 'functional' character (that is, the 'productive' and hence *mercantile* character) that it demands of every activity.

In this manner, we can circumscribe the character of the 'master' with more or less precision. The fact that it happens to coincide with the character of the adherent to the doctrine of the Eternal Return is merely one aspect of Nietzsche's description.

In the first place, the term 'master', which is borrowed from hierarchical societies, merely expresses, in Nietzsche's thought, an attitude of refusal with regard to a society founded on work, money and surplus production. If Nietzsche had remained here, his protest would have been purely oneiric, no different from the similar reactions of a Baudelaire, a Poe, a Flaubert and many others – those '*decadents*'.

But Nietzsche did not pursue his prophetic combat as a *dreamer* in revolt against the existing order of our industrial societies. The point of departure for his projects is the fact that the modern economy depends on science, and cannot sustain itself apart from science; that it rests on the 'powers of money', corporations, and on their armies of engineers and workers, whether skilled or not; and that *at the level* of production, these powers cannot develop their own techniques except through forms of knowledge required by the manipulation of the objects they produce, and through the laws that govern the exchange and consumption of these products.

It is not now a question of knowing whether this strict interdependence of science and the economy, and the methods this interdependence engenders and develops, are not themselves the result of a 'creative' impulse characteristic of the industrial phenomenon. Nietzsche insists above all on the fact that the latter is a highly gregarious phenomenon, which is what permits us to see today that, although it sustains a *morally new* organization of existence, it does so only under the constant threat that Nietzsche's prophecies make weigh heavily upon it – namely, that this industrially 'gregarized' power will monopolize all the means to existence by realizing them in its own manner.

This is why, of all the projects termed 'training and selection', among the most virulent are precisely those that present the greatest *contrast* with our own economic organization.

If these projects have an aggressive character, it is due less to Nietzsche's hostility against *progressive socialization* than to his apprehension of everything this industrializing spirit would go on to develop in the name of an extravagant gregariousness.

Nietzsche's 'aristocratism' has nothing to do with a nostalgia for past hierarchies, nor, in order to realize this aristocratism, does he appeal to retrograde economic conditions. On the contrary, convinced that the economy has an irreversible hold over the affects – and that the affects are exploited totally for economic ends – Nietzsche constantly interprets socialist systems as *pessimistic* negations of life's strongest impulses, even though some fragments go so far as to suggest that a socialist society might have the advantage of accelerating the massive saturation of mediocre needs – a process that would be indispensable to the *setting apart* of an unassimilated group, this group being the 'higher' caste. Consequently, he believes in the ultimate failure of the socialist experiment, and even expresses a desire to see the attempt be made, certain that it will end in an immense waste of human lives. This indicates that Nietzsche did not believe that any regime could escape the process of de-assimilated forces that must ultimately turn against it. Now the most remarkable thing about these fragmentary sketches – which always show the effects of an improvisation oscillating between utopic moods and reactions to factual states – is what they identify as symptomatic of our modern world: namely, the mercantilization of value judgements, which disparages any 'non-productive' state as a diverting of forces, for which a category of individuals could be found guilty not only in a material sense, but also in an affective and moral sense.

Here again, we are touching on the institutional confusion between the reality principle of science and the reality principle of gregarious morality.

Initially formulated by reason in reaction against non-reason, the *reality principle* has become a much more fragile thing today, since humanity has been subject to many consecutive catastrophes and the failure of many delirious experiments.

Because societies can no longer exist without an *excess* of experiments in every domain, the incongruity between institutional norms and the constantly revised norms of science and the economy provokes an alternation between individual and social instabilities. The more this incongruity is affirmed in modern *everyday life*, the more rigorous and severe this censure becomes (a censure that is exercised less in the name of anachronistic institutions than in the name of the productivity of exchangeable goods): the production and exchange of objects alone are identified as the domain of the *intelligible*; and the *ability* to produce exchangeable goods establishes a variable norm of '*health*' and '*sickness*' – indeed, a norm of social justification. Morally speaking, whoever happens to transgress this censure is either stricken with *unintelligibility* or stigmatized by *non-productivity*.

As if in reponse to this, other fragments evoke two castes *separated* by their different *manners of living*, and it is a pure criterion of value that assigns the higher status to the contemplative caste – a contemplation that entails complete licence with regard to one's actions – and the lower status to the poor, business, or mercantile caste, since it would be contrary to the interest of this caste to grant itself any licence that would be morally or materially costly.

In and of themselves, these projects have nothing conclusive about them and draw no consequences – insofar as they imply no strategy with regard to social processes. The projects of 'selection', on the contrary, are developed with the concrete realities of modern social life in mind, and although they appeal to the same criteria of *gregariousness* and the singular, exceptional case, they always survey the close relationship between the economic factor and the gregarization of affects. The idea of a 'caste', which had haunted every social theorist of the last century, is emphasized by Nietzsche, on the one hand, in his considerations of the *laws of Manu* (which he studied during this period in a very dubious French translation, in conjunction with everything his friend Deussen had taught him about Hinduism) – and, on the other hand, by taking issue with the hierarchical constructions of Auguste Comte. In return, Nietzsche more or less describes the 'aristocracy of the future' in terms of a behaviour that is at once aggressive with regard to the so-called ends pursued by economic (Anglo-Saxon) optimism, and complicit with every phase of the process that would lead to a generalized (and hence planetary) levelling. Nietzsche expects a movement of resistance to come from the extreme perfection of the mechanism – that is, from the progressive de-assimilation of 'surplus forces'. His belief that this de-assimilation will be accompanied by a material or moral catastrophe, since it would coincide with the disclosure of the doctrine of the *Vicious Circle*; or his suggestion that the 'initiates' of the doctrine will have to intervene in a hidden manner – all this is revealed in the fragments in a rather obscure and particularly incoherent fashion (as when, in certain sequences of the unpublished manuscripts, one finds no fragments that consider the economic process, the role of a superior caste still to be born, and a selection at the same time; even then, however, it is not always clear whether or not the selection proceeds morally from the disclosure of the doctrine).

In these considerations of the economic and strategic order, the principle put forward is always that certain forces should be kept in reserve for the future. It is here that the distinction he makes between *training* and *taming* intervenes:

What I want to make clear by all the means in my power:
a. that there is no worse confusion than the confusion of (disciplinary) *training* with *taming*: which is what has been done – Training, as I understand it, is a means of storing up the tremendous forces of mankind so that the generations can build upon the work of their forefathers – not only outwardly, but inwardly,

organically growing out of them and becoming something stronger –

b. that it is extraordinarily dangerous to believe that mankind as a whole will progress and grow stronger if individuals become flabby, equal, average –

Mankind is an abstraction: the goal of training, even in the case of a single individual, can only be *the stronger man* (– the man without training is weak, extravagant, unstable –).[114]

Here again, it is clear that Nietzsche is not concerned with the *fate* of humanity (a pure abstraction, in Stirner's sense); that he envisions humanity as something more like a raw material, and this always from a strictly 'artistic' point of view; and that future generations are and will only ever be valuable because of their rare *successes*, which are always *individual*. But how is this *bias* expressed here? Precisely as a certain *misgiving* with regard to the *human* quality, a misgiving that relies on the *moral adhesion to the fate of humanity* – when in fact it is only a question of the means of satisfying an idiosyncrasy, in itself spectacular: the blossoming of a sovereign *insolence*.

This idiosyncrasy cannot not be *insolent* with regard to resources, since it must find them in what, by definition, it denies: the gregarious context [*fond*]. Either it is the species that is conserved in all its mediocrity, this mediocrity being the very means it uses to economize its energies. Or else the individual, as the beneficiary of these energies, squanders them by consuming them for itself. The individual, if it is sovereign, can allow itself such waste and inconstancy. . . .

To the degree that humanity seeks consistency in and through its *conservation* alone, it falls ever further into inconsistency. The increase in the number of *agents* of existence is proportional to the decrease in the power of each of them. If power is already the violence of the absurd, then at the level of gregariousness it must find in the individual agent some meaning for the species. Hence, the more the species grows, the more it perpetuates itself for nothing. For the species, as a whole, cannot act as the *sole agent* of existence, which alone would account for the *singularity* of each individual.

At the level of the species, then, the unbridled power of propagation destroys the species' *raison d'être*: it cannot be its own justification. It is justified only in terms of the *differences* it is able to produce in relation to itself, that is to say, the different degrees of intensity of existence. But the greater the number of living beings becomes, the more these differences tend to be effaced, for each difference is *reproduced at the same rhythm*, and consequently they re-form a homogenous totality in which this difference is in turn annulled.

Thus the power at work in the propagation of the species, henceforth considered as the *sole agent* of existence, would have attained a state of equilibrium, insofar as the latter is verified by the fixity of the species. But (as Nietzsche tried to demonstrate using the theory of energy) every state of equilibrium is repugnant to power, which upsets this equilibrium by increasing. Similarly, as *propagation*, power also exceeds the human species as the *sole agent* of *existence*, and it is by exceeding it that power turns the species into a *teeming monstrosity*: at this stage, *the species is no longer the master of its own destiny*. It would be vain for power to try to exhaust itself in a new agent, and for this reason it must also come back to *itself*, until it is totally spent. Now the absurdity of the Eternal Return is opposed to this absurd reproduction, even though it is the same vicious Circle. The total devalorization of power through the propagation of the species, the *usurping agent of existence*, has as its counterpart the *singular case*, which is where surplus power finds its image: the image of chance. For if the *singular case* can be defined only negatively in relation to gregariousness, it is defined positively with regard to power. The singular case is not hereditary, and its originality cannot be transmitted; on the contrary, it is a threat to the species as species; in relation to it, gregariousness is nothing more than a raw and living *material*, characteristic of an elaboration of chance.

The concepts 'individual' and 'species' equally false and merely apparent. *'Species' expresses only the fact that an abundance of similar creatures appear at the same time and that the tempo of the further growth and change is for a long time slowed down*, so actual small continuations and increases are not very much noticed (– a phase of evolution in which the evolution is not visible, so an equilibrium *seems* to have been attained, making possible the false notion *that a goal has been attained* – and that this is the goal of evolution –).[115]

Nietzsche never considered the phenomenon of demography explicitly, yet it is implied in the role he wants to make the species play, namely, that of an *experimental material*. The conscious possibility of human *waste* is henceforth the order of his speculations.

The first point under this rubric is that, up to the present, it has been an error to treat the human species as an *individual* – and thus as the *sole agent* of existence.

The second point is that, since it is a question of instituting new tables of *values* – and thus a goal, a new meaning – these values must be taught only to individuals.

The third point is that, since it is also a question of his own doctrine, the doctrine's virtue can be exercised only on the condition of *extirpating* the *gregarious link* in each individual, and the reference to the *tutelary authorities* of the species as a whole.

Nietzsche abandons a moral selection of the doctrine according to the injunction, *Will to re-will life* as such. But he remains attached to the necessity of a hidden action which, in the name of the Vicious Circle, would induce *'despair'* in anyone who still lays claim to a 'gregarious' consciousness. From this fact, Nietzsche implies that a given state can be interpreted as violence from the viewpoint of gregariousness, or as experimental from the viewpoint of the *Vicious Circle*. In reality, this state of violence reigns sufficiently in fact: but in himself Nietzsche projects this *state of fact* as a criterion that would sanction his postulate.

The doctrine now seems to be an *interpretation* of the established reign of violence. But as *training and selection*, the doctrine institutes this reign as the *justice* of the universal economy. Consequently, whether it is a question of the 'Master' or the 'slave', their behaviour will change nothing in this economy; it will now be up to them to *change* themselves in order for the economy to remain a *justice* for one, and a *pure economy* for another. Who here is the Master, who is its slave? One of them represents the species that defends itself against exceptional cases, the other is one of these cases. Each of them contains the exploiter or the exploited of the other. Now this economy, which *the Vicious Circle of the Return* represents, thus the *justice of the Circle*, if it does not disappear totally in the projects of selection, gives rise to the outlines of an *experimental* selection derived from the economic processes of the modern world. So that Nietzsche presents an always equivocal interpretation, according to which the 'initiates' of the doctrine of the Return would be authorized by the absurdity of the 'Vicious Circle' to act without scruples, and would intervene, at a willed moment, in order to forge the new type of overman from the convulsions born out of a universal levelling.

> Slavery is universally visible, though no one wants to admit it; – we would have to be ubiquitous to know all its situations, to better represent all its opinions; it is only in this manner that we will be able to dominate and exploit it. Our nature must remain hidden: much like the Jesuits who established a dictatorship in the midst of universal anarchy, but who introduced themselves into it as a *tool* and a *function*. What is our function, our cloak of slavery? Our teaching? – Slavery must not

be suppressed, it is necessary. We would simply like that such (men) for whom we are working always be formed, so that we do not waste this enormous mass of political and commercial forces. If only for there to be *spectators* and *non-partners!*[116]

The importance of increasing gregariousness and the growth of populations is only the obverse side of the industrial phenomenon. If there are more and more needs to satisfy, even if new needs imply a so-called 'rise in the standard of living', they are vulgarized by their very multiplication as well as by their satisfaction – a new form of gregariousness.

Nietzsche registers the distant moral and social consequences of this phenomenon with the precision of a seismograph. As exploitation developed, it demanded, under the pretext of a *massive* (and thus *average*) *saturation*, that *completely conditioned reflexes* be substituted for the *appetitive* spontaneity of individuals on a vast scale. Consequently, it also arrogated to itself the 'moral' and 'psycho-technical' mission (inherited from the essentially *punitive* element of the economies of the two world wars, which were *prototypes* of planetary planning) of exterminating any impulse that might induce human nature to *increase its emotive capacity* – notably, the propensity of the individual to put its '*useful*' *specificity* at risk by seeking that which *exceeds* it as an agent: namely, the most subtle states of the soul, which are capable of inducing a *rapture* that surpasses its congenital servitude, and therefore of producing an intensity that corresponds to the impulsive *constraint* of its own phantasms – even if they are themselves due to this *congenital servitude*, thus magnified.

What Nietzsche calls, in another fragment, '*licence with regard to every virtue-imperative*'[117] is itself the very practice of these impulses, insofar as they find the forms of their blossoming either in a *lived culture* or in a sphere proper to their own way of living, acting, thinking and feeling.

Impulses that do not necessarily arise out of material riches, but flow from a *spiritual heredity* in the way they use 'riches',

namely, from a *knowledge*; and that, socially speaking, give rise
to an *isolated* human group, no longer defined by origins of
any kind, but by *affinities* whose long-standing habits form
the group's cohesion (offensive and defensive): such is the
'luxury' (but such is also culture) – the 'aristocratism' which,
according to Nietzsche, must be represented by at least *one*
group, *one* particular case, *not* as a *fraction* of humanity but
as its *surplus* (and hence, for the totality, as an exterminable,
shootable, odious leech). This group or particular case – if it
wants to assume a *surplus existence* – can live only in the *distance*
it *must* maintain, morally speaking, from the totality, drawing
its strength from the indignation, hostility and reprobation
heaped on it by the totality, which necessarily rejects its own
'surplus', since it is unable to see it as anything other than a
rebellious, sick, or degenerate fraction of itself.

The term 'surplus' points to the formation of new castes of
'masters and slaves' by the industrial process itself.

This notion already seems to underlie the projects of earlier
epochs that had sketched out – as if in anticipation of our
society of consumption – a new mercantile class that was
incapable of revolting, and for this reason was enslaved by
the satisfaction of its own needs. Those who are excluded
are excluded by their own moral non-satisfaction: superior
natures, living prostheses, austere and sober. But the 'main
consideration' is 'not to see the task of the higher species in
leading the lower (as, e.g., Comte does), but the lower as a
base upon which the higher species performs its *own* tasks –
upon which it alone can stand'.[118]

Another fragment dating from the period of *The Gay
Science* evokes the 'Surplus Men':

SURPLUS MEN. You, masters of yourselves! You,
sovereign men! All those whose nature is only an
appurtenance, all those who cannot be counted, they
are working for you, though it might not seem so from
a superficial glance! These princes, these businessmen,
these agriculturalists, these military men who perhaps

think of themselves as high above you – they are only slaves who, according to an eternal necessity, do not work for themselves! There are never slaves without masters – and you others will always be these masters for whom they are working: in a later century, one will be able to see more clearly this presently indiscernable spectacle! Leave them, then, their ways of seeing and their illusions, through which they justify and deceive themselves about their servile work, don't battle against opinions that constitute a remission for slaves! But always remember that this enormous effort, this sweat, this dust, this din of the labour of civilization is at the service of those who know how to use it all without participating in this work; that surplus men who are maintained by this universal surplus-labor are necessary, and that these men of surplus constitute the meaning and apology of all this fermentation! In the meantime, be millers and let these waters come to your watermills! Don't worry about their struggles or the wild tumult of these tempests! Whatever forms of the State or societies might result from it, *they will never be anything more than forms of slavery* – and you will always be the sovereigns, for you alone belong to yourselves, and the others will never be anything more than *accessories*![119]

The project that foresees a 'class' of *satiated slaves satisfied with their lot* who work to benefit *austere and sober masters*, in accordance with the latter's 'creative tasks', is nothing other than a systematization of what Nietzsche sees in the already existing order: namely, that the false hierarchy of the so-called ruling class, which believes it determines the fate of the rarest individuals, hidden among the masses, in reality frees an inverted and secret hierarchy from its most vile tasks – a hierarchy formed by 'surplus men' who are unassimilable to the general interest. The 'rulers' (industrialists, military men, bankers, businessmen, bureaucrats, etc.), with their various tasks, are merely effective slaves who *work unknowingly* on behalf of these *hidden masters*, and thus for a *contemplative* caste that ceaselessly forms the 'values' and the meaning of life.

But this is only a preliminary phase. What now exists in a hidden manner will one day be manifest in an event, when the sign of the Vicious Circle will shine forth in the firmament of universal consciousness in all the brilliance of its absurdity and the absolute non-sense of existence – at which time it will be the exclusive task of the masters to *determine*, not only the meaning, but the course of all things. How will this event be brought about?

There are two ways to foresee the constraint exerted by the thought of the *Vicious Circle*: either the thought of the Vicious Circle will become so *intolerable* at this point that the weakest will destroy themselves; or else, since it is unlikely that despair will replace indifference, Nietzsche imagines that the 'experimenters', under the sign of the Vicious Circle, will undertake certain initiatives which will make life impossible for the 'refuse', and will make the *'privileged' incapable of revolting*.

It might be tempting to think that this prophecy would have subsequently been fulfilled 'beyond all hope', were it not, once again, for these *false masters* – unconscious slaves – who, while working unknowingly for the hidden hierarchy, exempted the hierarchy from all the vulgarity that experimentation always entails; for the false masters were pursuing an *aim* and gave themselves a *meaning* that the hidden hierarchy laughed at.

This *meaning* and *aim* are what Nietzsche foresaw almost a century in advance: planetary planning or management. The hierarchies initiated during Nietzsche's era had no idea of this type of management; it is rather our present-day hierarchies that have fulfilled Nietzsche's prophecies. *Mutatis mutandis*, the relationship between the now-existing hierarchies and the hidden hierarchies remains the same: the former slave away, work, plan for the best or the worst; but the hidden, from one generation to the next, are awaiting the hour, the *willed moment*, at which they will overturn the final 'signification', and extract the consequences of this immense labour of 'unconscious slaves'. As Nietzsche said of the *Church* and of *Russia*, the hidden know how to *wait*.

The *need* to show that as the consumption of humans and humanity becomes more and more economical and the 'machinery' of interests and services is integrated ever more intricately, a *counter-movement* is inevitable. I designate this as the *secretion of a luxury surplus of humanity*: it aims to bring to light a stronger species, a higher type that arises and preserves itself under different conditions from those of the average human. My concept, *my parable* for this type is, as one knows, the word 'overman'.

On that first road which can now be completely surveyed, arise adaptation, levelling, higher Chinadom, modesty in the instincts, satisfaction in the dwarfing of humanity – a kind of *stationary level of humanity*. Once we possess that common economic management of the earth that will soon be inevitable, mankind will be able to find its best meaning as a machine in the service of this economy – as a tremendous clockwork, composed of ever smaller, ever more subtly 'adapted' gears; as an ever-growing superfluity of all dominating and commanding elements; as a whole of tremendous force, whose individual factors represent *minimal forces, minimal values*.

In opposition to this dwarfing and adaptation of humanity to a specialized utility, a reverse movement is needed – the production of a *synthetic, summarizing, justifying human being* for whose existence this transformation of humanity into a machine is a precondition, as a base on which he can invent his *higher form of being*.

He needs the opposition of the masses, of the 'leveled', a feeling of distance from them! He stands on them, he lives off them. This higher form of aristocracy is that of the future. – Morally speaking, this overall machinery, this solidarity of all gears, represents a maximum in the exploitation of man; but it presupposes those on whose account this exploitation has meaning. Otherwise it would really be nothing but an overall diminution, a value diminution of the type man – a regressive phenomenon in the grand style.

It is clear, what I combat is economic optimism: as if increasing expenditure of everybody must necessarily involve the increasing welfare of everybody. The opposite seems to me to be the case: *expenditure of everybody amounts to a collective loss*: humanity is *diminished* – so one no longer knows what *aim* this tremendous process has served. An aim? a new aim? – *that* is what humanity needs.[120]

A *division of labour* among the affects within society: so individuals and classes produce an *incomplete*, but for that reason *more useful*, kind of soul. To what extent certain affects have remained almost rudimentary in every type within society (with a view to developing another affect more strongly).

Justification of morality:

economic (the intention to exploit individual strength to the greatest possible extent to prevent the squandering of everything exceptional);

aesthetic (the formation of firm types, together with pleasure in one's own type);

political (the art of enduring the tremendous tension between differing degrees of power);

physiological (as a pretended high evaluation in favour of the underprivileged or mediocre – for the preservation of the weak).[121]

The strong of the future. – That which partly necessity, partly chance has achieved here and there, the conditions for the production of a stronger type, we are now able to comprehend and *consciously will: we are able to create the conditions under which such an elevation is possible.*

Until now, 'education' has had in view the needs of society: *not* the possible needs of the future, but the needs of the society of the day. One desired to produce 'tools' for it. Assuming the *wealth of force* were greater, one could imagine forces being *subtracted*, not to serve the needs of society but some future need.

Such a task would have to be posed the more it was grasped to what extent the contemporary form of society was being so powerfully transformed that at some future time *it would be unable to exist for its own sake alone*, but only as a *tool* in the hands of a stronger race.

The increasing dwarfing of man is precisely the driving force that brings to mind the training of *a stronger race* – a race that would be excessive precisely where the dwarfed species was weak and growing weaker (in will, responsibility, self-assurance, ability to posit goals for oneself).

The *means* would be those history teaches: *isolation* through *interests in preservation that are the reverse of those which are average today*; habituation to reverse evaluations; distance as a pathos; a free conscience in those things that today are the most undervalued and prohibited.

The *homogenizing* of European man is the great process that cannot be obstructed: one should even hasten it. The necessity *to create a gulf, distance, order of rank*, is given *eo ipso* – *not* the necessity to retard this process.

As soon as it is established, this *homogenizing species* requires a *justification*: it lies in serving a higher sovereign species that stands upon the former and can raise itself to its task only by doing this. Not merely a race of masters whose sole task is to rule, but a race with *its own sphere of life*, with an excess of strength for beauty, bravery, culture, manners to the highest peak of the spirit; an *affirming* race that may grant itself *every great luxury* – strong enough to have no need of *the tyranny of the virtue-imperative*, rich enough to have no need of

thrift and pedantry, beyond good and evil; a hothouse
for strange and choice plants.[122]

Of these three fragments, the first two read like an irrefutable
description of our present situation. The third examines the
consequences that will ensue after the final phases of an
irreversible process – already envisioned in the first two
fragments. The complementary fragments are summarized
in a postulate that is 'delirious' only to the degree that the
process of 'planetary management' is in itself *'reasonable'*.
Nietzsche's postulate lacks necessity: this is why it is
derisory, though for Nietszche this would be its own
justification. *Planetary management* is practicable: hence it
can do without justification. If Nietzsche nevertheless claims
one, it is because something must justify this servitude before
life. If life has no need of justice, it is strong enough to bear
the iniquity; but if the *servitude of everyone* is absurd, it must at
least be given a meaning.

Let us here recall the argument that, *on this side of* the *concrete* realization Nietzsche envisions, takes its inspiration from
a *petitio principii*. In the first place, there is Nietzsche's statement that henceforth we can *knowingly will* and thus *produce
the conditions necessary to* the formation of a *'higher' species*.

In the second place, there is his claim that *society is in the
midst of a powerful transformation that no longer allows it to exist
for itself*.

But what does this mean, if not that the economic mechanism of exploitation (developed by science and the economy)
is *decomposed* as an institutional structure into a set of means.
The result of this is:

on the one hand, that society can no longer fashion its
members as 'instruments' to its own ends, now that it has
itself become the instrument of a mechanism;

on the other hand, that a 'surplus' of forces, eliminated by
the mechanism, are now made available for the formation of
a different human type.

But it is here that Nietzsche's conspiratory phantasm

begins. *Who* is going to develop this human type? No one will be convinced of it simply by envisioning what Nietzsche calls the '*subtraction of forces*' or their *isolation*.

It remains to be seen if this human type can be developed by a mechanism that rejects the unassimilable (surplus production), or if it is necessary here to anticipate a deliberate intervention.

To attain this human type, says Nietzsche, we simply have to accelerate, rather than fight, the ever-expanding process that seems to be contrary to the goal: *equalization* (in the guise of the democratization practised by industrial society) – which implies, for Nietzsche, a reduction of the human being. The '*rise in the standard of living*' maintains a confusion between the *quality of needs* and the quality of the means to satisfy them. The more this *equalization* – that is, the satisfaction of the most frustrated – *spreads*, the greater will be the *base* that one has at one's disposal. This base will be constituted precisely through *an interest in conserving an average level*. And it is here that Nietzsche has an irrefutable premonition: *the total effacement of differences in the satisfaction of needs* and *the homogenization of the habits of feeling and thinking* will have as its effect a moral and affective numbing. Whether it is experienced or not, if Nietzsche speaks, here as elsewhere, of a *justification*, it is because he understands that the *human being will no longer feel itself*, nor its substance, nor its power – even though it will henceforth be capable of exploiting other planets.

This means that *the very impulse of the Eternal Return*, which keeps the secret of its law far from consciousness, would incite humanity *to live against this inexorable law*. When Nietzsche ponders the ultimate *justification* of the fate allotted to human beings by the economy, it is because this same law is still fulfilled in a way of life. Thus, if the existence of societies as such is put in question by the resources of culture and science – in and through a universally enslaving economy – and if this constitutes a moment of the Circle, its obscure phase, then this movement must be pursued to its starting-point – the point to which this enslavement, when pushed to its extreme, will lead us. If *the enslavement of everyone* coincides with *justice*, the only practicable justice, it is only because, somewhere, freedom bursts forth from an *iniquitous* and absurd flash that servitude alone can have an *equitable* meaning. It is in this relation, in this tension – in this final intensity – that the luminous achievement of the sinister Circle appears.

The thought that a *setting apart* or *isolation* of a human group could be used as a *method* for creating a series of 'rare and singular plants' (a 'race' having '*its own sphere of life*', freed from any virtue-imperative): – this experimental character of the project – impracticable – if it were not the object of a vast conspiracy – because no amount of 'planning' could ever foresee '*hothouses*' of this kind – would in some manner have to be inscribed in and produced by the very process of the economy. (And in fact, what regime today does not have, in some form or another, an 'experimental' character of just this kind, within which – whatever aims it may invoke for the method it practises – there exists a hierarchy of 'experimenters', a tiny fraction of humanity with 'its own sphere of life', who – although they are incapable of ever producing, by virtue of their familiarity with its cause – can at least claim for themselves the merit, with all the privileges that ensue, of having extirpated like so much chaff the smallest germs of those 'rare and singular plants' . . . a prevention that is undoubtedly less costly than their cultivation.)

But since Nietzsche insists on the *eliminatory* phase of the (economic) process, that is, on the *de-assimilation of affective types* (which this process rejects), the segregation of a 'caste' that Nietzsche claims to be 'sovereign' would already be implicit in the life of every society. The selection occurs spontaneously, in accordance with certain affinities grounded in the *unexchangeable* (*non-communicable*) character of certain ways of living, thinking and feeling *in the largest circuits*.

Now the idea that the only valid 'legitimation' of 'planetary management' would be the task of nourishing a human type whose attribute of sovereignty would be derived from its 'non-productive' way of living, in the context of a gregarious and hard-working totality, amounts to a kind of sanctification of *parasitism*.

This challenge is *anticipated* by every industrial morality, whose laws of production create *a bad conscience* in anyone who lives within the unexchangeable, and which can tolerate no culture or sphere of life that is not in some manner integrated into or subjected to general productivity. It is against this vast enterprise of *intimidating the affects*, whose amplitude he measures, that Nietzsche proposes his own *projects of selection*, as so many menaces. These projects must provide for the propitious moment when these rare, singular and, to be sure, poisonous plants can be clandestinely cultivated – and then can blossom forth like an insurrection of the affects against *every virtue-imperative*. Nietzsche knows that the advent of his 'sovereign' and sovereignly non-productive 'caste' is inscribed in the 'Vicious Circle'; consequently, he leaves it to the progressive 'functionalization' of gregariousness to prepare its prior conditions – unconsciously but inevitably.

But prior in what sense? In the sense that these conditions are the result of the very dilemmas that industrial power creates from the fact of gregarious proliferation. It matters little whether or not the sovereignly non-productive take the form of a 'caste', in accordance with Nietzsche's perspective, which in this regard is still too marked by the political aestheticism of his time. Rather, it would seem, its particular character would lie in the *unforeseeable force* of generations. The power of the propagation of the species is already turned against the *instrument that multiplied it*: the industrial spirit, which raised gregariousness to the rank of the *sole agent* of existence, will have thus carried the seeds of its own destruction within itself. Despite appearances, the new species, 'strong enough to have no need of the tyranny of the virtue-imperative',[123] does not yet reign; and unless it is already preparing for it on the backs of the classes, what it will ultimately bring about – the most fearful thing of its kind – is perhaps still sleeping in the cradle.

> The philosophical nihilist is convinced that all that happens is meaningless and in vain; and that there ought not to be anything meaningless and in vain. But whence this: there ought not to be? From where does one get *this* 'meaning', *this* standard? – At bottom, the nihilist thinks that the sight of such a bleak, useless existence makes a philosopher feel *dissatisfied*, bleak, desperate. Such an insight goes against our finer sensibility as philosophers. It amounts to the absurd valuation: to have any right to be, the character of existence *would have to give the philosopher pleasure.* –
>
> Now it is easy to see that pleasure and displeasure can only be *means* in the course of events: the question remains whether we are at all able to see the 'meaning', the 'aim', whether the question of meaninglessness or its opposite is not insoluble for us. – [124]

> Nihilism does not only contemplate the 'in vain'! nor is it merely the belief that everything deserves to perish: one helps to destroy. – This is, if you will, illogical; but the nihilist does not believe that one needs to be logical. – It is the condition of strong spirits and wills, and these do not find it possible to stop with the No of 'judgement': their nature demands the No of the deed. The reduction to nothing by judgement is seconded by the reduction to nothing by hand.[125]

From this point on, the *conspiracy* seems to be the true motive of this reversal of the doctrine of the Return into an experimental instrument. If there is a representation of a conspiracy in Nietzsche's thought, it is one that, in this regard, is no longer content to simply level a judgement against existence. Thought must itself have the same *effectiveness* as what happens *outside of it* and *without it*. This type of thought, in the long run, must therefore *come to pass* as an *event*. For Nietzsche's thought to conceive of itself as a conspiracy, it must have previously grasped the march of events as following the dictates of a *premeditated* action. If Nietzsche rejects Darwin's concept of natural selection as a falsification of the real selection, as a selection that ensures the reign of those who *compromise the meaning and value of life*, it is because he feels that the Darwinian selection *conspires with gregariousness* by presenting *mediocre* beings as *strong*, rich and powerful beings. The latter, from Nietzsche's point of view, are nothing other than the singular and exceptional cases that have been practically *eliminated* up to now. The selection expounded by Darwin coincides perfectly with bourgeois morality. This then is the external conspiracy – the conspiracy of the science and morality of institutions – against which Nietzsche projects the conspiracy of the Vicious Circle. This sign will henceforth inspire an experimental action – a kind of counter-selection that follows from the very nature of the interpretation of the Eternal Return, that is to say, from the *lived experience* of a singular and privileged case. The *unintelligible depth* of experience is thus in itself the challenge thrown up against the gregarious propensities, as they are expressed in everything that is communicable, comprehensible and exchangeable.

However, through its experimental intent, the conspiracy seems to repudiate the very authenticity of the 'Vicious Circle'. On the one hand, the *meaninglessness of existence* serves as an *argument* for the philosopher to free his hands and start pruning on the spot. On the other hand, the 'truth' of the Return is virtually *renounced* as a chimera, and considered as a pure phantasm. Hence it is the simulacrum of a doctrine invoked by those who pursue the simulacrum of a goal: namely, the 'overman'. In effect, the 'overman' must be identified with the Vicious Circle and, in this case, would be identified with a phantasm. For if the *Return* were only a chimera in Nietzsche, then 'giving the history of the human species a *goal* and a *meaning*', willing this goal, comprehending this meaning, would amount only to following the dictates of this second simulacrum of the overman. If it is *true*, on the contrary, that *all things return* in accordance with the *Vicious Circle*, then *the proposed meaning and goal would be chimerical* – and all the experiments would merely be an imposture.

When Nietzsche, at various points, speaks of a 'reconversion of politics', he alludes to the *experimental freedom* that, *were it not assumed by the philosopher* (the scientist and the artist), would risk being taken over *by the masses*. But at that point, this most audacious *experimentation* would again be decried in the name of the conservation of the species. The *meaningless* depth of existence must therefore prevail over the 'reasonable' progress of the species, but it can prevail only if the philosopher gives affective forces an *aim* in which they can find satisfaction, an aim that makes the *useless expenditure* of affectivity predominate over expenditures that are *useful* to the species, and hence to the organization of the world.

If the 'Vicious Circle' – to avoid speaking of a theology of the 'god of the vicious circle' – not only turns the apparently irreversible progression of history into a regressive movement (toward an always undeterminable starting-point), but also maintains the species in an 'initial' state that is entirely dependent on *experimental initiatives* that will decide in favour of '*singular cases*', then we can no longer refer to the criteria of what is true or false in the unpredictability of every decision (against which one might like to hold out). For *the reality principle disappears along with the principle of the identity of each and every thing.* The only reality is a perfectly arbitrary one, expressed in simulacra instituted (as values) by an impulsive state in which fluctuations change their meanings, depending on the greater or lesser interpretive force of *singular cases*. The *meaning* and *aim* of *what happens* can always be revoked as much by the success of the *experimentation* as by its failure.

Nietzsche, as he writes to Overbeck and later to Strindberg, wants *to break the history of humanity in two* – as well as humanity itself. In the course of events, the Eternal Return, as experience, as the thought of thoughts, constitutes the event that abolishes history. Nietzsche adopts the role of the Evangelist: *the kingdom is already among you*. But what is among you – this is the bad (or good) news – is the Vicious Circle that leads to the *'superhuman'*. Nietzsche should have said: the *inhuman*.

The conspiracy of the Vicious Circle must provide a perspective on the singular case and close off any outlet that leads to the species as species: everything that was intelligible for the species becomes obscure, uncertain, harrowing.

From this viewpoint, though Nietzsche never tried to describe the required methodological conditions, we can say not only that the conspiracy he outlined took place *without him*, but that it succeeded perfectly: neither through *capitalism*, nor *the working class*, nor *science*, but rather through the *methods* dictated by objects themselves and their *modes of production*, with their laws of growth and consumption. The industrial phenomenon, in short, is a concrete form of the *most malicious caricaturization* of his doctrine, that is to say, the regime of the Return has been installed in the 'productive' existence of humans who never produce anything but a state of *strangeness* between themselves and their life.

In this way, by realizing one aspect of Nietzsche's project, industrialism – which today has become a technique – forms the exact inverse of his postulate. It is neither the triumph of singular cases, nor the triumph of the mediocre, but quite simply a new and totally amoral form of gregariousness – the sole agent left to define existence: not the 'superhuman' but the 'super-gregarious' – the Master of the Earth.

7

The Consultation of the Paternal Shadow

The good fortune of my existence, its uniqueness perhaps, lies in its fatality: to express it in the form of a riddle, *I am already dead as my father, while as my mother I am still living and becoming old.*

This dual descent, as it were, both from the highest and the lowest rung of the ladder of life, at the same time a *decadent* and a *beginning* – this, if anything, explains that neutrality, that freedom from all partiality in relation to the total problem of life, that perhaps distinguishes me.[126]

Nietzsche, when he wrote *Ecce Homo*, knew both how a riddle *is constructed* and how a signification is constructed. The latter depends on a play of mirrors in which the *will to interpret* deliberately encloses itself, and simulates a necessity in order to flee the vacuity of its arbitrariness.

'*To be able to read a text without any interpretation*' – this desideratum of Nietzsche expresses his revolt against the servitude implied in all signification. What then is it that will free us from a given signification and restore us to *uninterpretable existence*? How is this to be 'understood' (*Verstehen*)? How can the fact of holding to [*se tenir dans*] what is to be understood be *intensified* without being subject to a determined intention?

This is the question that underlies Nietzsche's 'autobiographical' writings. He opened himself up to the act of understanding, he explicated himself by *implicating himself* in a preconceived *interpretation* of the 'text'.

Nothing could be more misleading than that which at first sight seems transparent in this riddle, the very *shadow* of a solution being able to serve as a key-word: *I am already dead as my father, while as my mother I am still living and becoming old.* This interiorization of a state of affairs cannot but have the same aspect as what was inscribed in the *oneiric experience* Nietzsche related to himself as a child. The *oneiric* experience concerns *his already dead father whom he sees raising his younger brother in a dream.* The child Nietzsche grows up in the shadow of his mother's mourning and bereavement, and becomes a young man brought up exclusively by women.

This *premonitory dream* of Nietzsche's childhood was written down afterwards, first at the age of thirteen or fourteen (1858), and then again at the age of seventeen.

THE PREMONITORY DREAM

First Version (1858)

At this time I dreamed that I heard the sounds of an organ coming from the church, as if at a burial. As I was looking to see what was going on, a grave suddenly opened, and my father, clothed in his death-shroud, arose from the tomb. He hurries toward the church and almost immediately comes back with a child in his arms. The mound of the grave reopens; he climbs back in, and the gravestone once again sinks back over the opening. The swelling noise of the organ immediately stops, and I wake up.

The day after this night, little Joseph is suddenly taken ill with cramps and convulsions, and dies within a few hours. Our anguish was immense. My dream was fulfilled completely.

> *The little cadaver, moreover, was laid in my father's arms.*[127]

Second Version (1861)

I seemed to hear the sound of a deadened organ coming from the nearby church. Surprised, *I open the window* that looks over the church and the cemetery. My father's tomb opens, a white form rises from it and disappears into the church. The lugubrious, disturbing sounds continue to bellow; the white form carries something under its arms that I cannot make out. The tumulus is raised, the form descends into it, the organs fall silent. I wake up.

The next day, my younger brother, a vivacious and gifted child, is seized with convulsions and dies within half an hour. He was buried *beside my father's tomb.*[128]

The second version, written three years after the first, adds some explanatory revisions: the organ-sounds coming from the church make the dreamer, in his dream, *open the window* looking over the cemetery and the church. The rest of the dream is related much more vaguely, the emphasis being placed on the *bellowing* of the organs; as in the first version, the essential elements of the scene are the rising movement of the gravestone, and the coming and going of the shadow. The child is no longer visible, but the commentary tells us that little Joseph was gifted and that he died within half an hour – which means that the young Nietzsche is relating the details and impressions of his family circle. In the first version, the child is laid to rest in the arms of his father; in the second, he is buried near the paternal tomb.

Later, Nietzsche seems to have forgotten that he had made note of this dream, and although he would always speak of his father and his premature death with veneration, up through *Ecce Homo*, he would never again speak of this nightmare. By contrast, he saw a link between his father's age at the moment of his death, and his own age during the period of his deepest depression: 'My father died at the age of thirty-six: he was delicate, kind, and morbid, as a being that is destined merely to pass by – more a gracious memory of life than life itself. In the same year in which his life went downward, mine, too, went downward: at thirty-six, I reached the lowest point of my vitality' (1879).[129]

During the writing of *Ecce Homo* in Turin, everything was reduced to a pure historical evocation: the events of his youth, of his family circle, of his ancestors.

If this dream really took place on the day before his brother's death, when Nietzsche was a child of six, it must have had the compensatory value of a reconstitution of the traumatism in order to make Nietzsche relate it, six or seven years later, in his journal, and to return to it one last time at the age of seventeen. What must retain our attention, however, is not the premonitory meaning that Nietzsche gave to it at this early age, but on the contrary, the underlying interpretation of this dream by the dream itself. The premonitory meaning will then take on a completely different scope.

First, the father's death gives way to an *auditory memory* (*funeral music*).

Next, there is the *vision* of the cemetery and the church.

The movement of the scene: *the tomb opens*, apparition of the dead father, his entry into the sanctuary, his exit with the child in his arms; new opening of the tomb, the stone sinks over the opening. The funeral music ends.

The presumed aim: death goes looking for a child in the church. The child *is not in the house*.

The music, source of the dream, lies at the origin of the action: Nietzsche says that, in his dream, he first heard the *sound of organs*.

I *open* the window and the *tomb opens*: I open the tomb of my father who is looking for *me* in the church. My dead father is looking for me and carries me off because I am trying to see my dead father. I am dead, the father of myself, I suppress myself, in order to awaken to music. My dead father makes me hear the music.

How did Nietzsche experience his own behaviour in relation to his dead father? First, through a negative identification that included his own judgement of himself as a *decadent*. But this merely concerned the intellectual order of his autobiography. *As my mother, I am still living and becoming old* – but not in the sense that, through symmetry, his mother would represent *vigour* [*essor*]. Nietzsche *substituted himself*, and *had always substituted himself, not for his father next to his mother* – following the Oedipal schema – but, in accordance with an inverted schema, *for his mother* next to his father, as being *his own mother*. This is what he later explained through his own self-cure.

For Nietzsche to have inverted the *Oedipal schema* in this way, that is, to have kept before him *the shadow of his dead father* opposite his still-living mother, he had to *distance himself further and further from his family, mother and sister*, and to reconstitute what he calls his 'dual descent': *decline* and *vigour* – terms that here imply a redistribution of his tendencies with regard to the past and to the future, and thus to his own fatality.

This inversion of the 'Oedipal schema' would not go unpunished. The *real* mother (along with Nietzsche's sister) became *the very image of life in its most despicable and detested form* – what Nietzsche condemned, what he suffered from, what suffocated him was *the mortal compassion for the sick son*. The *dead father* demanded such a condemnation for two reasons: on the one hand, because he had the *nobility* of the *decadent*, a detachment with regard to life; and on the other hand, because he *re-engendered* the true *son* from his own death, the one who, by *reproducing the decline of this father*, reached the lowest level of his existence, and received as compensation an *exuberance of the spirit*.

Nietzsche's identification (as a *decadent*) with his *defunct father* did not yet give him the strength to live, but it did provide him, in return, with the secret for achieving it. Never having been anything but the 'shadow of himself', he sought to grasp healthier concepts and values from the perspective of the sick, and from the perspective of a rich life, he probed the secret labour of the decadent instincts – an exercise that led him to *reverse perspectives*, and thus to the '*Revaluation of Values*'. The dual descent was at work here: *decadence* and *beginning* – he establishes a new genealogy. Nietzsche's living mother did not know what to do with the *dead father*, and could represent neither a *recommencement* nor an *ascending life* [*essor*]. It was through the *dead father*, even though he represented Nietzsche's *decadent heredity* and his propensity to ill-health, that the *initiation* of the sick son would take place – an initiation that would produce such a degree of lucidity that he could *reverse perspectives* in order to revaluate values.

If one objects here that Nietzsche was simply *compensating* for what his father had not given him (sound health), and that the search for this compensation was experienced as *a feeling of guilt toward his dead father*, since this search for life – for forces that repudiate the spiritual – profaned the *image of the deceased* ('*You are defiling your father's grave*', as his mother said during his liaison with Lou), one would simply be developing the same motif: the *presence of the dead father* as an explanation of Nietzszche's struggle with his own fatality. When Nietzsche writes that *the happiness of his existence* resides in this fatality, because it stems from his dual descent (decadence–vigour), he is interpreting his life, having reached the ultimate lucidity, as a crest from which the return of the night can already be seen. And in this way, *we can reinterpret Nietzsche's interpretation*, not only because we know what would follow, but because we are already warned by the young Nietzsche's revelations of what had shattered his childhood.

These dual tendencies (decadence and beginning), in his analogical reference (*as my father, as my mother*), were characterized by an *asymmetry*: *the dead father had become a phantasm*, whereas *the living mother* remained *external to this analogical elaboration*. For Nietzsche, she herself could only represent, not life, but the 'compromise of the *meaning and value of life*'. In his interpretation of his own destiny, Nietzsche corrected this asymmetry or imbalance by substituting himself *for the mother* beside the *father's shadow*. So that *the still-living mother*, who worried about his incomprehensible states, became for him, by the very fact that she wanted to care for him, *the sign of his sickness*, and not of the healthy life. She would never become *the sign of that exuberance of spirit* which was the destiny of her son. On the other hand, the dead father, the father's shadow – who by dying young was the sign of resignation, of the inability to live, of detachment from life – became the sign of the *meaning* of life, its *value*. But to recover *life itself*, Nietzsche, as his *own mother*, gave birth to himself anew and became his own creature.

Very early on, the young student of Schulpforta, the venerable Lutheran institution, sensing a solidarity with pagan Hellenism and invoking an unknown god, applied himself and, despite the pietist style he adopted in his journal, gave ample evidence, even in this conventional form, of a rhetorical precociousness whose virtuosity was astonishing.

Unconsciously, he first developed a mimetism, which little by little began to simulate the required accents of tenderness and exaltation, terror and lyrical jubilation. But then a precocious reflection intervened, and authentic emotions were liberated from the gangue he had received in an education typical of a pastoral milieu. A gift for 'introspective' analysis was awakened, and with it a defiance with regard to any effusiveness. With analysis came irony and conscious fabulation. Deep within himself lay the spectre of the father, who became the spectre of *madness* and the *abyss*, into which the gaze of the self-constructing youth fell, fascinated, especially since his ears were ringing with the chords of a funereal *music*. Mourning was turned into a voluptuous delight in sound, while libidinal images, which were beginning to haunt the adolescent, would eventually be expressed in the elaboration of a necrophilic cynicism.

AUTOBIOGRAPHICAL FRAGMENT OF 1860

The first of these tendencies was revealed in the '*dream of the false start*', *the day before the beginning of summer vacation*, which Nietzsche recounted in his childhood memoir (1860) – '*episodes*', he says, 'that *I will ornament in a rather fantastic manner*'. Nietzsche, during this time, was still a boarder at Schulpforta, in his sixteenth year, the approximate date of the writing.

As the sun is setting, the young Nietzsche and his friend 'Wilhelm' cross the courtyard of the Schulpforta institution and, hurrying away quickly from the 'lugubrious' city of Halle, head through the fields, breathing in the fragrances of a summer night. They hasten toward Naumburg.

> What greater joy, Wilhelm, than to explore the world together [cries Nietzsche]. A friend's love, a friend's faithfulness! Breathing in the splendid summer night, the perfume of flowers, the flushed faces of the evening! Don't your thoughts take flight from the jubilant meadowlark, and are they not enthroned on the gold-rimmed clouds! My life stretches before me like a marvelous nighttime landscape. How the days group themselves before me, now in a gloomy light, now in jubilant dissolution!
>
> Then a strident scream struck our ears: it came from the nearby insane asylum. We squeezed our hands tightly: the agonizing wings of an evil spirit seemed to have brushed against us. No, nothing could separate us from each other, nothing but a youthful death. Get back, powers of Evil! – Even in this beautiful universe, there are evildoers. But what is evil?[130]

Darkness falls, and 'the clouds gathered into a greyish, nocturnal mass'. The two boys quicken their pace and stop talking to each other. The paths fade in the darkness of a forest, and they are seized by fear. Suddenly, a far-off glimmer approaches them. They change their mind, go to meet it, and perceive the outlines of an individual holding a lantern, a rifle on his back, followed by a barking dog.

The stranger offers to guide them, asks them about their families, and then the walk continues, silently. Suddenly, the man lets out a shrill whistle: the forest comes to life, flaming torches emerge, and masked faces appear from all sides and surround the young boys. '*I lost consciousness, no longer aware of what was happening to me.*'[131]

This nightmare scene, which the young Nietzsche took delight in mixing with memories from his vacation – whether or not he really dreamed it, or if this is a simple embellishment – nonetheless contains elements that are no less premonitory than those in the dream of his brother's death.

The theme of the departure, preceding the real departure for vacation (the return to familial places) is made up of images that foreshadow the final events of Nietzsche's life: his definitive return to his sister and mother, emptied of this thought, this vacation from the vacations of the 'lucid' ego. We will never know how Nietzsche himself experienced it. In this text, the young Nietzsche is shown fleeing what are for him the tedious locales of Halle, and becoming intoxicated with the spectacle of a twilight landscape. *How the days group themselves before me, now in a gloomy light, now in jubilant dissolution.* Immediately thereafter, *a strident scream rings out from the nearby insane asylum.*

How could this lugubrious note, chosen here to create the ambience of puerile terror in these pages, not take on its signification at the end of Nietzsche's lucid life? As imagined here, the *scream of insanity in general* ([es kam aus dem nahen Irrenhaus] *which comes from the nearby insane asylum*) puts the emphasis on the preceding sentence: *How the days group themselves before me, now in a gloomy light, now in jubilant dissolution.*

The nocturnal encounter with the terrifying face of the hunter, the *whistle* that provokes the apparition of masked physiognomies, the *loss of consciousness* – these are all so many melodramatic details that form the self-punishing nuance of the imagined dream: 'self-punishing' merely for having attempted to *anticipate the future* — this future that will lead to the *jubilant dissolution.*

But here is a fragment that shows the other face of the young Nietzsche. It is the outline for a 'horror story', a story that the pupil of Pforta — according to those who have rescued the sketch from oblivion — must have written during a vacation stay at Pastor Oehler's, his maternal uncle. Just as the preceding fragment brings to light the vision of 'the *jubilant dissolution*', so the following fragment, through the wild imaginings of a juvenile, already reveals the depth of *morose delight* through which the young Nietzsche — under the name of 'Euphorion', an imaginary medical student — gives vent to his hatred for the human species. Not only does he want to demonstrate his skill (as a future experimenter) at various practices (impregnating skinny nuns, thinning fat people down to a cadaverous state, autopsying the human automaton as a disabused 'physiologist' of the future); but again and above all, he wants to be judged a master in the art of changing young people into old people *quickly.* From the first lines, Nietzsche's eye is already showing through.

Here again, *the funereal dependence on the paternal shadow,* on the plane of the function of living, becomes a cruel irony: the libidinal forces of the adolescent are given free rein only through a puerile and macabre wager, as much toward his *own ego* as toward his familial surroundings (namely the presbytery of the Pastor Oehler). Already the theme of the double (mask and complicity) is here affirmed: hatred of himself as the product of a milieu from which he dissociates himself, and the search for a group of affinities.

(EUPHORION)

A flow of tender and soothing harmonies ride the waves of my soul — what then has made it so bitter? Ah, to weep and then die! Then nothing! Lifeless — my hand is trembling . . . .

The mottled nuances of the early-morning reddening play on the sky, a daily fireworks that bores me. My eyes sparkle with another passion, at the risk, I fear, of piercing the celestial vault. Here I am, I feel totally exposed, I know myself right through – but if only I could find the head of my double! To dissect his brain or my own childhood head with golden curls . . . ah . . . twenty years ago . . . childhood . . . what a strange word rings in my ear. Have I myself, then, also been fashioned in every respect by the old, rusty mechanism of the world? Me – the winch of the mill – who henceforth winds and unwinds, comfortably and slowly, the rope we call *fatum* – until the knacker buries me and some bluebottles secure me a little immortality.

At this thought, I almost feel like laughing – however, another idea is bothering me – perhaps little flowers will then sprout from my bones, maybe a 'tender violet' or even – at which point, by chance, the knacker will satisfy his needs on my tomb – a forget-me-not. Then lovers will come . . . . How disgusting! What rot! While I thus wallow in similar thoughts of the future – for it seems more agreeable for me to corrupt myself under the humid earth than to vegetate under the blue sky, more pleasant to slither like a fat little worm than to be a man – wandering question mark – what always worries me is to see people strolling in the streets, flirtatious, delicate, happy. What are they? whited sepulchres, as some Jew said in times past. – In my room, the silence of death – only my pen scratches away at the paper – for I like to think while writing, since we have not yet invented a machine that could reproduce our unexpressed and unwritten thoughts on some sort of material. In front of me, an inkwell to drown my black heart in, a pair of scissors to sever my neck, manuscripts to wipe me with, and a chamberpot.

Opposite me lives a nun, whom I visit from time to time to enjoy her decency. I know her very well, from head to toe, better than I know myself. She was once a thin, skinny nun – I was a doctor, and made sure she soon got fat. Her brother lives with her. They got married just in time. He was too fat and flourishing for me; I've made him lean – as a corpse. He will die shortly – which pleases me, for I will dissect him. But first I will write the story of my life, for, apart from its intrinsic interest, it is also instructive in the art of making people age quickly, of which I am a master. Who is to read it? My doubles. There are still plenty of them wandering in this vale of sorrows.

Here Euphorion leaned back slightly and groaned, for he had a consumptive disease in the marrow of his spine.[132]

While summing up his adolescence at the age of nineteen, the young philology student wrote:

'I can cast a grateful glance on anything that could happen to me, whether joy or suffering; events have led me to this point like a child.

'Perhaps it is time to grasp the reins of the events and to leave life.

'And thus, as long as he believes, man manages to free himself from everything that had hitherto embraced him; he doesn't need to break his connections; without knowing it, these connections fall away, when a god orders it; and where then is the ring that embraces everything at the end? Is it the world? Is it God?'[133]

Much later, the answer was given in an equally interrogative retrospection:

'*Around the hero everything turns into tragedy; around the demi-god, into a satyr play; and around God – what? perhaps into "world"?*'[134]

The retrospective explanation Nietzsche himself provided simply shows us the importance of *the father*, who would reappear when Nietzsche wrote his own apologia.

If we again consider the tomb scene – the *opening* of the tomb, the emission of the paternal shadow, its *coming and going*, its *re-descent*, with everything accompanied by *funeral music* – we see a new suggestion emanating from this oneiric experience related by the child. The father was being united with something *indistinct*: the womb of the earth was *half-open*, an abyss which in Greek is called Chaos. (For Nietzsche, this name remained so powerful in his thought that, during his *experience of the Return*, he would note that the *cyclical movement of the universe* and *Chaos* are not irreconcilable.)[135]

If we examine not only the linguistic but also the affective etymology of these terms, the irrational stratification of the vocables and their superposition, an explanation seems to appear, which can be ascribed not only to Nietzsche's exegetical ingenuity, but to his unique vision – the paternal shadow and the image of the tomb are merged into a single sign: Chaos.

On the other hand, there was the autobiographical symbol through which Nietzsche *made the deterioration of his thirty-sixth year coincide with the thirty-sixth and final year of his father's life*, and thereby designated this lowest level of his vitality as a new point of departure, a *new beginning* – an exegesis that retrospectively brings to light a pathological apparatus that would lead to two fundamental utterances. The first concerned the relationship between Chaos and *becoming*, which implied a *re-becoming*.

The other utterance, the *death of God*, concerned Nietzsche's relationship with the guarantor of his *ego's* identity – namely, the abolition, not of the divine itself, which is inseparable from *Chaos*, but of an identical and once-and-for-all individuality.

The obsession with authenticity, namely, with his unexchangeable and irreducible depth, and all his efforts to attain it – this is what constituted Nietzsche's primary and ultimate preoccupation. Hence his feeling of *not having been born yet*.

Fundamental discovery: what I have been told about my private life, about my inner life, is a lie. There must therefore be an 'outside of myself' [*hors de moi*] where my authentic depth would lie.

Two possibilities: either it lies in history and the past (Greece, or some other period of history); or else it lies in whatever the *contemporary world*, experienced as an *absence* of *myself*, creates as my future; I do not exist for my contemporary friends.

Either science (the physiological investigation of the body, this unknown reality); or else the economy of the universe (Chaos), which reveals to me the laws of my own behaviour (the *simulation of Chaos*).

Two ways of conceiving my own temporality: *my constitutive elements are dispersed in past time and in the future.*

I am confined *somewhere* and I will never manage to *find* myself again: the message the prisoner sends to me is unintelligible; I am shut up inside language, and what belongs to me lies on the *outside*, in the time which the universe follows and which history recounts: the *memory* that outlives humans is *my mother*, and the *Chaos* that turns around on itself is my *father*.

It remains an open question whether or not Nietzsche, on the 'conceptual' plane, ever managed to free himself from this vision; or whether *his father's shadow*, as his *interlocutor* concerning his chances of life and death, already determined, at the beginning of Nietzsche's career, what he himself called his first aberration – the spiritual paternity that Wagner seemed to want to exercise over the young philologist. Nietzsche here gave in to an obscure propensity: he was unaware that he had reinterpreted the *paternal shadow*, that he had created an *erroneous* version of it; that several years would have to pass before he could come back and consult the *shadow*, and become a shadow himself – in order to smash the simulacrum of Wagner's paternity.

And after this rupture, because he was already *dead* as his father, he would act as *his own mother*, he would *take care* of himself and even *feign his own cure* out of hostility toward the uncomprehending mother, overwhelmed by her constant concern. Hence also his assiduous observation of himself, and of everything that was related to the functioning of his corporeal machine (the promotion of the body to the rank of a higher intelligence). The persistent headaches and the threat of imbecility, both of which recalled his father's collapse, were taken to be the sign of a possible heredity.

It was then that my instinct made its inexorable decision against any longer yielding, going along, and confounding myself. Any kind of life, the most unfavourable conditions, sickness, poverty – anything seemed preferable to that unseemly 'selflessness' into which I had got myself originally in ignorance and *youth* and in which I had got stuck later on from inertia and so-called 'sense of duty.'

Here it happened in a manner that I cannot admire sufficiently that, precisely at the right time, my father's *wicked* heritage came to my aid – at bottom, predestination to an early death. Sickness *detached me slowly*: it spared me any break, any violent and offensive step. Thus I did not lose any good will and actually gained not a little. My sickness also gave me the right to change all my habits completely; it permitted, it *commanded* me to forget; it bestowed on me the necessity of lying still, of leisure, of waiting and being patient. – But that means, of thinking. – My eyes alone put an end to all bookwormishness – in brief, philology: I was delivered from the 'book'; for years I did not read a thing – the greatest benefit I ever conferred upon myself. – That nethermost *self* which had, as it were, been buried and grown silent under the continual pressure of having to listen to other *selves* (and this is after all what reading means) awakened slowly, shyly, dubiously – but *eventually it spoke again*. Never have I felt happier with myself than in the sickest and most painful periods of my life: one only need look at *The Dawn* or *The Wanderer and*

His Shadow to comprehend what this 'return to myself'
meant – a supreme kind of recovery.[136]

The break with Wagner and its possible effects have been
interpreted, especially by Lou Salomé, as shedding important
light on Nietzsche's later perplexities. If a provisional equilibrium was broken at that moment, perhaps it was because
his contact with Wagner's *false* paternity, which Nietzsche
submitted to and accepted, pointed to the outlines of an
Oedipal schema, though it was a delayed outline: the *conquest
of the mother in the guise of the prestigious Cosima* – an *intention*
that was nonetheless censured, postponed, and buried in
the folds of Nietzsche's heart, dissimulated on the outside
as a victorious retreat. Wagner, as the paternal phantasm,
was beaten – and some of Wagner's personal statements,
which were not above suspicion in this regard, were indeed
confirmed, three years after Wagner's death, by Nietzsche's
final utterance: *Ariadne, I love you.*[137]

(But these are *a posteriori* reconstructions, and in this
context, the interchangeable vocable *Ariadne* was equivalent
to that of *Cosima* only at the moment when these two names
plainly covered a single object, capable of satisfying a libidinal
mood – since Nietzsche as Nietzsche no longer existed.)

That his intention to conquer the *Mother* in the guise
of Cosima was aborted and buried is in keeping with the
predominance of the first schema sketched out by Nietzsche
himself: *dead as his father, still living as his mother* (and growing
old) – which leads one to believe that he had no other choice
than to interpret this as a *fundamental constraint.*

That Nietzsche wanted to take in hand the reconstitution
of his dual descent (decline and vigour), initially in order to
unify these two tendencies; that in this effort he tried to
project himself on his friends; that he met with the resistance
of his most esteemed schoolmates, notably Rohde – all this
is what first led him to seek support in couples, first with
Overbeck and his wife, and then with the 'adventurers'
couple' formed by Paul Rée and Lou Salomé.

Certainly the Overbecks, at whose home he was often a guest, and with whom he lived for long periods of time, were essentially interlocutors who, because of their intellectual orientation and their moral and material support, were often disarmed by the confidences Nietzsche placed in them – especially when these confidences concerned the other couple, Lou and Rée, who, in terms of their origins, differed totally from the Overbecks. But with both couples, Nietzsche always acted in accordance with an obscure need whose urgency could explain both his hesitations and his *faux pas*: *his need to give birth to himself through himself, and his consequent tendency to give himself over to a double presence, both feminine and virile* – a tendency he had already contracted with the Wagner couple.

Speech was here used as a subterfuge that veiled his idle virility, even if this meant confiding his secrets (or the semblance of secrets) to the woman's heart, living in her memory, defining himself in terms of the man's reactions, and finally extracting his own unified substance from their respective impressions.

The marriages of his friends Rohde and Overbeck affected his own existence in the sense that his celibacy sometimes weighed on him, but at other times strengthened him: a companion could have been both his nurse and his disciple.

Whenever he gave himself over to a couple in this way, he abandoned the creation of himself: that is, he did not dare to create himself with all his impulses, but instead expected to receive the meaning of life from the *couple's reaction*, and thus from the 'gregarious' law of the species. But whenever he detached himself or broke with them, he began to work on his own image, his own consistency: *the paternal tomb again opened* (the music began again). He denied the gregarious meaning of life, and at the same time, he exalted the father as *Chaos*, and the *relationship with the father* as the *Eternal Return*. This *relationship* was, in short, simply a *self-maternity*, a giving-birth to himself. *Weiderkunft* (feminine subst.) is close to *Niederkunft* (lit. 'to come from below', to give birth, to bring to light).

Hence, Nietzsche was never the father of himself because *he was dead as his father* – the *dead God* always remained *God* – as the unique God. But as a multiple God (Chaos), he was the essence of metamorphosis, and was made manifest in as many divine figures as there were fortuitous individualities in the implicit circle of the Return.

In referring to biographical facts – since we are here trying to grasp the content of one statement among so many others in *Ecco Homo* – we run the great risk of confusing different planes and structures. However, the motif – as *already interpreted by the autobiographer*, who is here only a *pseudo-autobiographer* – betrays, by this very interpretation, a certain constraint: the constraint of lived facts that he was unable to bring to term. This is what the words say: *I am still living and growing old as my mother.*

In his dependence on the paternal shadow, Nietzsche never ceased to feel the effect of his own *non-birth*: nor was his oeuvre the 'son' that should have been born, but rather its 'substitute'. Hence the *portrait* he gave of himself in *Ecce Homo*, his *double* apologetic, which had to compensate for the *sterile ageing* of the *mother* he was *to himself.*

Faced with the Rée–Salomé couple, Nietzsche failed lamentably in his virility and *through* his virility. For him, this couple did not have a 'parental' character analogous to that of the Wagners; this was rather a 'sister and brother' couple, 'lost children' with whom he tried to integrate himself as a *third party.* If he could not succeed in doing so, it was because he wanted to *act as a spiritual father, lover, and rival* all at once.

He could not impose himself as a father (even less as a *dead father*). Nor could he propose himself as a *master of thought*, the doctor of the 'thought of thoughts', because the doctrine of the Return still kept him in the obscure relationship that linked him to the paternal shadow. He confided its secret to Lou, but without possessing her either as a *woman* or as a *disciple*. Even worse, he was unable to act against Rée, to whom he was linked by a quasi-fraternal intimacy, and to whom he owed an attention and an exchange of thoughts which had fortified him when he was at his lowest – and in whom he discovered, in what followed, a invincible rival: he let himself be manipulated by Rée when he thought he was his surest intermediary to get to Lou.

The fact that Nietzsche was unable personally to form a disciple for himself was in keeping with this confusion of motifs: in keeping, not only with the character of his doctrine, which was incomprehensible to his contemporaries, but with his own affective disarray.

The adventure with Lou, at the moment when Nietzsche was about to draw the consequences of the revelation of the Eternal Return, constituted a test. Just as he was about to reach the final metamorphosis, the encounter with Lou gave rise to an obstacle within himself: *a pride in his own virility*, a final boost to his 'ego'. Lou was a trap in the sense that she flattered his need to possess – and flattered it under the guise of a feminine disciple the like of which he would never again encounter.

If the period that saw the birth of *Zarathustra*, and the works that followed, was a *'complete misery'*, since *'immortality costs dearly'* and *'one dies several times over from one's living'*, one could say that the Lou experience was the price Nietzsche paid for it. Nietzsche survived this test only by killing that part of virility in himself that would lay claim to its object. Not Eros, *but that which had 'normalized' Eros in him*: his reflections on marriage, on the union of lovers 'who erect a "monument" to their passion', coincide almost word for word with those that Lou developed in her memoirs. During this adventure, Nietzsche could not distinguish between the motif of his *singular case* and the 'gregarious' need to reproduce oneself. Thus, he was unable to avoid confusing the emotion, experienced with a nature whose resources were highly analogous to his own, with the desire to impregnate – both morally and physically. To want to explain the creation of *Zarathustra* as a compensation for his desire to 'have a son' is literally insane. Nietzsche's later behaviour toward Lou, the fact that he sometimes adopted his sister's point of view, going so far as to insult Rée and nearly provoke him to a duel – all this was supposed to have made him *break down* to the point of annihilation. It would not be going too far to say that he died to himself. No doubt the creation of *Zarathustra* was, in this regard, something of a miracle – but it was an ostentatious miracle. Because Nietzsche at this point felt humiliated and offended, he adopted the *role of an ambiguous character*, as ambiguous as the circumstances that gave birth to it. The new Nietzsche, the penultimate one, re-created himself with a strong build, with a ferocious aggressiveness toward both himself and others. Under the mask of *Zarathustra*, the profound wound Lóu had inflicted on him was scarified – his virility divested itself from its socially and humanly communicable forms. Once again, his thought had cast off a false representation of itself, one that had rendered it vulnerable. Thrown into a total affective isolation, the new Nietzsche was sustained by a boundless cynicism in which his mind, purified of all cloudy sentiments, consented to a final afflux of animal impulses. Nietzsche adhered fully to this afflux, which he termed *Dionysus* and affirmed with all the more energy now that his health was deteriorating anew. Long and difficult were the stages of his convalescence.

On 11 February 1883, he had written to Overbeck:

> I will not conceal it from you: I am in a bad way. It is night all around me again; I feel as if the lightning had flashed – I was for a short time completely in my element and in my light. And now it has passed. I think I shall inevitably go to pieces, unless something happens – I have absolutely no idea *what* . . . .
>
> *My whole life has crumbled under my gaze*: this whole eerie, deliberately secluded secret life, which *takes one step* every six years, and actually wants nothing but the taking of this step, while everything else, *all my human relationships, have to do with a mask of me* and I

must perpetually be the victim of living a completely hidden life. I have always been exposed to the cruellest coincidences – or rather, it is I who have always turned all coincidence into cruelty.[138]

A strange phrase: a 'deliberately secluded secret life'. What was he dissimulating under the mask? 'I think I shall inevitably go to pieces, unless something happens – I have absolutely no idea *what.*' Was it the fact that he lived masked in his relationships to others that would cause him to perish? Or, on the contrary, would it be caused by what he was hiding? He notes: 'It is I who have always turned all coincidence into cruelty.' The moment to *unmask* himself arrived *fortuitously*, and thereby became a cruelty toward himself.

To say that he turned everything that happened fortuitously into 'cruelty' was a reinterpretation on Nietzsche's part. The 'mask' he had to bear was already the result of a suggested interpretation. How could the randomness of the encounter not provoke an interpretation? Is not chance always reinterpreted in terms of continuity? The word of Zarathustra comes to mind here: '*I am only a fragment, a riddle, and a dreadful chance*' – out of which he wants to create a unity.[139] If the mask, then, was only a false unity in relation to others, does that mean that the *secret life Nietzsche was dissimulating would only be dreadful chance, fragment, riddle?* Where then did the cruelty of chance come from? How did it turn into the cruelty suffered by Nietzsche? How did it occur in relation to Lou? By revealing himself to her, Nietzsche thought he had recovered his unity. But he compromised this revelation, and the bond that resulted from it, by taking a thoughtless step: the desire to take possession of Lou personally arose in a disastrous fashion. Rather than overcoming chance, Nietzsche here got caught in the trap of his own fatality. He was driven by the fear of his own solitude, which he hid from himself by proposing marriage. From this viewpoint, the phrase at the beginning of the letter becomes clearer: 'I think I shall inevitably go to pieces, *unless something happens – I have absolutely no idea what.'* This mask, which Nietzsche rejected as a falsification of the self, concealed the dreadful chance that Nietzsche was to himself – until Nietzsche started to adhere to discontinuity, and chance ceased to be dreadful and became a joyful fortuity.

CORRESPONDENCE

To Overbeck

Summer 1883 (Sils-Maria)

My dear friend Overbeck:

I would like to write you a few forthright words, just as I did recently to your dear wife. I have an *aim*, which compels me to go on living and for the sake of which I *must* cope with even the most painful matters. *Without this aim* I would take things much more lightly – that is, I would stop living. And it was not only this past winter that anyone seeing and understanding my condition from close at hand would have had the *right* to say: '*Make it easier for yourself! Die!*'; in previous times, too, in the terrible years of physical suffering, it was the same with me. Even my Genoese years are a long, long chain of self-conquests for the sake of that aim and *not* to the taste of any human being that I know. So, dear friend, the 'tyrant in me', the inexorable tyrant, *wills* that I conquer this time too (as regards *physical torments*, their duration, intensity, and variety, I can count myself among the most experienced and tested of people; is it my *lot* that I should be equally so experienced and tested in the torments of the soul?). And to be consistent with my way of thinking and my latest philosophy, I must even have an absolute victory – that is, the transformation of experience into gold and use of the highest order.

Meanwhile I am still the incarnate *wrestling match*, so that your dear wife's recent requests made me feel as if someone were asking old Laocoön to set about it and vanquish his serpents.

My relatives and I – we are too different. The precaution I took against receiving any letters from them last winter cannot be maintained any more (I am not hard enough for that).

But the danger is *extreme*. My nature is so concentrated that whatever strikes me moves straight to my center. The misfortune of last year is only as *great* as it is in proportion to the aim and purpose which dominates me; I was, and have become, terribly *doubtful* about my *right* to set myself such an aim – the sense of my weakness overcame me at just the moment when everything, everything should have given me courage!

Think of some way, dear friend Overbeck, in which I can take my mind off it *absolutely*! I think the strongest and most extreme means are required – you cannot imagine how this madness rages in me, day and night.

That I should have thought and written this year my *sunniest* and most serene things, many miles above myself and my misery – this is really one of the most amazing and inexplicable things I know.

As far as I can estimate, I *need* to survive *through next year* – help me to *hold out* for another fifteen months. But every contemptuous word that is written against Rée or Frl. Salomé makes my heart bleed; it seems I am not made to be anyone's enemy (whereas my sister recently wrote that I should be in good spirits, that this was a 'brisk and jolly war').

I have used the strongest means I know to take my mind *off* it, and in particular have determined on the most intense and personal productiveness. (In the meantime, I have finished the sketch of a 'Morality for Moralists.') Ah, friend, I am certainly a cunning old moralist of praxis and self-mastery; I have neglected as little in this area as, for instance, last winter when treating my own nervous fever. But I have no support from *outside*; on the contrary, everything seems to conspire to keep me imprisoned in my abyss – last winter's terrible

weather, the like of which the Genoese coast had never
seen, and now again this cold, gloomy, rainy summer.
Loyally,
   Your Nietzsche[140]

Nietzsche's intimate ordeal took on its full weight only in
proportion to the *aim* he had prescribed for himself. What
was this aim? Was it the doctrine of the Eternal Return,
the revaluation – the perfect instrument through which his
thought could act on posterity? Or was it *something else*? Was it
not rather a question of Nietzsche's own *metamorphosis*, which
would be achieved *through* this work, or which in any case *had
to be completed*? '*My nature is so concentrated that whatever strikes
me moves straight to my center.*' Thus every event of importance,
in life, since it came from the outside, put the *centre* of his
nature in question again, either threatening it or enriching it.
Nietzsche loved himself only for his *aim*; he *hated* himself as a
victim of the *traps of life*, and the adventure with Lou, given its
consequences, was the *worst* he had ever known. The extent
of the failure was such that he required an incommensurate
compensation: humanly, his distress drove him to seek out
every possible expedient.

Nietzsche staked the entire weight of his thought on his
adventure with Lou. If it had taken a 'happy turn', perhaps
Nietzsche would have reconciled himself with gregarious
necessities. Lou would have been their *mediator*, and life
would have thereby preserved the 'centre' of his nature.
But it was part of Nietzsche's nature that the act of creating
hastened his *decentring*. *Creation (every creation) entails a disequilibrium*: only experience can re-establish an equilibrium by
accumulating new forces. If experience remains sterile, it
cannot unleash the forces appropriate to the act of creation,
and the latter becomes nothing but a reaction – which is, in
turn, sterile. For it uses up the reserves of and weakens the
status quo.

Are not many creations born out of the experience of a
failure, as if the failure were its indispensable condition? Such

indeed is often the case. But a completely different operation entered into play here, one which presupposed a completely different organization. *The phantasm was produced only as the result of a failure. A positive experience ran counter to the phantasm that conditioned this organization.* In such a case, an economy of the phantasm is developed, which determines in advance the supply and demand between the alienating forces and their writing. The mad are those who chose their alienated states as stereotypes. They know what they are expressing through these stereotyped states, and that they are making use of these states as *means of expression.* But at bottom, a means of expression is merely a way of *putting in an appearance [faire acte de présence],* and hence of upsetting the order of things. Whatever their *experiences* may be, they are not the object of an *exchange* between *life* and *thought,* but between their *vision of life* and their *art.* They know that what determines their experiences are phantasms, which are captured in their *art* – at the willed moment.

Now this willed moment lay in wait for Nietzsche beyond even the region of art. Once he realized he had been separated from his unique and irreplaceable interlocutor, he started down a path which, in the eyes of witnesses, led to a catastrophe – namely, the willed moment of his own metamorphosis. After his failure with Lou, not only was the master without a disciple, but the virility of the man remained unassuaged. In 1883, this frustrated virility constituted a profound wound, a *hiatus* in which Nietzsche's ego was de-actualized and broken. The creation of *Zarathustra* was merely an external compensation – and in terms of its reception by those around him, it was not even a compensation. From then on, Nietzsche, owing to the very distance of the past, would reconstitute this past on the ruins of his present ego. He would reinterpret the idyll of Tribschen and, by diminishing Wagner, would relive more freely the feelings he had experienced in the presence of Cosima. But let us leave behind the coarse and easy outlines of an analysis that would make use of Nietzsche's childhood memories (the dream), the memories of his youth (the spectre), Euphorion's morose delight – and instead sketch out a 'complex' in which the father (God the Father) becomes the Minotaur (with Wagner's features), and in which the Mother (not Franziska Nietzsche) and the sister (not Elisabeth) are named *Ariadne* (with Cosima's features) – whereas Nietzsche's mother and his sister Elisabeth would be the competitive and punitive representatives of this regression.

8

The Most Beautiful Invention of the Sick

I set down here a list of psychological states as signs of a full and flourishing life that one is accustomed today to condemn as *morbid*. For by now we have learned better than to speak of healthy and sick as of an antithesis: it is a question of degrees. My claim in this matter is that what is today called '*healthy*' represents a lower level than that which under favorable circumstances *would be* healthy — that we are relatively sick — The artist belongs to a still stronger race. What would be harmful and morbid in us, in him is nature — But one objects to us that it is precisely the *impoverishment* of the machine that makes possible extravagant powers of understanding of every kind of suggestion: witness our hysterical females.

An *excess* of sap and force can bring with it symptoms of partial constraint, of sense hallucinations, susceptibility to suggestion, just as well as can impoverishment of life: the stimulus is differently conditioned, the effect remains the same — But the after-effect is not the same; the extreme exhaustion of all morbid natures after their nervous eccentricities has nothing in common with the states of the artist, who *does not have to atone* for his good periods — He is rich enough for them: he is able to squander without becoming poor.

As one may today consider 'genius' as a form of

neurosis, so perhaps also the artistic power of suggestion – and indeed our *artists* are painfully like hysterical females!!! But that is an objection to 'today', not to 'artists.'[141]

In fragments such as these, Nietzsche's own reflections never took shape without first *reflecting* in themselves the perspective that was opposed to his own. Some fragments develop one aspect in isolation, such as *resistance* or *non-resistance*; but these terms could just as easily have been used for a contrary demonstration by an adversary as by Nietzsche himself. He thus made use of the notion of *decadence*, along with its opposite *vigour* [*essor*], every time *strength* or *weakness* had to be proved in terms of these criteria. Language, by consequence, threw Nietzsche back into the opposing camp (health, norm, gregariousness), since the *symptoms* of strength, of the powerful singularity, could be determined only negatively (as illness, insanity, unintelligibility). The symptoms of strength as well as weakness, of health as well as sickness, were disconcerting insofar as they looked the same.

In Nietzsche's own declarations, the gregarious criterion of health perpetually intruded on that of the morbid singularity. The term '*will to power*', given the ambiguity of its accepted meaning, was primarily addressed to the 'social' intelligence, since the content and orientation that Nietzsche gave to it, from the viewpoint of the singularity, could not take shape otherwise than through a compromise detrimental to its affirmation. To take another example: the idea of a *resistance or non-resistance* to harmful invasions would be comprehensible only if one presumed that the individual, in the traditional moral sense, maintains its durable identity; but it becomes unintelligible if the individual is only a fiction – as it was for Nietzsche – and if the principle of identity is abolished.

The situation was different with a term such as the *Eternal Return*, which strictly speaking was an *acceptation* that referred to the *singular case*, first as a *lived fact*, then as a *thought* – and which was no longer addressed to the social intelligence, but to sensibility, emotivity and affectivity, thus to the impulsive life of each and every person. The same could be said of any term which refers to the conceivable states of this latter sphere. Once Nietzsche examined them in the light of criteria such as *health* or *sickness*, which imply a desire to *endure*, he was again caught up in the designations of institutional language, and again became subject to the reality principle.

To what extent can the insane or the monstrous – which are cases of degeneration, or accidents with regard to the norms of the species – be compared socially with the exceptional cases that 'enrich' human life? What does *enrich* mean here? Are natural processes impoverished in the *sterility* characteristic of the ordinary monster? What border must be respected or crossed for the monster to become a Mozart? Conversely, how did Mozart manage to avoid monstrosity? What if the same emotions had been exercised in a manner that was at once *cruel and sterile* – sterile for society?

We have absolutely no criteria for determining when the sick, the insane, and the monstrous would be cases of sterility, as opposed to exceptional cases, nor when the latter would be considered fecund, under the pretext that they allow the mass of normal (mediocre) beings to enjoy moments when they emerge from their mediocrity. The terms fecundity and mediocrity, even if they merely concern the cases in question, are still criteria of utility and are instituted entirely by the gregarious spirit. By consequence, here again Nietzsche argues both for and against – involuntarily against himself and for the mass. For if he wants *fecund individuals*, which alone could justify existence (the existence of the species, and thus of the mass), he has to believe in *fecundity* – but this requires an interpretation that can discern between what is *useful to the other person* (and thus to a representative of the species) and what is simply an *overabundance* of existence. This overabundance, even if it eludes the species and the other individuals that represent the species, nonetheless remains an overabundance and, notwithstanding this overabundance, something unexchangeable and thus *without price*.

Did Nietzsche ever manage to rid himself of the notion of *decadence*? Did he even try to get rid of it? Did he feel the complexity of existence so strongly that this notion itself seemed impoverishing? Is this the reason why the *revaluation of values* – the '*magnum opus*' – did not get written? And yet Nietzsche would continue to use the term *decadence*, along with the criteria of health and morbidity, right up until the end – no doubt because this complicity with all the 'positive' qualities of morbidity and decadence required, as their counterpart, a criterion that would place these same qualities in doubt: the essential point is that lucidity never abandons or betrays life, but always remains subordinate to it, it exalts life even in its blindest forms. Nietzsche therefore submitted himself to '*the most beautiful invention of the sick*' – that is, to a sovereign *malice*, and thus to his own aggressiveness.

Why the weak conquer.

In summa: the sick and weak have more sympathy, are 'more *humane*' – :

the sick and weak have more *spirit*, are more changeable, various, entertaining – more malicious: it was the sick who invented *malice*. (A morbid precociousness is often found in the rickety, scrofulous and tubercular – .)

Esprit: quality of late races: Jews, Frenchmen, Chinese. (The anti-Semites do not forgive the Jews for possessing 'spirit' – and money. Anti-Semites – another name for the 'underprivileged.')

The fools and the saint – the two most interesting kinds of man –

closely related to them, the 'genius', and the great 'adventurers and criminals',

the sick and the weak have had *fascination* on their side: they are more interesting than the healthy.

All individuals, especially the most healthy, are *sick* at certain periods in their lives: – the great emotions, the passions of power, love, revenge, are accompanied by profound disturbances. And as for decadence, it is represented in almost every sense by every man who does not die too soon: – thus he also knows from experience the instincts that belong to it:

– almost every man is decadent for half his life.

Finally: woman! One-half of mankind is weak, typically sick, changeable, inconstant – woman needs strength in order to cleave to it; she needs a religion of weakness that glorifies being weak, loving, and being humble as divine.

Or better, she makes the strong weak – she rules when she succeeds in overcoming the strong. Woman has always conspired with the types of decadence, the priests, against the 'powerful', the 'strong', the *men*.

Finally: increasing civilization, which necessarily brings with it an increase with the morbid elements, in the neurotic-psychiatric and criminal.

An intermediary species arises: the *artist*, restrained from *crime* by weakness of will and social timidity and not yet ripe for the *madhouse*, but reaching out inquisitively toward both spheres with his antennae: this specific culture plant, the modern artist, painter, musician, above all novelist, who describes his mode of life with the very inappropriate word 'naturalism.'

Lunatics, criminals, and 'naturalists' are increasing: sign of a growing culture rushing on *precipitately* – i.e., the refuse, the waste, gain importance – *decline keeps pace*.

Finally: the social hodgepodge, consequence of the Revolution, the establishment of equal rights, of the superstition of 'equal men.' The bearers of the instincts of decline (of *ressentiment*, discontent, the drive to destroy, anarchism, and nihilism), including the slave instincts, the instincts of cowardice, cunning, and *canaille* in those orders that have long been kept down, mingle with the blood of all classes: two, three generations later the race is no longer recognizable – everything has become a mob. From this there results *a collective instinct against selection, against privilege of all kinds, that is so powerful and self-assured, hard, and cruel in its operation, that the privileged soon succumb to it.*[142]

Nietzsche, in this fragment, has certainly not freed himself from the criteria of the *morbid* and the *healthy*. Insofar as he knows himself to be sick and weak, however, he revalorizes these states of existence and thus modifies his own distinction, enriching it by adding certain nuances. The sick are rehabilitated for having a greater compassion and, at the same time, for having 'invented' malice; ageing, decadent races are rehabilitated for possessing more spirit; the *fool* and the *saint* are rehabilitated – and opposed to the 'genius' and the 'criminal adventurer', who are here united in a single affective genus. Such revisionism, in Nietzsche, was due in large part to his discovery of Dostoevsky. For even if they derived opposite conclusions from their analogous visions of the human soul, Nietzsche could not help but experience, through his contact with Dostoevsky's '*demons*' and the '*underground man*', an infinite and incessant solicitation, recognizing himself in many of the remarks the Russian novelist put in his characters' mouths.

Toward the end, the theme of the affinity between the artist and the criminal became ever more frequent. The idea that the creator of simulacra makes use of aggressive and asocial forces in his own representations gave rise to a singular passage in *Ecce Homo*. It is not the idea of 'sublimation' that emerges here, he says, but a reproach against those who necessarily consent to sublimation through pusillanimity. It is obvious that, for Nietzsche, art cannot compensate for action, nor can it substitute for an impulse. If art reproduces violence and distress, pleasure and its satisfaction, it cannot be a pretext for mutilating the integrity of a strong nature whose *exuberance* is expressed as much in its differences and aberrations as in the imaginative representations from which both the 'crime' and its simulacrum are derived. 'Sublimation' in no way guarantees the 'morality' of an individual. Nietzsche will admit that sublimation can be a source of creative bliss only insofar as it attests to the presence of a surplus force that comes from its own overabundance – in the same way that *'God himself, who at the end of his six days' work lay down as a serpent under the tree of knowledge'.*[143]

★   ★   ★

'No doubt, *certainty* is what drives one insane. – But one must be profound, an abyss, a philosopher to feel that way. – We are all *afraid* of truth . . . .But the strength required for the vision of the most powerful reality is not only compatible with the most powerful strength for action, for monstrous action, for crime – it even presupposes it' (*Ecce Homo*).[144]

Certainty takes on the offensive characteristic of delirium. How can certainty make the mind delirious? What kind of *certainty* is in question here? It is the certainty of the irreducible depth whose muteness has no equivalent. For if certainty produces delirium, it is because the *imagined monstrosity* is only the obverse side of a criminal act.

Lord Bacon would have concealed *monstrous dispositions* under the mask of Shakespeare. If Nietzsche 'had published *Zarathustra* under another name – for example, that of Richard Wagner – the acuteness of two thousand years would not have been sufficient for anyone to guess that the author of *Human, All-Too-Human* is the visionary of Zarathustra'.[145] But Wagner was neither Shakespeare nor Bacon, although Nietzsche did not hesitate to assign Wagner the role of a priest in relation to himself – a name comparable to the one Shakespeare would have adopted with regard to Francis Bacon. In this way, he assimilates the agonies of the latter to his own. Nietzsche, then, is here identifying himself with

Lord Bacon. Because he is *certain*, he accepts the delirium: the *visionary reality* presupposes the strength to realize the vision *in reality*. Delirium does not lie in the *monstrous act*, but in the *certainty* that the *strength to bring it about* is prior to the power of representing it. The terms *monstrous* and *criminal* express the presumptuousness through which the vision gives rise to power.

On the one hand, the power *to act in reality* must *dissimilate itself* under the power of *the most real* of visions. On the other hand, what makes one mad is the *certainty* that each of these presupposes the other: the constraint is not resolved in the simulation. Thus there is no longer anything that separates two different domains of the real – the simulacrum of the act, and the act itself.

'What must a man have suffered to have such a need of *being a buffoon!*'[146] By consequence, the 'histrionic' must dissimulate the *certainty of his double power* and *turn in derision* against what he is by *merely feigning to be it* (Shakespeare, Caesar).

Nietzsche thus situates the philosopher and the 'abyss' on the same plane: *knowledge is an unacknowledged power of monstrosity*. The philosopher would be a mere histrionic if he did not have this power, if he refused monstrosity. And Bacon, under the mask of Shakespeare, attributed to the creative imagination 'peculiar intrigues' of which we know nothing. But neither Bacon nor the 'histrionic' Shakespeare was mad: they became, as the *certainty* uttered by Nietzsche, his own madness.

But suppose that Shakespeare had merely been the living pseudonym of Lord Bacon. In this case, the 'dissatisfaction' felt by both of them was used by Nietzsche to express his own uneasiness: namely, his 'inability' to exist as a character of historical action, and his moral authority, to which he wanted to find an equivalent in events for which he could claim responsibility. He well knew that he harboured such events in himself, that he was hastening their advent. But he had reached the point where he was compensating for the silence or incomprehension of his Germanic public by evoking concrete situations that could only be a caricature of his thought. We others can now measure the burden of this uneasiness in a mind that wanted to demonstrate to itself the riddle of his own fate through the expedient of this very problematic Shakespeare–Francis Bacon identity. It was the viewpoint of *visionary* power (that is, the viewpoint of his own work) that swept him up in this game of arbitrary pseudonymity – a game which, apparently, was a long way from his theory of the fortuitous *case*, of the fortuitous individual of the Return. Here, on the contrary, it was he himself who became a pseudonym for a moment – and for no more than a moment. For in the next moment, it quickly changed content and signification.

But the term *madness* merely denotes an operation grounded in the abolition of the principle of identity, which Nietzsche now introduces into the domain of his personal declarations, thereby reducing all the mechanisms of thought to the procedures of deception. Since the latter is attributed to language, the personal behaviour that results from it simply reproduces a verbal metonymy. The disorder it provokes in the relationships between individuals and the surrounding world has something of the character of an 'opportunistic' discontinuity as well as a scrambling of the code of everyday signs. Both imply a kind of 'slippage' of reality, which never apprehends itself except as a *being-equivalent-to-something*.

But since the event also changed nature – whether it was a ceremonious occasion, a social incident, a scandal, or a criminal trial – Nietzsche would always be able to find himself again in it. His interest in murderers, for example, and the manner in which he spoke of them, demonstrated that he no longer sought to argue except insofar as everything that happens happens to himself. Strangely, the rubric of *'faits divers'* or the *'society gossip column'*, whose fortuitousness gave his language a peremptory tone, became an important dimension of his thought: a refusal to limit his discussions to his vision of the world. When making personal declarations, he presumed that his interlocutor would register the *fact* of 'Nietzsche', and would orient himself around this fact so as to live in Nietzsche's perspective. His entire correspondence of 1887–8 is filled with declarations of this type. They would even affect the demonstrations of his simplicity, his discretion, his modesty, his prudence, and his circumspection, which Nietzsche provides in *Ecce Homo*. He had now become his own 'propagandist': somewhere in the contemporary world there exists an authority who will decide both the future and the moral and spiritual orientation of his generation.

9

The Euphoria of Turin

JOURNAL OF THE NIHILIST. The shudder caused by the 'false' discovery – emptiness: no more thought: the powerful affects revolve around objects with no value:

– spectator of these absurd inclinations for and against

– reflective, ironic, cold with regard to oneself

– the strongest inclinations appears as lies: as if we had to believe in their objects, as if they had wanted to seduce us –

– the strongest force asks 'What's the use? . . . '

– all things remain, but serve no useful purpose –

– atheism as the absence of an ideal.

Phase of a 'no' and a passionate doing-'no': accumulated desire is discharged in it, seeking a link, a relation, an adoration . . .

Phase of mistrust even of the 'no' . . .

even of doubt
even of irony
even of mistrust.

Catastrophe: Is not the lie something divine . . .

Does not the value of all things consist in the fact that they are false . . .

Is not despair simply the consequence of a belief in *the divine nature of truth* . . .

Do not the *lie* and *falsification* (the

conversion to the false) imply the introduction of a meaning, do they not themselves have a value, a meaning, a goal . . .
Should we not believe in God, not be-
cause he is true, but *because he is false* – ?[147]

And how many *ideals* are, at bottom, still possible! –
Here is a little ideal I stumble on once every five weeks
on a wild and lonely walk, in an azure moment of sinful
happiness. To spend one's life amid delicate and absurd
things; a stranger to reality; half an artist, half a bird and
metaphysician; with no care for reality, except now
and then to acknowledge it in the manner of a good
dancer with the tips of one's toes; always tickled by
some sunray of happiness; exuberant and encouraged
even by misery – for misery *preserves* the happy man;
fixing a little humorous tail even to holiest things: this, as
is obvious, is the ideal of a heavy, hundredweight spirit
– a *spirit of gravity*.[148]

And how many new gods are still possible! As for myself,
in whom the religious, that is to say god-forming,
instinct occasionally becomes active at impossible times
– how differently, how variously the divine has revealed
itself to me each time!
    So many strange things have passed before me in
those timeless moments that fall into one's life as if from
the moon, when one no longer has any idea how old
one is or how young one will yet be – I should not
doubt that there are many kinds of gods – There are
some one cannot imagine without a certain halcyon
and frivolous quality in their make-up – Perhaps light
feet are even an integral part of the concept 'god'
– Is it necessary to elaborate that a god prefers to
stay beyond everything bourgeois and rational? and,
between ourselves, also beyond good and evil? His
prospect is *free* – in Goethe's words. And to call upon

the inestimable authority of Zarathustra in this instance: Zarathustra goes so far as to confess: 'I would believe only a God who could *dance*' –

To repeat: how many new gods are still possible! – Zarathustra himself, to be sure, is merely an old atheist: he believes neither in old nor new gods. Zarathustra says he *would*; but Zarathustra says he *will* not – Do not misunderstand him!

The type of God after the type of creative spirits, of 'great men.'[149]

When one considers the final period of Nietzsche's activity, particularly his last 'lucid' year, there is a strong temptation to say to oneself: this is what the twenty years of his career had to lead to – the abyss. Or one can distance oneself from this statement in order to oppose to it a viewpoint that is as rash as the first is banal: what these twenty years had slowly and silently prepared for was a singular apotheosis, one that was celebrated, acted out and commented on by Nietzsche himself. But the abyss and the apotheosis here seem to be inseparable.

What did it all mean? Nietzsche, speaking of the crucifixion, in this way expressed the astonishment of the disciples as he imagined them, unable to comprehend Jesus's words and gestures. And in the *Antichrist*, he himself provided the response: it was the greatest *irony* of universal history.[150]

All the interpretations and commentaries that Nietzsche's collapse may give rise to must remain under the sign of this same irony that Nietzsche pointed to at the moment of his departure. At what point did he reach the edge of the abyss? He collapsed suddenly, between the end of 1888 and the beginning of 1889, say some, including his closest friends. No, say others, the illness had obviously been affecting him since *Zarathustra*, and certainly since the end of 1887. Both groups believe in the reality of the professor of philology, they both take the reality of the philosopher seriously. Neither group wants to admit that Nietzsche's understanding was being exercised to its fullest extent, nor are they willing to take at their word his successive and sometimes contradictory declarations, which are examined only as a means of classifying Nietzsche in the context of contemporary thought. Both groups approach the final spectacle that Nietzsche offered of himself in Turin from these points of view, enviously seeking some trace of incoherence in the final works that immediately precede the 'closure', or identifying those works that are most exempt from any suspicion of 'imbalance' – all without ever speaking of Nietzsche's valetudinary antecedents.

The various witnesses of Nietzsche's life held firm opinions about his supposedly unhealthy propensities. Overbeck, his most trustworthy and honest confidante during the ten final 'lucid' years, examined the motives for the collapse scrupulously and with the greatest circumspection. It undoubtedly seemed conceivable to him that the madness had simply been the product of Nietzsche's particular way of life. But this is still a rather timid hypothesis. For if madness as madness could be the product of a way of life (when it more certainly would lie at its origin), it would function in a completely different manner: if, from the start, a mind regarded the boundary between reason and unreason, from the viewpoint of knowledge, as a flagrant error, it would consent to reason only if it could also reserve for itself the use of unreason.

Among the 'monuments' of his illness that I possess in my collection of Nietzsche's letters, one of the most telling is the call of distress, half (in) German, half (in) Latin, which he addressed to me from Sils (Hte Engadine) on 8 Sept. 1881. The two languages – German and a less-than-perfect Latin – revealed to me the state of his reason's health, though I could do nothing to help him. My own conclusions, after examining my own memories as well as Miss Forster's narrative – particularly the contrast between Nietzsche's unhealthy state in 1884, when I myself visited him here

in Basel at the Croix Blanche Hotel, and the impression
of her brother's health that his sister says she had a few
weeks later (in September or October of that same year,
in Zurich), most notably his cheerfulness during their
reconciliation – have convinced me that, during this
period, Nietzsche was subject to violent oscillations
between the deepest depression and euphoric exal-
tations – oscillations which in this form generally
characterize candidates for madness – and that, at that
time, I had visited such a candidate. Moreover, I had
similar impressions during the preceding year when I
spent time with Nietzsche at Schuls, near Tarasp. And
if I sometimes felt I was in contact with a mentally
ill person, during these years, the very manner in
which Nietzsche, bedridden and suffering gravely from
a migraine, one day tried to initiate me, for the first and
last time, into his secret doctrine, could leave me with
no doubt whatsoever that he was no longer master of
his reason.

Nietzsche confided his revelations of the Eternal
Return to me during a visit to Basel, in the summer of
1884 (at the Croix Blanche Hotel), in the same mysteri-
ous fashion he had revealed it to Mme Andreas Salomé,
according to her own testimony. Bedridden, suffering,
in a hoarse and sinister voice, he communicated to me
part of his esoteric doctrine. He may have spoken with
me about the doctrine before, but only in passing, as if
it were merely a well-known doctrine of ancient philosophy, without there being anything to draw attention
to the fact that it was a matter that concerned him
personally. At the very least, I have an obscure memory
of our discussions on this subject prior to 1884.

Since these communications of 1884 were so totally
incomprehensible to me, I also concluded that he was
undoubtedly talking about some kind of link with
ancient philosophy. It was also to this effect that,
some years after Nietzsche's collapse, I spoke with

Rohde, who shared completely my opinion as to the origin of this doctrine, but who, for the rest, refused to speak of Nietzsche's use of it as anything other than a symptom of his morbid state.[151]

When Nietzsche spoke of his thought of the Return, his interlocutors presumed that his representation of it was *borrowed* from the systems of antiquity. But Nietzsche's own experience at Sils-Maria was enveloped in this representation, and it provoked the impression of strangeness felt by his friends. Overbeck was not quite sure if it was a mystification or a delirious idea. He emphasizes the state Nietzsche was in when he spoke with him (bedridden, suffering from a migraine), the disturbing tone of his hoarse voice, the spectacular character of the communication – all of which contrast sharply with the 'objective' tone Nietzsche would have used to speak of Hellenic conceptions of the Return.

Although Overbeck attributed the inexplicable content of the doctrine to Nietzsche's unhealthy state, he refused to see in it the slightest indication of madness itself; consequently, he did not recognize in his 'lucid' productions any obscure influence of madness, prior to the explosion of delirium at Turin. Nothing seemed more erroneous to him than to reinterpret Nietzsche's thought retrospectively from the collapse. Nietzsche himself, at the beginning of 1888, had written to Deussen:

I have lived, willed, and perhaps also *obtained* this and more, so that a kind of violence is necessary for me to distance and separate myself from myself. The vehemence of my interior oscillations were prodigious: and I have concluded *epithetis ornantobus* that, in some manner, this is also perceptible from a distance, which seems to be gratifying to German critics ('eccentric', 'pathological', 'psychiatric', and *hoc genus omne*). These men, who have no notion of *my center* or the great passion my life is devoted to, will for that reason have difficulty seeing *where* I have hitherto been *outside my center*, where I really *was* 'eccentric.' But what does it matter they distrust my subject and my contact! The worse that can happen is that no one does anything (– which would make me distrustful with regard to myself).'*

Recalling the passage from this letter (to Deussen), Overbeck concluded: 'The only thing that must be taken into account is the fact that Nietzsche himself admits his own "excentricity", and that he thereby affirms the inaccessibility of the latter to any judgment other than his own. In any case, this judgment retains the force of argument with regard to any judgment of the knowledge of oneself – namely, that

---

* *Nietzsche Briefwechsel*, Dritte Abteilung, 5. Bd. (Berlin/New York, 1984), p. 221 ff. Nietzsche had written to Carl Fuchs (14 December 1887) in terms almost identical to those in his letter to Deussen: '. . . almost without willing it, but in accordance with an inexorable necessity, right in the midst of settling my accounts with men and things, and putting behind me my whole life hitherto. Almost everything that I do now is a 'drawing-the-line under everything.' *The vehemence of my inner oscillations* has been terrifying, all through these past years; now that I must make the transition to a new and more intense form, I need, above all, a new estrangement, a still more intense depersonalization. So it is of greatest importance what and who still remain to me.

What age am I? I do not know – as little as I know how young I shall become . . . . In Germany there are strong complaints about my 'eccentricity.' But since people do not know where my center is, they will find it hard to know for certain where and when I have still not been 'excentric' – for example, being a classical philologist; this was being outside my center (which, fortunately, does not mean that I was a bad classical philologist). Likewise today it seems to me an eccentricity that I should have been a Wagnerite. It was an inordinately dangerous experiment; now that I know it did *not* ruin me, I know also what meaning it has had for me – it was the strongest test of my character. To be sure, one's inmost being gradually disciplines one back to unity; that passion, to which no name can be put for a long time, rescues us from all digressions and dispersions, that task of which one is the involuntary missionary' (*Nietzsche Briefwechsel*, Abt. 3/5, a.a.O., S. 209 ff. = Middleton, Letter 161, pp. 280–1, translation modified).

The reasons Nietzsche gives for his 'eccentricity' are still of a polemical order, and if he had already let it be known many times that his rupture with Wagner had tested his character, he still does not say what his *centre* is, nor does he identify the *task* for which he is the involuntary missionary. This in no way invalidates the manner in which Overbeck discusses and poses the question of Nietzsche's 'centre'.

it provides no proof and yet is the supreme proof. At least Nietzsche proved that he had not found his own center.'

No matter how justified Overbeck's warning against any retrospective interpretation of the oeuvre from the collapse may be, however, his discussion still seems to depend upon an *optimistic conception of the understanding* in general that Nietzsche himself did his utmost to destroy. It presumes certain norms of the intellect, in the name of which, for example, Dr Podach today refuses to grant Nietzsche the rational or 'objective' capacity 'indispensable to a philosopher' – a lack that would already have been painfully obvious in Nietzsche's inability to construct a coherent system of his thought. The claim that Nietzsche was unable to find 'his own centre' is also dependent on such a conception of the understanding.

But if Nietzsche admitted his own excentricity, what did he mean when he said, '*where I really was*' '*outside my center*'? Had he not said to the same Overbeck that he had '*a nature so concentrated that everything that struck or touched him was directed toward his center*' – whence his vulnerability to *cruel chance*, which stemmed from the very fact of being too concentrated? If his centre was identified with the 'great passion' to which his life was dedicated, if he needed to remain alive a few more years in order to pursue a goal – what then was this goal? The work? Or something else that would be accomplished in what was to come? Was it not his concentration that kept his *will* from achieving this goal? If the goal was the work, then as long as he remained focused on the idea of the work, and thus on communication, in reality he created an obstacle to the experience, for he still conceived of it as something communicable; 'his centre' was no longer his passion, but was still conceived of in terms of his understanding. By eluding the vehemence of his oscillations in this manner, he postponed the experience of *being outside his centre*. Now this experience – which was something his previous work demanded, and thus something he demanded of himself – was his own metamorphosis. How was Nietzsche led to deny the serenity of the understanding, if not through the centrifugal forces of Chaos? Not that he had invoked these forces: the more he feared their imminent irruption, the more he fought against incoherence, and the more he submitted to the allure of the discontinuous and the arbitrary: '*Thoughts are the signs of a play and combat of affects; they always depend on their hidden roots.*'[152] In the consciousness he acquired of them, there appeared, from the start, little by little, the outlines of the seductive smile of the sphinx.

Intensity, excitation, tonality: such is thought, independent of what it expresses or could express, and its application in turn arouses other intensities, other excitations, other tonalities. From then on, Nietzsche wanted to exercise his thought from the viewpoint of the emotional capacity, and no longer the conceptual capacity: at that limit where knowledge offers itself as a resource for acting, no longer for the peace of the understanding, but at the mercy of the alluring forces of Chaos.

What overcame these centrifugal forces in order to communicate them was not the understanding; these forces were themselves communicated one day, at Sils-Maria, in the form of a movement around something whose approach remained for ever forbidden, as if in accordance with a secret accord or liaison. First the *ring*; then the *wheel of fortune*; and finally the *circulus vitiosus deus* – so many figures that, in themselves, presuppose a centre, a focus, a void, perhaps even a god which inspires the circular movement and is expressed in it, yet which is *kept at a distance*. The centrifugal forces never flee the centre for ever, but approach it anew only in order to retreat from it yet again. Such are the vehement oscillations that overwhelm an individual as long as he seeks only his own centre, and cannot see the circle of which he himself is a part. For if these oscillations overwhelm him, it is because each corresponds to an individuality *other* than the one he believes himself to be, from the point of view of the unfindable centre. As a result, an identity is essentially fortuitous, and every identity must pass through a series of individualities in order for the fortuitousness of a particular identity to render them all necessary. What the Eternal Return implies as a doctrine is neither more nor less than the insignificance of the *once and for all* of the principle of identity or non-contradiction, which lies at the base of the understanding. If all things come to pass once and for all, then, lacking intensity, they fall back into the insignificance of meaning. But because intensity is the *soul* of the Eternal Return, all things acquire signification only through the intensity of the circle.

But this is still only one possible statement of the thought of the Return: the lived experience of the intensity of the circle, which is substituted for the principle of the *once and for all*, opens itself up to a number of individualities through which it passes, until it returns to the only one to whom the Eternal Return was revealed . . . .

This experience became obscure once Nietzsche tried to initiate his friends into it, as if into a semblance of a doctrine that required the understanding – and they *felt* the delirium. If the event at Turin proved them right, it also explained why they understood nothing of his whispered words – the only ones through which he could transmit to them the vertigo he experienced at Sils-Maria.

'First *images* – to explain how images arise in the mind. Then *words*, applied to images. Finally *concepts*, possible only when there are words.'[153]

A word, once it signifies an emotion, passes itself off as identical to the experienced emotion, which in turn had strength only when it had no word. A signified emotion is weaker than an insignificant emotion.

Whenever a communicative designation intervenes in an exchange of words with others (subjects), there is therefore a discrepancy between what was experienced and what was expressed.

This experience knowingly determined Nietzsche's relationships with all those around him: his friends did not reflect

on the emotional genesis of a thought. And when Nietzsche
invited them to think with him, he was really inviting them
to feel, and thus to feel his own prior emotion.

But this discrepancy between the designation and the designated emotion in the constitution of *meaning* (the meaning
of the emotion) – thus this movement of the word toward
the emotion and of the emotion toward the *choice of the word*
– thus the fact that the expression is itself an emotion – all of
this has relevance only in relation to an agent [*suppôt*] who
undertakes this operation, who can maintain its continuity in
the midst of all this coming-and-going, and who undertakes
it as much in relation to itself as to others. Nietzsche never
ceased to be preoccupied with this phenomenon, it *underlay*
his contact with the friends and acquaintances around him.
The agent *unmakes* and remakes itself in accordance with
the receptivity of other agents – agents of comprehension.
Through their own *fluctuations*, the latter continually modify
the system of designations. Once the need to designate the
emotion to others (to those capable of feeling it) ceases, the
emotion is no longer designated except through itself – in
the agent: either through a code of designations (once the
emotion is *thought* as designatable), a code on which the
agent depends – or else through non-designatable states, and
thus as something non-designatable: a rise or fall (euphoria –
depression) in which the agent is contradictorily unmade and
remade: for it disappears in the euphoria and is remade in the
depression as if it were an agent only through the absence or
incapacity of the euphoria.

The consequences Nietzsche drew from these situations
were developed in terms of the following argumentative
scheme. First, it is our needs that interpret the world: every
impulse, as a need to dominate, has its own perspective that
it constantly imposes on other impulses. Second, given this
plurality of perspectives, it not only follows that everything
is an interpretation, but that the subject that interprets is itself
an interpretation. Third, the intelligibility of everything that
can only be thought (since we can form no thought that

is not constrained by the rules of institutional language) is derived from the gregarious morality of truthfulness – and in this sense the principle of truthfulness itself implies gregariousness. '"You shall be knowable, express yourself by *clear* and *constant* signs – otherwise you are dangerous; and if you are evil, your ability to dissimulate is the worst thing for the herd. We despise the secret and the unrecognizable. – Consequently you must consider yourself knowable, you may not be concealed from yourself, you may not believe that you change." Thus: the demand for truthfulness presupposes the knowability and stability of the person.'[154]

Given this moralization of the intelligible (or of the intelligible as the foundation of gregarious morality), Nietzsche developed an ambiguous inquiry both into the forces of conservation and into the forces of dissolution. He ceaselessly oscillated between fixation (in clear and constant signs) and his propensity to movement, to the dispersion of himself – to the point where the tension provoked a rupture between the *constancy of signs* and *that which* they are unable to signify other than through their *fixity*: as if inertia itself were inverted into the *obstinacy* of words, as if the constancy of signs were replaced by a word that would be equivalent to an *obstinate gesture*, recuperating the unknowable, dispersed under the appearance of incoherence. And in this manner, Nietzsche came to recapitulate for himself the stages that had led him to a *theory of the fortuitous case*:

1. My endeavor to oppose decadence and the increasing weakness of personality.

I sought a new *center*.

2. Impossibility of this endeavor recognized.

3. Thereupon I advanced further down the road of dissolution – where I found new sources of strength for individuals.

We have to be destroyers! . . .

I perceived that the state of dissolution, in which individual natures can perfect themselves as never before – is an image and isolated example [*cas singulier*] of existence in general.

Theory of the *fortuitous case*, the soul, a being that selects and nourishes itself, strong, crafty, and creative – continually

(this creative force normally passes by unseen! it is conceived solely as 'passive')

I recognized *active force*, created out of the fortuitous!

– the fortuitous case itself is only the mutual collision of creative impulses

Against the paralyzing sense of general dissolution and incompleteness, I opposed

the eternal return![155]

He would incarnate the fortuitous case. At the same time, he would *reproduce* the world, which is merely a combination of random events. Thus he would train himself in the practice of the unforeseeable.

The 'incoherence' that certain people thought could be found only in the final messages from Turin exists *at the start* of Nietzsche's career – his paralysing confrontation. Over the years he had painstakingly disguised and dissimulated this confrontation before producing it on the squares of Turin. The fact that there was an unhealthy psychological disposition underlying the initial dilemma, making it the pitiless accomplice of this debilitating quarrel, did not suppress the struggle, as if it had been decided in advance. On the contrary, it pushed the struggle to an extreme by making Nietzsche's own organism its battlefield.

But the collapse would never have occurred if the seduction exerted by Chaos – that is, by incoherence – had not still and always been present in Nietzsche, except that it would not have taken place in full view in such a striking fashion. In a certain sense, the premonition of evil, of the disproportion between *the time of the pathos* and *the time granted to his organism*, gave rise to an exchange, a transaction: this organism (this instrument, this body) was the *price* of the pathos. In order to inscribe itself in the depths of his organism, the law of the Eternal Return of all possible individuations, as the justice *of the universe*, required the destruction of the very organ that had disclosed it: namely, *Nietzsche's brain*, a fortuitous product, realized by the randomness that constitutes the *Law* of all the possible (but limited) combinations of the Return of all things. – But once again, this is nothing but a *formulation* of the event using terms forged by this same brain. If Nietzsche had not had a premonition of his decline, he would not have given at one blow (in a few days, in a few messages) the totality of what it signified through himself. It was first of all necessary for him to acquire, through successive efforts, the signification of a sign. But once he acquired it, his efforts and even their fruits mattered little to him; he was now certain of his authority. From this 'position of strength', the challenge he would throw in the face of our era also mattered little to him: he himself had become its undreamt-of measure. But this authority did not have to rely on the *previous declarations* in which it had been grounded. If Nietzsche had taken a single one of his declarations to be absolute, the whole operation would have been compromised. His authority *was not that of an individual* – as his most sympathetic commentators still delude themselves in claiming – but that of a *fortuitous* case, which is nothing other than the expression of a *law* – and thus of a justice.

Had Nietzsche not been prey to this premonitory vertigo, perhaps he might have risked confusing the meaning of his message with that of an immutable philosophical system. But Damocles's sword was dangling above him: you could be struck with imbecility *at any moment*, and everything you have said that is just, true and authentic will be marked by the stamp of *mental debility*. Because of this threat, he admitted this debility as if it were already a *fait accompli*. The threat became his own ruse, or his own genius: let us express what lies at the *depth* of all things in a monstrous form. For if we declare that this depth is unknowable, we will always cut the figure of a *easy-going agnosticism*, which will change nothing in the behaviour of humanity, nor in its morality, nor in its forms of existence. But if we speak the language of a imposter-fool, everything will be completely different; and therefore we will say this absurd thing: *everything returns!*

Nietzsche was a metaphysical 'propagandist' for Wagner during the time when Bayreuth was still a difficult project to realize. But once the undertaking turned into an idolatrous cult of the old master, under Cosima's auspices, Nietzsche realized that he had devoted himself to an art that had diverted his own aspirations, that had monopolized and falsified them in favour of a revival of Teutonic virtuism. He would later blame the Wagnerian movement for his books' lack of success, and for the incomprehension he noted in his old friends, especially in those he had introduced to Wagner, but also in others he had met at Bayreuth. Nietzsche would henceforth seek the reasons for his repugnance: Wagner corrupted music through his dramatic musical conception, 'an impossible synthesis of spoken drama and a music given over and subordinated entirely to the expression of affects'.

He then revealed all the traits of false genius in Wagner, who relied on the nervous vulnerability of the listener. Intoxication, ecstasy, the tonality of the soul, excess, delirium, hallucination – these were what this *Cagliostro* seemed to look for in order to abuse the crowds and heighten the hysteria of his female listeners. Worse yet, these dubious means were put in the service of what was the evil *par excellence* of his generation: a pseudo-mysticism, a 'return to Rome', chastity – the worse things that Nietzsche could ever condemn, excoriate, or abominate. Because of this, he called Wagner a *histrionic*, and therefore the very symptom of *decadence*. Nietzsche in this way revealed the ambiguity of his attacks: even before Wagner had composed *Parsifal* (the work that is the primary example of the process he ascribes to the old master), he had deliberately ascribed to Wagner what he himself was developing in his thought: Wagner expressed *Dionysianism* (or what this term refers to) in its essential form. But he was not content to express it: he could not sustain it as a pure musician; *he exploited it toward ends that are incompatible with what Dionysianism represents*. Now for Nietzsche, neither the philosopher nor the scientist can ever communicate Dionysianism; in effect, only the *histrionic* is able to give an account of it – and this is what he criticizes Wagner for being.

Only the histrionic is capable of communicating Dionysianism. But if Wagner was a histrionic, why was he merely a *decadent* and not a true and pure musician? Wagner seemed 'to confuse himself with Shakespeare, when he insisted on the *actor* in Shakespeare'. Neither an authentic artist nor even an actor is a histrionic; every authentic artist is conscious of producing something that is *false*, namely, a *simulacrum*. Yet Wagner claimed to be a reformer, a regenerative philosopher; but he was only a musician and therefore, according to Nietzsche, he was a *bad* musician: 'vain, greedy, sensual, perverse', he did not even have the strength of his impudence. Thus, because he used the simulacrum while remaining *totally unconscious* of the false, he was merely a *histrionic*. Now for Nietzsche, the histrionic was the formula for a secret weapon that would explode the traditional criteria of knowledge – the *true* and the *false*. The phenomenon of the *actor* became, in Nietzsche, an analogue for the simulation of being itself.

Nietzsche wanted to reserve the means of exploiting this weapon for himself alone. He was amply furnished with its substance and possessed the necessary instrument to set it free, to develop it, to give it form. In Nietzsche, histrionism was strictly related to his own secret labour of decomposing the person. He projected on to Wagner's physiognomy – three years after the latter's death – everything that, while authentic in himself, appeared as tainted and corrupt in Wagner.

Nietzsche developed the phantasm of the mask from this same motif (of unconscious dissimulation and the conscious simulacrum of the authentic). The mask is not only a metaphor of universal importance, but something to which Nietzsche had recourse in his own behaviour toward his contemporaries. *The mask hides the absence of a determinate physiognomy*, it parallels his relationship with the unforeseeable and unfathomable Chaos. But the mask is nonetheless an *emergence from Chaos* – the limit-point where necessity and chance confront each other, where the arbitrary and the 'just' coincide.

The mask, which forms a determined physiognomy all the same, even when it hides its absence, *belongs to external interpretation*, but corresponds to an internal desire of suggestion. Even more, it reveals that the person who appears to wear the mask must also have *decided* on such-and-such a face with regard to 'himself'. But – and this is the process he was pursuing, or that Chaos was pursuing through him – Nietzsche would treat his own necessary ego as a mask (what he has become in order to be such-and-such an ego). He could then vindicate himself in the same way that he interpreted Dostoevsky's *Underground Man*: 'A cruel way to *know myself* was to look at myself with derision, but with such a reckless, voluptuous, and offhanded sovereign power that I was drunk with pleasure.'[156]

If Nietzsche, from his adolescence onward, was preoccupied with the recovery of his own past, and thus with its autobiographical construction, it is because he was seeking in this inventory of his existence the movement that would justify the *fortuitousness* of his being. *Ecce Homo*, as an autobiography, does not glorify an exemplary ego, but rather describes the progressive disengagement of an idiosyncrasy at the expense of this ego, insofar as this idiosyncrasy is imposed on the ego, and disintegrates the ego into what it itself constitutes.

Just as the mask hides the absence of a determinate physiognomy – and thus conceals Chaos, the richness of Chaos – so *the gesture that accompanies the mask* (the *histrionic* gesture) is strictly related to the designation of the lived emotion before it is signified by speech. This improvised gesture, in itself devoid of meaning, but a simulator and thus *interpretable*, signals the barely perceptible demarcation *where the impulses still hesitate to be ascribed any identification, where necessity, which is unaware of itself, appears to be arbitrary, before receiving an externally necessary signification.* On the one hand, there is the possibility of a gesture that, in itself, is devoid of meaning; on the other hand, there is the continuity of this gesture, its consequences in an action that itself acquires meaning only if the *refusal of Chaos*, of the *plurality* of meaning, is accomplished in the form of a decision, in favour of exteriority, in order to intervene in the 'course' of events. During Nietzsche's sojourn in Turin, such an 'insane' gesture would increasingly come to prevail over any explanation. It expressed more directly the coincidence of the *fortuitous case* (*Zufall*) with the *sudden idea* (*Einfall*).

After publishing *The Case of Wagner*, Nietzsche started to write the first part of the *Revaluation of All Values*. According to certain posthumous plans, this work was the *Antichrist*, the whole of which he wrote in *Turin* (at the same time as *Nietzsche Contra Wagner*, *The Twilight of the Idols* and *Ecce Homo*). None of these four works would be published prior to his internment in Jena. But by the time he completed the *Antichrist*, Nietzsche was no longer concerned with the *Revaluation*. Lacking a systematic elaboration of his so-called *magnum opus*, Nietzsche instead entered into the perspective of a *conspiracy*. This (paranoiac) vision of the world and of his own situation, which began in Turin, constituted a dictated system, organized by the Nietzschean pathos. During this period, gesture would be substituted for discourse; and his own speech, far surpassing the merely 'literary' level, would henceforth have to be handled like dynamite. Nietzsche now believed he was pursuing, not the realization of a system, but the application of a programme. What pushed him in this direction was the extraordinary euphoria of his final days in Turin.

We will follow the histrionic development of this euphoria (apart from the ongoing composition of *Ecce Homo*), in more or less brief or extended forms, by examining Nietzsche's correspondence from Turin during the last six months of 1888. These forms vary, however, depending on the sphere that his various correspondents represented for Nietzsche: his friends, intimates (Overbeck, Gast), and former acquaintances (Burckhardt, Cosima) already belonged to a more or less stable past, but because of the Turin hallucinations, they would now be seen in a new light. Strindberg's appearance in Nietzsche's life, by contrast, would enrich this hallucinatory state. For the first time, Nietzsche could dialogue (if only in letters) with an equal, a *genius* whose own temporary delirium had had the same scope as Nietzsche's – now embryonic but soon to become definitive. Strindberg not only provided Nietzsche with evidence, along with Brandes's lectures, of the growing recognition of his authority; even better, Strindberg – unwittingly, it is true – confirmed Nietzsche in his Turinesque vision of the world, and thereby helped prepare for Nietzsche's own transfiguration and his elevation into an absolutely fabulous region. Strindberg's pathos sustained Nietzsche's paranoia.

To what degree might the correspondence with Strindberg have influenced Nietzsche's predisposition to gesture, and thus to a gestural speech, which reached its height toward the end of 1888 in his final messages?

During this exchange of letters, Strindberg's acerbic irony, through a singular coincidence, happened to correspond with the tonality of Nietzsche's soul, at once violent and euphoric – a coincidence that (had Strindberg agreed to translate *Ecce Homo* into French) would have been, as Nietzsche himself said, '*the miracle of a fortuitous case pregnant with meaning*'.

Strindberg, who already had a long experience with his own paranoiac crises, and who, toward the end of 1888, was enjoying one of the most sober periods of his existence, had not yet realized the state of Nietzsche's soul in Turin. He interpreted his final remarks as nuances of style, if not as pure movements of humour. Since he was one of the few people not only to have admired Nietzsche since *Zarathustra*, but to have been influenced by him – most notably, by his psychology of women – he received Nietzsche's latest works (*The Case of Wagner, The Twilight of the Idols* [no doubt he had received page proofs of *Twilight*, since the work was not published until 1890]) as a coherent continuation of what Nietzsche already represented in his eyes.

CORRESPONDENCE

Strindberg to Nietzsche

End of November 1888

Dear Sir,

You have certainly given mankind the deepest book they possess, and not the least of your achievements is that you have had the courage and perhaps also the irrepressible impulse to spit all these magnificent words into the face of the rabble. I thank you for it. Nevertheless it strikes me that with all your intellectual candor you have somewhat flattered the criminal type. Just look at the hundreds of photographs that illustrate Lombroso's 'Criminal Man', and you will agree that the criminal is an inferior animal, a degenerate, a weakling, not possessing the necessary gifts to circumvent those laws that present too powerful an obstacle to his will and his strength. Just observe the stupidly moral appearance of these honest beasts! What a disappointment for morality!

And so you wish to be translated into our Greenlandish language. Why not into French or English? You can form an estimate of our intelligence from the fact that they wanted to put me into a nursing home on account of my tragedy, and that a spirit as subtle and rich as that of Brandes is silenced by this 'majority of duffers'.

I end all my letters to my friends with, 'Read Nietzsche!' That is my *Carthago est delenda*.

At all events our greatness will diminish the moment you are recognized and understood and the dear mob begins to hob-nob with you as if you were one of themselves. It would be better if you maintained your noble seclusion and allowed us others, 10,000 higher men, to make a secret pilgrimage to your sanctuary in order to partake of your riches to our hearts' content. Let us guard the esoteric doctrine so as to keep it pure and unimpaired and not spread it broadcast without the instrumentality of devoted disciples among whom is

August Strindberg[157]

Strindberg, who feared his own deliriums – from which he had learned to free himself, with great strength, by dividing in two – could not see how his own tone, which would never have permitted itself to feel such a state, could nonetheless precipitate the progressively delirious interpretation that was being formulated in Nietzsche's mind. He was aware neither of Nietzsche's euphoria at Turin, nor of the way Nietzsche was beginning to experience events around him. The passionate interest in his play *Married People* that Nietzsche expressed, as well as the importance Nietzsche seemed to attach to a possible performance of *Father* at Antoine's Théâtre Libre, seemed perfectly natural to him.

When, under the pretext that Strindberg himself was responsible for the French translation of *Father*, Nietzsche asked him to undertake the translation of *Ecce Homo* – which itself seems rather extraordinary – Strindberg accepted in principle, provided that Nietzsche was willing to bear the cost.

Nietzsche to August Strindberg

Turin, December 7, 1888

My dear and honored Sir:

Has a letter of mine been lost? The moment I had finished reading your *Père* for a second time, I wrote you a letter, deeply impressed by this masterpiece of hard psychology; I also expressed to you my conviction that your work is predestined to be performed in Paris now, in the Théâtre Libre of M. Antoine – you should simply demand it of Zola!

The hereditary criminal is *décadent*, even insane – no

doubt about that! But the history of criminal families, for which the Englishman Galton (*Hereditary Genius*) has collected the largest body of material, points constantly back to an excessively strong person where a certain social level is the case. The latest great criminal case in Paris, that of Prado, presented the classic type: Prado was superior to his judges, even to his lawyers, in self-control, wit, and exuberance of spirit; nevertheless, the pressure of the accusation had so reduced him physiologically that some witnesses could recognize him only from the old portraits.

But now a word or two between ourselves, very much between ourselves! When your letter reached me yesterday – the first letter in my life to reach me – I had just finished the last revision of the manuscript of *Ecce Homo*. Since there are no more coincidences in my life, you are consequently not a coincidence. Why do you write letters that arrive at such a moment!

Ecce Homo should indeed appear simultaneously in German, French, and English. Yesterday I sent the manuscript to my printer; as soon as a sheet is ready, it must go to the translators. *But who are these translators?* Honestly I did not know that you yourself are responsible for the excellent French of your *Père*; I thought that it must be a masterly translation. If you were to undertake the French translation yourself, I would be overjoyed at this miracle of a coincidence pregnant with meaning. For, between ourselves, it would take a poet of the first rank to translate *Ecce Homo*; in its language, in the refinement of its feeling, it is a thousand miles beyond any mere 'translator.' Actually, it is not a thick book; I suppose it would be, in the French edition (perhaps with Lemerre, Paul Bourget's publisher!) priced at about three francs fifty. Since it says unheard-of things and sometimes, in all innocence, speaks the language of the rulers of the world, the number of editions will surpass even *Nana*.

On the other hand, it is anti-German to an annihi-
lating extent; throughout, I side with French culture
(I treat all the German philosophers as 'unconscious
counterfeiters'). Also the book is not boring – at points
I even wrote it in the 'Prado' style. To secure myself
against German brutalities, I shall send the first copies,
before publication, to Prince Bismarck and the young
emperor, with letters declaring war – military men
cannot reply to that with police measures. – I am a
psychologist. –

Consider it, *verehrter Herr!* It is a matter of the first
importance. For I am strong enough to break the history
of humanity in two.

There is still the question of the English translation.
Would you have any suggestion? An anti-German book
in England. . . .

Yours very devotedly,
Nietzsche[158]

Strindberg to Nietzsche

Copenhagen, mid-December 1888
My dear Sir,

I was overjoyed at receiving a word of appreciation
from your master-hand regarding my misunderstood
tragedy. I ought to tell you, my dear sir, that I was
compelled to give the publisher two editions gratis
before I could hope to see my piece printed. Out
of gratitude for this, when the piece was performed
at the theatre, one old lady in the audience fell dead,
another was successfully delivered of a child, and at the
sight of the strait-jacket, three-quarters of the people
present rose as one man and left the theatre amid
maniacal yells.

And, then, you ask me to get Zola to have the piece
played before Henri Becque's Parisians! Why, it would
lead to universal parturition in that city of cuckolds. And
now to your affairs.

Sometimes I write straightaway in the French language (just glance at the enclosed article with its Boulevard, though picturesque, style), but at times I translate my own works.

It is quite impossible to find a French translator who will not improve your style according to the rhetorical 'Ecole Normale', and rob your mode of expression of all its pristine freshness. The shocking translation of *Married People* was done by a Swiss-Frenchman (from French-Switzerland) for the sum of 1,000 francs. He was paid to the last farthing and then they demanded, in Paris, 500 francs for revising his work. From this you will understand that the translation of your work will be a matter of a good deal of money, and as I am a poor devil with a wife, three kids, two servants, and debts, etc., I could not grant you any diminution in the matter of fees, particularly as I should be forced to work not as a literary hack but as a poet. If you are not appalled at the thought of what it will cost you, you can rely upon me and my talent. Otherwise I should be happy to try and find a French translator for you who would be absolutely as reliable as possible.

As regards England, I really do not feel in a position to say anything whatever; for, as far as she is concerned, we have to deal with a nation of bigots that has delivered itself up into the hands of its women, and this is tantamount to hopeless decadence. You know, my dear Sir, what morality means in England: Girls' High School libraries, Currer Bell, Miss Braddon and the rest; Don't soil your hand with that offal! In the French language you can pierce your way even into the uttermost depths of the negro-world, so you can safely let England's trousered women go to the deuce. Please think the matter over and consider my suggestions and let me hear from you about it as soon as possible.

Awaiting your reply, I am yours sincerely,
August Strindberg[159]

But Nietzsche did not seem to follow up this counter-proposition, though he did send Strindberg a copy of the *Genealogy of Morals*. Strindberg responded by sending him a package containing his *Swiss News*, one of which, notably, recounts the 'Tortures of Conscience' of a German officer who, mad with regret for having given the order to shoot some thieves, deserts and becomes a Swiss citizen in order to avoid being the instrument of an imperialist power.

Nietzsche reacted briefly:

[Undated]

Dear Sir:

You will soon have an answer about your novella – it sounds like a rifle shot. I have ordered a convocation of the princes in Rome – I mean to have the young emperor shot.

Auf Wiedersehen! For we shall see each other again.

Une seule condition: Divorçons . . .

Nietzsche Caesar[160]

It was at this moment that Strindberg began to fear for Nietzsche. For this penultimate message from Turin, signed 'Nietzsche *Caesar*', betrayed the total upheaval that had taken place since Nietzsche solicited Strindberg as a translator (7 December) – an upheaval which, in the context of the letters and messages to his other correspondents (while writing *Ecce Homo*), was rigorously linked to his gestures and speech since the beginning of 1888; and in any case, they demonstrate that the upheaval had been imminent since the middle of November. From his Danish retreat in Holte, Strindberg could not follow the various phases of Nietzsche's metamorphosis; he had been corresponding with him only since autumn.

Upon receiving this brief message signed *Caesar*, Strindberg hesitated, rather than taking it to be merely facetious. He could not avoid an initial feeling of anguish, but he disguised its expression by seeming to raise the stakes: he signed his own response, written in Latin and Greek, *Deus optimus maximus*.

Holtibus pridie Cal. Jan.
MDCCCLXXXIX

Carissime doctor!
Thelo, Thelo manenai!
Litteras tuas non sine perturbatione accepi et tibi gratias
ago.
'Rectius vives, Licini, neque altum.
Semper urgendo neque, dum procellas
Cautus horrescis nimium premendo
    Litus iniquum.'
Interdum juvat insanire!
    Vale et Fave!
        Strindberg
        (Deus optimus maximus)[161]

Nietzsche responded immediately and, given his present
state, with an astonishing continuity:

Herr Strindberg!
Eheu . . . not *Divorçons* after all? . . .
        The Crucified[162]

The citation of the verses from Horace may have merely
impressed Nietzsche. By contrast, the *Thelo manenai* ('I want,
I want to be mad') and the *interdum juvat insanine* ('meanwhile
let us rejoice in our madness') could have either encouraged
Nietzsche's state or added nothing to the euphoria. What is
clear, however, is that his state did not prevent Nietzsche
from conforming to the spirit of compassion expressed in
this final homage to his histrionics. The *Deus optimus
maximus*, which had just become part of his turmoil (*non
sine perturbatione*, 'not without a severe shock'), prompted him
to sign his return message not as *Caesar* but as *the Crucified*. At
the moment he signed his letter in this way, and chose the
physiognomy of Christ to mask the loss of his own identity,
he had already used this attribute-name to sign messages to
other correspondents (notably Brandes and Gast). Strindberg

was among those to whom, in his double apotheosis as *Dionysus* and *the Crucified*, Nietzsche revealed his face as the Christ. His euphoric state thus had *two perspectives* that stemmed from the confrontation established in *Ecce Homo*: *Dionysus versus the Crucified*.

The *perspective of the Crucified* was the perspective of the *conspiracy*; it was the logical continuation of the paranoiac system. From this perspective, the Crucified was substituted for Caesar; the *victim* became the force of judgement – hence the punitive execution of his enemies. Strindberg, Brandes and Gast, for various reasons, were chosen to be his accomplices. The conspiracy had begun in *Nietzsche Contra Wagner* and would eventually be directed against the leaders of imperial Germany, which formed an obstacle to Nietzschean sovereignty. But as the idea of a conspiracy developed, his 'actual' goal began to merge with the much greater project of 'breaking the history of humanity in two'. All that remained of Nietzsche himself was the face and the voice, which were lent to the two authorities presiding over the loss of his own unity: a double theophany was being expressed through Nietzsche. The extraordinary tension this required, however, never seemed to exclude from Nietzsche's consciousness the enormity of abruptly switching his allegiance from Dionysus to the Crucified, and vice versa.

Thus, even as he wrote his final message, Nietzsche was well aware to *whom* he was addressing himself, and correctly signed it *the Crucified*. He was counting on Strindberg's correct *interpretation*. Nietzsche never seemed to lose sight of his own condition: he *simulated* Dionysus or the Crucified and took a certain delight in the enormity of his simulation. The madness consisted in this delight. No one will ever be able to judge to what degree *this simulation was perfect and absolute*; the sole criterion lies in the intensity with which Nietzsche experienced the simulation, to the point of ecstasy. To reach this ecstasy of delight, an immense and liberatory state of derision must have carried him, for a few days, the first of the year 1889, through the streets of Turin, as an overcoming of his moral suffering: an attitude of mockery with regard to himself, with regard to everything he had been in his own eyes, thus with regard to Mr Nietzsche – an attitude that led to the casualness with which he wrote to his correspondents, "'Once you discovered me, it was no great feat to find me: the difficulty now is to lose me. . . .'" The Crucified' (to Brandes).[163]

If the process that destroys 'the reality principle' consists in a suspension or extinction of the consciousness of the external world, it would then seem that Nietzsche, on the contrary, had never been more lucid than during these final days in Turin. *What he was conscious of was the fact that he had ceased to be Nietzsche,* that he had been, as it were, emptied of his person. But this *absence* of identity was made known in an enormous and inconsistent declaration, which attributed a divine physiognomy to this inconsistency – a declaration that was equivalent to the universal gesture of divine figures. How could he knowingly give himself over to such a spectacle, if not because he *knew* that *no one* would believe what he was saying? Two different kinds of motives had led him to this point: on the one hand, there was the *authority* by which he felt he could hold both himself and his contemporaries up to ridicule; and on the other hand, there was the voluptuous delight he experienced in acting out the fortuitous case ('the Nietzsche case'), which was in fact a lived Chaos, a total vacancy of the conscious ego. The director of play indeed remained the *Nietzschean consciousness,* but it was no longer the *Nietzschean ego,* it was no longer the *I* that signed itself 'Nietzsche'. The Nietzschean mode of expression and the Nietzschean vocabulary still subsisted for this consciousness, but they were related directly to the impulses and their fluctuations, which were liberated from the *censure* of the reality principle exercised by the *I,* and actualized this consciousness in the form of *residues* of the Nietzschean discourse. In a certain manner, these residues contained the entire repertory of Nietzsche's histrionicism, which made use of certain props depending on the fluctuating tonalities of his soul. Histrionics thus became the practice of the fortuitous case. The censure exerted by the reality principle could only tolerate, in accordance with this same principle, the conventional play of metaphor (language) or the simulacrum (the gesture of the actor). Now, the practice of the fortuitous case here became a way of abolishing the reality principle, but it presumed that this principle was still intact for others, on whose behalf the *effect* of the *mise-en-scène* was produced, just as language, even when it is used *arbitrarily*, presupposes the interpretation of others. The censure of the reality principle was linked externally to the judgements and reactions of others, who were now the guardians of the Nietzschean *ego*, which had been abandoned to their discretion by a consciousness that no longer had an agent. It was up to these others, to his friends, to the addressees of his messages, either to find Nietzsche again, or else, once they had found him, to lose him – which is much more difficult, as he said to Brandes. For these others may only be conserving a false Nietzsche, or fragments of his shattered ego. Whether Nietzsche would be restored in his totality or remain for ever dispersed (as Dionysus Zagreus), he had, in the course of these days in Turin, passed through the looking-glass of pure and simple objective reality, whose context limits the scope of an individual's words and gestures. As he had constantly affirmed, the fortuitous case, and hence the arbitrary case, is the only reality – or the total absence of a knowable reality. His authority was such that it could merge at will with the unknowable itself and establish its reign.

But given this conspiratorial perspective of the Crucified, how could Nietzsche also situate himself in the *perspective of Dionysus* – who not only addressed himself to different correspondents, but corresponded to different *emotive associations*?

The Crucified and his antagonist Dionysus no doubt entered into a certain equilibrium during the Turin euphoria. But, independent of the fact that, in order to sustain the euphoria, this equilibrium implied a reduction of the antagonism so forcefully affirmed in *Ecce Homo* ('*Have*

I been understood? Dionysus versus the Crucified'), Dionysus himself participated in the conspiracy, as a letter of 7 January to Overbeck made clear, since Dionysus was also the *signatory* of a 'decree' in accordance with which Wilhelm and all anti-Semites *had been shot*.

The *perspective of Dionysus* seemed to concern both a settling of scores with Wagner and, on a completely different plane, a kind of singular combat in which Cosima was the stake. The triumph of Dionysus would lead to the abandonment of the perspective of the conspiracy. Whenever Nietzsche signed 'Dionysus', the conspiracy itself was already overcome, liquidated, forgotten, and because of this fact, Nietzsche's euphoria was entirely reabsorbed into itself.

The signature *Dionysus* is in itself much less astonishing on Nietzsche's part than that of the Crucified, since in his prior work, Nietzsche had long used the figure of this god in order to identify it with the chaos of the universe. It was when he associated Dionysus with its opposite the *Crucified* that the need for an equilibrium became remarkable – not in the sense of a reabsorption of what he had rejected, but *in* the sense of an emotional equilibrium. However, this equilibrium, thus this association in the conspiracy, would be abandoned for another. This was, on Nietzsche's part, a defence against the paranoiac representation. With Dionysus, the histrionism tended to compensate for the conspiracy, and could achieve its ends only through libidinal representations.

How these libidinal forces attained a final equilibrium in which Nietzsche could have sought his 'cure' was revealed in the first message to Burckhardt, dated 4 January 1989, in which Nietzsche himself spoke of an *equilibrium*.

[Postmarked Turin, 4 January 1889]
Meinum verehrungswürdigen Jakob Burckhardt
    That was the little joke on account of which I con-done my boredom at having created a world. Now you are – thou art – our great greatest teacher; for I, together

with Ariadne, have only to be the golden equilibrium
of all things, everywhere we have such beings who are
above us. . . .
        Dionysus[164]

But this fragile equilibrium, which could last only a few
days, can be considered an instance of what Freud called, in
the paranoic process, *the irruption of the repressed*: repression
forms the primary mechanism of the paranoia, and the
irruption constitutes the final phase in which the patient,
having experienced this phase as a universal catastrophe, seeks
to reconstitute the world in a manner that will allow him to
live in it.

Nietzsche's behaviour in Turin could be 'explained' or
demonstrated by the irruption of a 'repressed' *counter-
Nietzsche* (after the loss of Tribschen and the break
with Wagner and Cosima). This *counter-Nietzsche* emerged
alongside the previously lucid Nietzsche, but he revised his
previously held – and apparently definitive – positions by
reinterpreting them. He *made use of Nietzsche's declarations*
(the penultimate works: *Nietzsche Contra Wagner* and *The
Antichrist*), and juxtaposed to them everything he had
repressed in order to declare, not only his anti-Wagnerism
and his anti-Christianism, but also the affective reality that
had been denied in the name of the previously lucid position.
This affective reality referred back, beyond all the explana-
tions, to the obscure motifs of his childhood (cf. Nietzsche's
premonitory dream at age six, the dead Father, etc.).

But if a *counter-Nietzsche* emerged alongside the lucid
Nietzsche (in accordance with the mechanism of repression),
there was nonetheless a strong link between the aphasia of the
counter-Nietzsche and the Nietzsche *who continued to speak* in
the terms of his previous declarations. The emergence of the
counter-Nietzsche was experienced as a *liberation* by the lucid
Nietzsche – hence the *euphoria*. In a way, the ruin of the
lucid Nietzsche worked to the *benefit* of the whole of the
Nietzschean pathos: the *transfiguration of the world*; the *rejoicing*

of the heavens; the reconciled confrontation of Dionysus and the Crucified, which, though a victory over *Ecce Homo*, was impossible to live – all this is what constituted the ecstasy of Turin.

(Whatever 'clinical' definitions might be ascribed to Nietzsche's behaviour before and during the Turin period [1887–8] – paraphrenia, dementia praecox, paranoia, schizophrenia – these definitions themselves have been established from the *outside*, namely, through institutional norms. It is obvious that psychiatrists attribute a purely *relative* objectivity to the *criteria* of the cure – and that, from a scientific point of view, *they do not believe in these criteria* any more than do their patients. From a purely artistic point of view, such *criteria of objectivity* had been exploited by Dostoevsky and Strindberg as resources for an infinite *irony*. In fact, as Freud said, psychiatrists approach these phenomena armed with the hypothesis that even *such singular manifestations of mind*, though far from the habitual thought of humans, *are derived from the most general and most natural processes of the psychic life*, and they would like to learn to comprehend these motives as the paths of this transformation.)*

In the first of the two missives that Nietzsche addressed to Burckhardt from Turin, that of 4 January 1989, he began by alluding to the relationship between a *joke* and his *boredom at*

---

* See *The President Schreber Case*, in Sigmund Freud, 'Psycho-Analytic Notes upon an Autobiographical Account of a Case of Paranoia (Dementia Paranoides)', in *Collected Papers*, trans. Alix and James Strachey (New York: Basic Books, 1959), Vol. 3, pp. 385–470. First illness: Autumn 1884–5. The illness ran its course '*without the occurrence of any incidents bordering upon the sphere of the supernatural*' (p. 390). Second illness: October 1893. '*He went through worse horrors than anyone could have imagined, and all on behalf of a sacred cause*' (p. 392). '*The patient is full of ideas of pathological origin, which have formed themselves into a complete system; they are now more or less fixed, and seem to be inaccessible to correction by means of any objective valuation of the actual external facts*' (p. 393). Schreber was released in 1902, and published *Memoirs of My Nervous Illness* in 1903. (The salvation of humanity depends on Schreber's transformation into a woman.) See Daniel Paul Schreber, *Memoirs of My Nervous Illness*, trans. Ida MacAlpine and Richard A. Hunter (Cambridge, Mass.: Harvard University Press, 1988).

having to create a world. The joke was a way of *'pardoning'* himself for all this boredom. For the first time, it was a question of the *creation of the world* (a divine act) – a theme taken up in the second missive – and of the function of histrionism: the joke *compensated* for this divine creation (thus, for the 'paranoiac', it compensated for the boredom of having to reconstruct a livable world for oneself). What this ('Dionysian') joke *consisted* of was precisely this *devotion to a 'divine' act of creation* (as Nietzsche Dionysus). This was the first indication of a new phase in Nietzsche's metamorphosis. Then (as if to excuse himself for the joke), he told Burckhardt that the latter was 'our great, our greatest master', and he continued by saying that he himself merely wanted to establish *an equilibrium with Ariadne: the happy equilibrium of all things (according to which) Ariadne and Dionysus–Nietzsche everywhere have such beings who are above them. . . .*

For the first time during this euphoria, the image of Ariadne emerged, inseparable from Dionysus, an image that had already been mentioned at several places both in the books and the posthumous fragments. Early in January, Nietzsche sent Cosima the message: *Ariadne, I love you – Dionysus.*[165]

Nietzsche suddenly reactualized his period in Basel and the 'idyll of Tribschen'. With the memory of Cosima–Ariadne, a new form of equilibrium made itself felt. The *Dionysus–the Crucified* equilibrium disappeared, in the sense that the perspective of the *conspiracy* suddenly seemed to be abandoned in favour of the reactualization of a distant past. Specifically *libidinal*, this reactualization had as its object the prestigious image of Cosima. Why, in this context, did he write to Professor Burckhardt – as 'our greatest master' – of *the equilibrium of all things* he was creating, and *which he said he had with Ariadne?* This was both an appeal to the *authority* of the famous historian – he had never ceased to venerate him, though his veneration was without reciprocity – and an appeal to a judge, to an authority that was in many respects paternalistic. Simultaneously, a need to mystify the old academic was expressed. At this moment, no one could have known (with the exception of Cosima herself) that he was implying Cosima when speaking of Ariadne. This appeal was no doubt an aspect of Nietzsche's final resistance to the impending madness, the last effort of his consciousness to hang on to its identity in the midst of the euphoria.

Through the expedient of a pure and simple *histrionics*, Nietzsche attempted to float on the shipwreck of his identity as the lucid Nietzsche. But it was only through the *memory of the personality of his correspondents* that he could feel the euphoric movement of this shipwreck. The euphoria was too violent for him to be compelled by its movement to communicate it to those who had *known* the person who was foundering; the liberation from his lucid ego was too strong for it to become the *enjoyment* of his self-mockery. Nietzsche always (1) *admitted* his histrionism, and (2) presented it as a way of *pardoning himself*, and thus of *distracting himself from the boredom of having to create a world*. This final motif – the need to re-create the world and to act as God – could be interpreted as an allusion to his works. In any case, the creation of the world was invoked as the meaning of his sojourn in Turin in an analogous phrase, the first line in the long letter dated 5 January, to the same Burckhardt.

CORRESPONDENCE

To Burckhardt

5 January 1889

Dear Professor,

Actually I would much rather be a Basel professor than God; but I have not ventured to carry my private egoism so far as to omit creating the world on his account. You see, one must make sacrifices, however and wherever one may be living. Yet I have kept a small student room for myself, which is situated opposite the Palazzo Carignano (in which I was born as Vittorio Emanuele) and which moreover allows me to hear from its desk the splendid music below me in the Galleria Subalpina. I pay twenty-five francs, with service, make my own tea, and do my own shopping, suffer from torn boots, and thank heaven every moment for the *old* world, for which human beings have not been simple and quiet enough. Since I am condemned to entertain the next eternity with bad jokes, I have a writing business here which really leaves nothing to be desired – very nice and not in the least strenuous. The post office is five paces away; I post my letters there myself, to play the part of the great *feuilletonist* of the *grande monde* [*sic*]. Naturally I am in close contact with Figaro, and so that you may have some idea of how harmless I can be, listen to my first two bad jokes:

Do not take the Prado case seriously. I am Prado, I am also Prado's father, I venture to say that I am also Lesseps. . . . I wanted to give my Parisians, whom I love, a new idea – that of a decent criminal. I am also Chambige – also a decent criminal.

Second joke. I greet the immortals. M. Daudet is one of the *quarante*.

Astu

The unpleasant thing, and one that nags my modesty, is that at bottom every name of history is I; also as regards the children I have brought into the world, it is a case of my considering with some distrust whether all of those who enter the 'Kingdom of God' do not also come *out of* God. This autumn, as lightly clad as possible, I twice attended my funeral, first as Count Robilant (no, he is my son, insofar as I am Carlo Alberto, my nature below), but I was Antonelli myself. Dear professor, you should see this construction; since I have no experience of the things I create, you may be as critical as you wish; I shall be grateful, without promising I shall make any use of it. We artists are unteachable. Today I saw an operetta – Moorish, of genius – and on this occasion have observed to my pleasure that Moscow nowadays and Rome also are grandiose matters. Look, for landscape too my talent is not denied. Think it over, we shall have a pleasant, pleasant talk together, Turin is not far, we have no very serious professional duties, a glass of Veltiner would be come by. Informal dress is the rule of propriety.

        With fond love,
          Your Nietzsche

    I go everywhere in my student overcoat; slap someone or other on the shoulder and say: *Siamo contenti? Son dio, ho fatto questa caricatura.* . . .

[On the margins of the letter are the following four postscripts.]

    Tomorrow my son Umberto is coming with the charming Margherita whom I receive, however, here too in my shirt sleeves.
    The *rest* is for Frau Cosima . . . Ariadne . . . From time to time we practice magic . . .
    I have had Caiaphas put in chains; I too was crucified at great length last year by the German doctors. Wilhelm, Bismarck, and all anti-Semites done away with.
    You can make any use of this letter which does not make the people of Basel think less highly of me.[166]

★   ★   ★

Siamo contenti? Son dio,
ho fatto questa caricatura.[167]

The extraordinary wealth of 'meaning' that plays in such a scintillating manner in this final letter to Burckhardt, though to psychiatrists it attests to the collapse of the philosopher, constitutes nothing less than the full apotheosis of the Nietzschean 'intellect'. The fullness of everything that Nietzsche's life had accumulated appears here in a flash of histrionism. The various themes, gathered together and overcome in so many *abridgements*, form a unique vision. It is no longer a question of the *will to power* or the *Eternal Return*, which are terms destined for reflection and philosophical communication, but of the obverse side of the *death of God*: namely, the kingdom of Heaven, out of which emanates *creation of the world*. The teaching of philology had been merely a pretext for escaping the divine condition. As long as the professorship seemed secure, *creation* (the creation of the world) was for Nietzsche a fearsome task. But once he assumed this task, it turned out – because of the modest conditions required to bring it about – to be as easy as being the *feuilletonist* of the *grande monde* [*sic*]: to create the world, and to spread the gossip of this world, were both the result of his histrionism, and were related in bad jokes. Bad, no doubt, in the eyes of Professor Burckhardt, who was chosen as confidant and judge. The seriousness of science, as the guardian of the reality principle, here served as Nietzsche's foil. Stupefaction or scandalized reason still formed the background against which the joke could be formulated and stated. Now in order to provide entertainment for the next *eternity*, the joke here took on the appearance of a perpetual reincarnation: it was extended to events and characters which, *at bottom*, were only projections and gestures of Nietzsche himself. '*Everything that enters the kingdom of God also comes out of God.*' Which amounts to saying that in the kingdom of God all identities are exchangeable, and that none of them is stable once and for all. This is why *informal dress is the rule of propriety* (literally, informality in dress is the condition that demands a 'proper' response). *Informal dress*, in other words, was the infinite availability of the divine histrionism. It was what allowed him to witness his own burial on two occasions, and to walk the streets of Turin slapping the shoulders of passersby and breaking his *incognito* with an air of familiarity: *Siamo contenti? Son dio, ho fatto questa caricatura.* It was also what allowed him *to receive his son Umberto and the charming Margherita in his shirt sleeves.* Informal dress represented the suppression of the 'impropriety' of the principle of identity – on which not only science and morality are based, but the behaviour that follows from them, and thus all communication based on the distinction between reality and the unreal.

The final paragraph of the letter and the first of the five postscripts still formed an integral part of the euphoria – as did the second, which made note of his intention to receive Prince Umberto and Princess Margherita in his shirt sleeves.

But a change occured in the third and fourth postscripts. Nietzsche suddenly left the ambience of Turin and once again entered the sphere of bygone realities. For one last time, his shattered ego recognized itself in the names it evoked, and in the near and distant episodes he had participated in as Nietzsche. A word intervenes: *magic*, thanks to which these bygone realities were reactualized. The third paragraph states, 'The *rest* is for Frau Cosima . . . Ariadne . . . From time to time we practice magic . . . .' The *rest* is for Madame Cosima . . . : this confidential insinuation made to Burckhardt, which hinted at some sort of secret (though there had never been even the slightest intimacy between Nietzsche and Cosima), was undoubtedly due to the euphoria. But it altered the strength of the euphoria and dissipated it in favour of this libidinal reactualization, which could already be felt in the first message of the day before. The evocation of Cosima (to whom he had just addressed the message, 'Ariadne, I love you') – the same Ariadne who had already figured in *Beyond Good and Evil, Ecco Homo,* and the *Sketch for a Satyr Play* – leads one to presume that Cosima had long been the object of the *magic* practised by Nietzsche. What was this *magic* (which has nothing in common with the creation of the world)? Was Nietzsche practising exercises of morose delight aimed at resurrecting, in a magical fashion, the prestigious image of Tribschen, having already survived the now long-distant break with Wagner (1878)? It seems that, as he wrote the words of this third postscript, Nietzsche was expressing a prodigious *interval* between what he had just related of the ambience of Turin and the confession that *from time to time he devotes himself to magic*. The object of this magic, Cosima, projected him back into a bygone *past* that had become his labyrinth, and into which, as the 'creator of the world' (which he was the instant before), he now descended anew as a 'magician'. He held Ariadne's thread in a different manner than did Theseus. The various associations are all presented at one and the same time: as Ariadne, Cosima was not only forsaken by Wagner (who died in 1883), but was doubly forsaken (Wagner–Judith Gautier); Nietzsche took Theseus's place in the role of Dionysus: Wagner was destroyed as the Minotaur who had devoured all the German youth (possible disciples of Nietzsche); Nietzsche thus substituted himself not only for Wagner–Theseus, but for Wagner–Minotaur. The identification with Dionysus was now established, and the satyr play could begin. The histrionic euphoria of Turin now became localized in the *names* of the Greek tragedy, and for an instant the mythical schemes offered a possible splitting in two. But the euphoria led Nietzsche back to contemporary life, to the present, and he was once again caught up in the histrionics. For his play, Dionysus–Nietzsche needed a satyr, and this satyr also came from the sphere of Tribschen. Now there were two satyrs who were designated to play this role: the first was Catulle Mendès (Judith Gautier's ex-husband, a couple with whom Nietzsche could have had only fleeting relationships); the second, his friend the painter von Seydlitz, to whom he had recently written about the Judith 'of Tribschenian memory'.

The search for a *satyr* (which he thought he had finally found in the person of Catulle Mendès) amounted to a delegation of libidinal powers. In this case, it was an old friend of the Wagner couple – and consequently, *the greatest satyr of all time* (whom he called the 'poet of Isoline') and '*not only of all time*' – who must put the previously faithful Cosima, entrenched in the cult of Beyreuth and resistant to Nietzsche, in the mood to give herself to Dionysus. All of this entered into the *magic* that Nietzsche practised 'from time to time'.

ARIADNE AND THE LABYRINTH
Satyr play at the end:
brief conversation between Dionysus, Theseus, and Ariadne
– Theseus is becoming absurd, said Ariadne, [–]
Theseus is becoming virtuous –
Theseus jealous of Ariadne's dream
The hero, admiring himself,
himself becomes absurd

Ariadne's Complaint

Dionysus without jealousy: 'That which I love in you, how could a Theseus love that . . .'
Last act. Wedding of Dionysus and Ariadne.
'One is not jealous when one is God',
said Dionysus, 'unless it be of gods.'168

'Ariadne', says Dionysus, 'you are a labyrinth: Theseus has gone astray in you, he has lost the thread; what good is it to him that he is not devoured by the Minotaur? That which devours him is worse than a Minotaur' (Dionysus). 'You are flattering me', Ariadne replied, 'I am weary of my pity, all heroes should perish by me (one must [be] become God for me to love). – 169

'O Ariadne, you are yourself the labyrinth: one cannot escape from it. . . .'
Dionysus, you flatter me, you are divine. . . .170

O Dionysus, divine one, why do you grasp me by the ears?
– I find a sort of humor in your ears,
Ariadne, why are they not longer? . . .'171

Be wise, Ariadne! . . .
You have little ears, you have ears like mine:
let some wisdom into them! −
Must we not first hate each other if we are to love each
other? . . .

I am your labyrinth. . . .[172]

The transfiguration of the world at Turin, and of Cosima into
Ariadne, was completed by a final transfiguration of history.
Nietzsche, having been successively incarnated as '*Alexander
and Caesar, Lord Bacon, the poet of "Shakespeare", Voltaire and
Napoleon, perhaps in Wagner*', would now manifest himself as
'*the triumphant Dionysus who will make the earth a festival . . .*',
as he tells 'my beloved princess Ariadne'.[173] A reflux toward
bygone years, and an afflux from the latter toward his present
situation in Turin.

A solemn day which rang out one more time in the
statement Nietzsche made while being admitted to Dr
Binswanger's clinic at Jena: *My wife Cosima brought me here.*
Not long before, at Turin, he had noted to himself, '*It is
a unique case in that I have found someone who resembles me.
Madame Cosima Wagner is by far the most noble [−] that there
has ever been, and in relation to myself, I have always interpreted her
union with Wagner as an adultery. . . . The Tristan case . . .*'[174]

Beyond his adventure with Lou, the physiognomy of
Cosima − that is, the trace of the young philologist's first
emotion − was resurrected, enriching all of Nietzsche's
subsequent emotions.

In one of the final sketches for the *satyr play*, Dionysus says
to Ariadne, *You are yourself the labyrinth*, and then, *I am your
labyrinth*.

Nietzsche was here expressing, not the course of his life
but the mazes of his soul, and he found no other exit in it
and for it than its starting-point. The soul has its own space
and its own itinerary, and all its multiple networks must
be traversed. If the soul, in traversing itself as a labyrinth,

merely makes progress in an irreversible error, as Virgil says, it is because it rediscovers a memory that requires the progression of life to be forgotten, just as the consciousness of the progression of life required this regressive movement to be forgotten. Autobiography is an attempt to reconcile these two opposing movements. But it must equally be on its guard against external biography – the narration of witnesses, their interpretation, the interpretation of posterity.

'Ariadne', 'Dionysus', the 'labyrinth': these were now the only names that remained in Nietzsche to convey that implacable regressive movement toward a region where the meaning and historical outlines of the figures would disappear.

The fourth paragraph (in the margin of the letter [the third postscript]) had a new and completely different inspiration. Abruptly, we are again back in the perspective of the *conspiracy*. It is as the *Crucified* that Nietzsche states that he has had the high priest, Caiaphas, placed in chains. He seems, however, to give to this identification an analogical value, since *he himself*, he says, would have been *crucified by the German doctors*. (Was this an allusion to the ophthalmologists who thought he would soon be condemned to blindness? Rather, he seems to be alluding to the state he was in as he writes to Burckhardt: his *dementia* would have required a *treatment*, whereas the way he had been persecuted – that is to say, not understood and ignored in Germany, the *flat country* of Europe – *amounted to* a treatment that led to his dementia: his crucifixion.) It was from this same dementia that he received the power, as a divine victim, to *punish* Caiaphas, which was a total reversal of his own (lucid) position as the *Antichrist*. But Caiaphas was the high priest of the Jews, and Christ was the king of the Jews. Hence the statement, as if it described a fait accompli: *Wilhelm, Bismarck, and all anti-Semites done away with* (those who prevented Nietzsche from reigning in Germany).

In this final paragraph, everything he had suffered at the

hands of the reigning Teutonism is mixed together one last time – and measured against his own 'sovereignty'. One of Nietzsche's last fragments, partly mutilated, declared that his *natural allies* were Jewish officers and bankers – who were, he says (according to the meaning of what remains of the mutilated sentence), the *sole power* capable of doing away with 'nationalist arrogance and the politics of popular interest'.[175] In what constitutes the last deciphered fragment, his hatred was concentrated against those close to him, his mother and sister, who compromised both his Polish origins and, in the end, 'his own divinity'.

> I touch here the question of race. I am a Polish gentleman, *pure blood*, in whom not a drop of impure blood is mixed, not the slightest German blood. If I seek my most profound opposite . . . – I always find my mother and my sister: to see myself allied with such German riff-raff was a blasphemy against my divinity. The ancestry on the side of my mother and sister to this very day [–] was a monstrosity [–] – I recognize that the deepest objection to my thought of the Eternal Return, which I call an abysmal thought, was always my mother and sister. . . . But then again, Pole that I am [–] a formidable atavism: one would have to go back several centuries to [–] find a human mixture with the degree of instinctive purity that I represent. I have, with regard to everything noble, a [–] sentiment of distinction [:] I could not tolerate having the young emperor as the coachman on my carriage.[176]

Thus, in the course of this final message, Nietzsche was dispersed and reassembled at different levels, and at different intervals of time. Whereas the greatest suffering was evoked one last time in order for Nietzsche to sign his own name, the greatest delight was made manifest at the level of the impulsive fluctuations: namely, the freedom to designate themselves at last, according to their own interpretation.

Nietzsche's obsessive thought had always been that events, actions, apparent decisions, and indeed the entire world have a completely different aspect from those they have taken on, from the beginning of time, in the sphere of language. Now he saw the world beyond language: was it the sphere of absolute muteness, or on the contrary the sphere of absolute language? The agent no longer led anything back to itself, but led itself into all things, which all designated themselves with the same swiftness as so many 'in-themselves'. . . .

Was this a matter of that *inversion of time* of which Nietzsche spoke in a previous fragment? '*We believe in the external world as the cause of its action on us – but in fact it is precisely this action, which takes place unconsciously, that we have transformed into the external world: our work is whatever the world makes us confront, which will henceforth react upon us. Time is necessary for it to be achieved: but this time is so short.*'[177]

In *no time at all*: the external world, 'our work' – this is what his euphoria recuperated. How can the world again become internalized? How can we again become externalized so that we are ourselves the effective action of the world? Where in us would the world end? Where would it begin? There is no limit to one and the same action.

The euphoria of Turin led Nietzsche to maintain, in a kind of *interpretive* availability, the residues of everything that constituted the past in the context of his present experience. What everyday life normally holds at a distance, so as to receive only the bare fact of the *day after day* – this is what suddenly irrupted in Nietzsche: the horizon of the past crept closer until it merged with the everyday, until they both occupied the same level. In return, everyday things abruptly receded into the distance: *yesterday* became today, the day before yesterday spilled over into tomorrow. The landscape of Turin, the monumental squares, the promenades along the Po River, were bathed in a kind of 'Claude Lorraine' luminosity (Dostoevsky's *golden age*), a diaphanousness that removed the weight of things and made them recede into an infinite distance. The stream of light here became a stream of laughter − *the laughter from which truth emerges*, the laughter in which all identities explode, including Nietzsche's. What also exploded was the meaning that things can have or lose for other things, not in terms of a limited linkage or a narrow context, but in terms of *variations of light* (despite the fact that this light is perceived by the mind before it exists for the eye, or that a reminiscence emanates from its rays).

'I thank heaven every moment for the *old world*, for which human beings have not been *simple* and quiet enough.'[178] The 'simplicity' of Nietzsche's vision at Turin almost had a Hölderlinian accent to it − being precisely the irony of the *society gossip column*.

Because it was a 'jubilant dissolution', Nietzsche's euphoria could not last as long as Hölderlin's contemplative alienation. Hölderlin's desolation elevated him to a high place of peace and forgetfulness where he was constantly visited by silent images, with which he could dialogue in the same simple, calm and melodious language. The silence of Hölderlin's poems of 'madness' has nothing in common with Nietzsche's menacing silence, the price of the histrionic explosion at Turin. The vision of the world accorded to Nietzsche was not unveiled in a more or less regular succession of landscapes and still lifes, extending over a period of forty years. It was a parody of the recollection of an event. It was mimed by a single actor during *one solemn day* − because everything was said and then disappeared in the span of a *single day*, even if this day had to last from 31 December to 6 January, beyond the rational calendar.

Such is the world as it appeared to Nietzsche under the monumental aspect of Turin: a *discontinuity of intensities* that are given *names* only through the *interpretation of those who receive his messages*; the latter still represent the *fixity of signs*, whereas in Nietzsche *this fixity no longer exists*. That the fluctuations of *intensities were able to assume the opposite name* to designate themselves − such is the miraculous irony. We must believe that this *coincidence* of the phantasm and the sign has existed for all time, and that the strength required to follow the *detour* through the intellect was 'superhuman'. Now that the agent 'Nietzsche' is destroyed, there is a festival for a few days, a few hours, or a few instants – but it is a sacrificial festival:

FIRE AND CONSUMMATION, THIS IS WHAT OUR ENTIRE LIFE MUST BE, OH YOU WIND-BAGS OF TRUTH! AND THE VAPOUR AND INCENSE OF THE SACRIFICES WILL LIVE LONGER THAN THE VICTIMS.'[179]

10

Additional Note on Nietzsche's Semiotic

In the posthumous fragments, we see Nietzsche reflecting on the substratum of his pathos – an always mobile substratum. Face to face with himself, however, his prospecting makes no claim to master what is moving within him; on the contrary, he seeks to conform himself to the subterranean mobility. For no one has *chosen* to be born *as such*; the choice was made outside of us – the 'outside' we designate as fate.

But once he begins to formulate his thinking in order to speak to his contemporaries, Nietzsche turns away from this gaping substratum, and almost immediately readopts the everyday habits of discussion – habits that are all based on '*the prejudices of the sentiments*'.

By spontaneously readopting the language of these *prejudices*, however, he cannot avoid developing his own prejudices or treating them apparently as *concepts*. His discourse, siding with a depth that is *incoherent* and arbitrary in relation to the intellect, must pretend to defend this *constraining coherence at the level of intellectual receptivity*.

In *Beyond Good and Evil*, Nietzsche says that *intellectual constraint, and not freedom*, is the true creative law of nature. The intellect is a constraining and selective *impulse – because of its very illusions*.

Nietzsche in this way likens the *will to power* – as the primordial impulse (in which there is neither incoherence nor coherence) – to the coherent forms of classicism as the hitherto supreme expression of the will to power.

In 'classicism' or the 'grand style' – which for Nietzsche encompasses the cold gaze of 'psychologists' and 'Machiavellian' despots as well as the rigour of artists – this coherence was able to prevail only because it was thought to be *guaranteed by the intellect*. The intellect, then, was by no means considered to be a selective *impulse*, but was at the opposite pole of the world of the impulses. But what happens to conceptual coherence when the intellect becomes a mere tool in the service of the unconscious?

Nietzsche's thought relentlessly examines the competition between the *arbitrary* constraint imposed by the freedom of the impulses, and the *persuasive* constraint of the intellect – the latter in turn being defined as an impulse.

But what type of discourse can reconcile 'coherence' with the fact of the impulses – especially if the impulses are *invoked* as an *end*, whereas the producer of the 'concept', namely the intellect, is used as a *tool* by this arbitrary 'incoherence'? For we can speak of incoherence only *in the terms of the intellect*.

How could Nietzsche translate the arbitrary freedom of the unintelligible depth into a *persuasive* constraint? Will not discourse simply become arbitrary and devoid of any constraint? No doubt, if the conceptual form were maintained. It is therefore necessary for this form to reproduce – under the constraint of the impulsive fluctuations and in a completely *desultory* manner – the discontinuity that intervenes between the coherence of the intellect and the incoherence of the impulses. Rather than pursuing the birth of the concept at the level of the intellect, it comes to interpret the concept. Such is the form of the aphorism.

> One should not conceal and corrupt the *fact* that our thoughts come to us in a fortuitous fashion. The profoundest and least exhausted books will probably also have something of the aphoristic and *unexpected* character of Pascal's *Pensées*. The driving forces and

the evaluations lay below the surface a long time; what comes out is effect.[180]

To prevent discourse from *being reduced to the level of a fallacious coherence*, it must be compelled toward a type of thought that does not refer back to itself (i.e., to the intellect), in a kind of edifice of subsequent thoughts, but is pushed to a limit where thought puts a *stop to itself* [*mette un terme à elle-même*]. Insofar as thought turns out to be efficacious, it is not as an utterance of the intellect but as the *premeditation* of an action. In the latter case, what thought retains from the intellect is only the representation of a possible event – a (premeditated) action in a double sense. Since thought is the act of the intellect, this *act of premeditating* – which is no longer a *new* intellectual act but an act that *suspends* the intellect – seeks to produce (itself in) a *fact*. It can no longer even be referred to as a thought but as a fact that *happens* to thought, as an event that brings thought back to its own origin. There is something resistant in thought that drives it forward – toward its point of departure.

Nietzsche, following this process to its source, thus discovers that of which thought is only a shadow: the *strength to resist*. How then is the intellect constituted so that the agent [*suppôt*] is capable of producing only representations?

Representations are nothing but the reactualization of a prior event, or the reactualizing preparation for a future event. But in truth, the event in turn is only a moment in a *continuum* which the agent isolates in relation to itself in its representations, sometimes as a *result*, sometimes as a *beginning*. As soon as the agent reflects on it, it is itself only the result or beginning of something else.

Every meditation that happens to us is only the trace of something prior, a 'pre-meditation' incorporated into ourselves – namely, a *premeditation of the now-'useless' acts* that have constituted us, so much so that our representations only *reactualize* the prior events of our own organization. This would be the origin of the intellect's representations and its products, of our thoughts that keep us from *pre-meditating* anew. But perhaps there is a different origin to the organization that is *particular* to each of us: something in that organization has *resisted* certain external actions. Something in us was therefore able to *resist until now*, though not at the level of the intellect's coherence. Would this not be a new *pre-meditation of acts to come . . .* ?*

Nietzsche's aphorisms, by consequence, tend to give to the *very act of thinking* the virtue of resistance to any 'conceptualization', to keep it beyond the 'norms' of the understanding, and thus to substitute for 'concepts' what he called *values*, since every 'concept' has never been anything

---

* 'The life process is possible only because it is not necessary always to start over again with numerous experiments, which in some manner have already been *incorporated.* – The real problem of organization is the following: "*How is experience even possible?*" We have only one form of comprehension: the concept, – the general case that contains the special case. In one case, the general, the typical seems to us to belong to experience; – in this sense, everything that is "living" seems comprehensible to us only through an intellect. *However, there is another form of comprehension*: – the only existing forms of organization are those *that can conserve and defend themselves against a great quantity of actions exerted against them*' (KSA, Vol. 11, p. 190, 26[156], Summer–Fall 1884).

'We must reformulate our notion of memory: it is the living sum of all the experiences of all organic life, organizing and forming themselves reciprocally, struggling among themselves, condensing and changing in numerous unities. We must suppose a process that acts like the formation of concepts *from particular cases*: the act of drawing and circumscribing the fundamental schema, and of cutting out the marginal traits. – Insofar as something can still be invoked (recalled) as an isolated factum, this something has not yet been merged into the whole: the most recent experiences are still floating on the surface. Feelings of inclination, repugnance, etc., are symptoms of already-formed unities; – our so-called "instincts" are similar formations. Thoughts are the most superficial things; appreciations that survive and impose themselves in an incomprehensible manner have more depth: pleasure and displeasure are complex actions of appreciation regulated by the instincts' (KSA, Vol. 11, p. 175, 26[94], Summer–Fall 1884).

These two fragments are closely related to each other, though they may not seem to be so at first sight. The first insists on the incorporation of experience, giving place to a 'concept' of generality: conceptual *comprehension* – which makes the renewing of certain experiences superfluous – would be the only form of comprehension. But Nietzsche envisions *another form of comprehension* which would lie precisely at the origin of the only organizations capable of subsisting: namely, the *resistance* to any action that would be exerted on it from the outside.   [*continued next page*

other than the trace of an *efficacious* act – not for thought itself but for the triumph of an unknown force [*une force quelconque*].

Strictly speaking, the terms 'coherence' and 'incoherence' are inapplicable to the activity of the impulses; in return, when the impulse exerts its constraint on the agent, *a coherence is established between the impulse and the agent agitated by its activity.* For the impulse to be constraining, there must be a *repressive force* that is opposed to the impulsive discharge and denounces this coherence as a threat to the agent – and thus as an incoherence with regard to this *repressive* force. This repressive force is nothing other than the *intellect*, which more or less ensures the coherence of the agent. But it can maintain this coherence only as long as the agent accepts the *signal of threat* that it receives from this repressive force, which is likewise impulsive, though it has a completely different origin. Without this signal of threat, despite the intrusion it represents – and thus without this very intrusion – the agent would not 'conceive' *the coherence that is established*, in a constraining manner, *between itself and a contrary impulse.*

The coherence felt by the agent between 'itself' and a state of the impulses is never anything but a redistribution of the impulsive forces at the expense of the *agent's coherence with itself as an intellect.*

There is neither 'coherence' nor 'incoherence' in the activity of the impulses; yet if we can nonetheless speak in

---

The second fragment, on the nature of memory, in a sense takes up again the arguments of the first, on the basis of incorporated experience – impulsive memory orders and eliminates in the same way as conceptual formation, *no longer as a concept* but as the formation of *impulsive unities.* It is precisely on the basis of impulses thus grouped together (giving place to inclination, to repugnance) that appreciations appear – namely as value judgements – whose genesis is incomprehensible at the superficial level of thought. Finally, both fragments explain Nietzsche's aphoristic form of expression. The aphorism gives an account of the active impulsive unities, of their battles and their amalgams: it is the very language of what resists, the comprehension of what is incorporable, without passing through the intellect.

these terms, it is thanks to this other *impulsive force* which is also *the intellect*. There is thus a coherence between this impulse and the agent, of which the agent admits it is itself the *end*, insofar as it submits to the constraint of this impulse. And there is, on the other hand, *a coherence between the agent and this other impulse* which is the *intellect*, inasmuch as it is the intellect that maintains *the coherence of the agent as agent*. There is thus a *total discordance* between the agent's own coherence as maintained by the intellect, and the coherence of the impulse *with* the agent. Sometimes the impulse seems to exist only *because of* the intellectual *repulsion* exerted by the agent to preserve the agent; and sometimes this *repulsion* turns against the intellect, which denounces this impulse. The intellect is thus nothing but the *obverse* of all other impulses, the *obverse* of *every coherence between the impulse and the agent*, and thus an incoherence in relation to the coherence of the agent with itself. But because the intellect is the obverse of the impulse, it is, as a *repulsion*, the *thought of this same impulse*; it is the thought that, in relation to this impulse, *constitutes the agent* outside of its coherence with the impulse as an *end*. The agent, whenever it thinks this impulse, turns its repulsion into this *thought impulse*, and likewise with every impulsive force. But this coherence of the agent with itself is constraining only because it corresponds to its own conservation: the intellect in this way appears as a means, insofar as it maintains *identity in coherence, as an end*. But as soon as a coherence can be established between the agent and another impulse as an *end*, the impulsive and repulsive condition renders this intellectual identity fragile. For if this coherence is felt to be *more constraining* for the agent than the coherence of its intellect (as when the intellect remains impotent, or, on the contrary, when it conceives of itself completely as a repulsion), the agent rejects this tutor, which merely conserves it in a sterile state: whereas it feels at ease with the impulsive movement – no matter how fantastic may be the coherence it believes it has found there. If it feels at ease with the phantasm that results from this, however, it will in turn want to express it, and can do so only as a function of the intellect: it must speak of it as an *idea*, and must admit that it would also be *valuable* for *another intellect*. The phantasm, as the source of this 'false' idea, makes it *false* only because it is compelled to *borrow* the means of its *own repulsion* – namely the intellect – if only in order to make it *thinkable for another intellect*.

How can the coherence of the agent with a determinate impulse – once this coherence, which in a certain manner is adulterous with respect to the intellect, *puts in question the agent as agent* – be transmitted as an *idea* to another intellect? *Idea* means that the intellect conceives it – reconstructs it – even before judging it true or false. Must it not, at the moment of its transmission, awaken the other intellect as an impulse (adhesion) or a *repulsion* (negation, disapproval) – and immediately set in motion what, in the other intellect, constitutes *its coherence as agent*? Must it not bring its own organization back to the level of *resistance* or *non-resistance*?

The phantasm – the phantasmic coherence of the agent with a determined impulse – is thus produced at the *limit-point* where this impulse is turned *into a thought* (*of this impulse*) as a *repulsion* against the *adulterous coherence* – precisely so that it can appear at the level of the intellect, no longer as *a threat to the agent's coherence with itself*, but on the contrary as a legitimate coherence. In this way, it can retain its *thinkable character* for another intellect. But nothing of the phantasm remains in the *idea* thus transmitted, or rather created according to totally different dimensions.

From the mood (impulse and repulsion) to the idea, from the idea to its declarative formulation, the conversion of the mute phantasm into speech is brought about. For the phantasm never tells us why it is willed by our impulses. We interpret it under the constraint of our environment, which is so well installed in us by its own signs that, by means of these signs, we never have done with declaring to ourselves what the impulse can indeed *will*: this is the phantasm. But under its own constraint we simulate what it 'means' for our declaration: this is the simulacrum.

As the mediator of this conversion, language is first of all the simulacrum of the external resistance of others (inasmuch as we cannot make use of them as simple objects); as the impartial arbitrator between this external constraint and our own phantasm, it organizes for us a sphere of *declarations* in which we believe ourselves to be *free* with regard to the resistance of the *real*. But on the other hand, language is the simulacrum of the obstinate singularity of our phantasm. For if we have recourse to language, it is because, through the fixity of signs, it also offers an equivalent to our obstinate singularity; and because the fixity of signs at the same time simulates the resistance of the institutional environment, we can also, through language, have an idea that is 'false' for ourselves be taken for a 'true' one – an idea whose only 'truth' is our repulsion at exchanging our phantasm for some institutional idea.

If the phantasm is what makes each of us a singular case – in order to defend it against the *institutional* signification given to it by the gregarious group – the singular case cannot avoid resorting to the simulacrum as something that is *equivalent* to its phantasm – as much as for a fraudulent exchange between the *singular case* and the *gregarious* generality. But if this exchange is *fraudulent*, it is because it is *willed as such* by both the generality and the singular case. The singular case *disappears* as such as soon as it *signifies* what it *is for itself*. In the individual there is only *a particular case of the species* that assures its intelligibility. Not only does it disappear as such as soon as it formulates its phantasm to itself – for it can never do this except through *instituted signs* – but it cannot reconstitute itself through these signs without at the same time excluding from itself what has *become intelligible* or exchangeable in it.

Notes

Klossowski himself provides no references for the sources of his citations from Nietzsche's notebooks. At the conclusion of the French text of the book, he simply appends the following note: 'All the citations from Nietzsche are taken from the posthumous fragments – and in particular, from those of his final decade (1880–1888).' We have attempted to locate the sources for as many of the citations as possible, both in the standard German editions and in existing English translations. With regard to the German citations, we are indebted to the bibliographic apparatus provided in the German translation of the work *Nietzsche und der Circulus vitiosus deus*, trans. Ronald Vouillé (Munich: Matthes & Seitz, 1986). Where no English translation exists, we have translated the Nietzsche citations directly from Klossowski's French renditions. On occasion, we have introduced minor alterations in the English translations to make them accord with Klossowski's French versions. The footnotes included in the text itself are Klossowski's own. The following abbreviations are used in the notes:

GS = Friedrich Nietzsche, *Gesammelte Schriften: Musarion-Ausgabe* (Munich: Musarion, 1920–9).
KSA = Friedrich Nietzsche, *Sämtliche Werke: Kritische Studienausgabe*, 15 vols, ed. Giorgio Colli and Mazzino

Montinari (Berlin: Walter de Gruyter, 1980).
Leidecker = *Nietzsche: Unpublished Letters*, ed. and trans. Kurt F. Leidecker (New York: Philosophical Library, 1959).
Levy = *Selected Letters*, ed. O. Levy, trans. A. N. Ludovici (London: Soho Book Company, 1985).
Middleton = *Selected Letters of Friedrich Nietzsche*, ed. and trans. Christopher Middleton (Chicago: University of Chicago Press, 1969).
Schlechta = Friedrich Nietzsche, *Werke in drei Bänden*, ed. Karl Schlechta (Munich: Carl Hanser, 1960).
WP = Friedrich Nietzsche, *The Will to Power*, trans. Walter Kaufman and R. J. Hollingdale (New York: Random House, 1967).

Translator's Preface

1 See Martin Heidegger, *Nietzsche* (1961), 4 vols, trans. David Farrell Krell, Frank A. Capuzzi and Joan Stambaugh (San Francisco: Harper & Row, 1981–7); and Gilles Deleuze, *Nietzsche and Philosophy* (1962), trans. Hugh Tomlinson (London: The Athlone Press, 1983).

2 Michel Foucault, letter to Pierre Klossowski, 3 July 1969, reproduced in *Cahiers pour un temps* (Paris: Centre Georges Pompidou, 1985), pp. 85–8. See also Michel Foucault, *Remarks on Marx: Conversations with Duccio Trombadori*, trans. R. James Goldstein and James Cascaito (New York: Semiotext(e), 1991), pp. 29–30: 'As far as I'm concerned, the most important authors who have, I won't say formed me, but who have enabled me to move away from my original education are Nietzsche, Bataille, Blanchot, and Klossowski.'

3 Alain Arnaud, *Pierre Klossowski* (Paris: Seuil, 1990), p. 186. Arnaud's book is perhaps the best introduction to Klossowski's work, and includes an extensive bibliography.

4 Pierre Klossowski, 'La création du monde', in *Acéphale 2* (January 1937); 'Deux interprétations récentes de Nietzsche', in *Acéphale, 1936–1939* (Paris: Jean-Michel Place, 1980); 'Sur quelques thèmes fondamentaux de la "Gaya Scienza" de Friedrich Nietzsche', in *Le Gai Savoir et Fragments posthumes, 1880–1882* (Paris: Club français du Livre, 1954); 'Nietzsche, le polythéisme et la parodie', in *Revue de métaphysique et de morale*

63, 2–3 (1958): 325–48. The latter two essays were reprinted in Pierre Klossowski, *Un si funeste désir* (Paris: Gallimard, 1963), pp. 7–36, 185–228. For Deleuze's assessment, see his *Difference and Repetition*, trans. Paul Patton (London: The Athlone Press, 1994), p. 312, note 19.

5   Pierre Klossowski, 'Oubli et anamnèse dans l'expérience vécue de l'éternal retour du même', in *Nietzsche*, ed. Gilles Deleuze, Les Cahiers de Royaumont-Philosophie, No. 6 (Paris: Minuit, 1967). Chapter 3 of *Nietzsche and the Vicious Circle* is a revised version of this essay.

6   See 'La période turinoise de Nietzsche', in *L'Éphémère* (Spring 1968); 'Le plus grave malentendu', in *Les Cahiers du chemin* (January 1969); 'Le Complot', in *Change* 2 (1969).

7   See the representative texts collected in David B. Allison's influential anthology, *The New Nietzsche* (New York: Delta, 1977).

8   See Gilles Deleuze and Félix Guattari, *Anti-Oedipus*, trans. Robert Hurley, Mark Seem and Helen R. Lane (New York: Viking Press, 1977), pp. 20–2, 367–8; and Jean-François Lyotard, *Libidinal Economy*, trans. Iain Hamilton Grant (London: The Athlone Press, 1993), pp. 66–94.

9   'Circulus vitiosus', in *Nietzsche aujourd'hui?*, 2 vols (Paris: Union Générale d'Editions, 10/18, 1973), vol. 2, pp. 91–121. The discussion that follows Klossowski's presentation includes what is, to my knowledge, the only published encounter between Jacques Derrida and Gilles Deleuze.

10 Pierre Klossowski, *Sade My Neighbor*, trans. Alphonso Lingis (Evanston, Ill.: Northwestern University Press, 1991).

11 Pierre Klossowski, *La Vocation suspendue* (Paris: Gallimard, 1950).

12 Pierre Klossowski, *Les Lois de l'hospitalité* (Paris: Gallimard, 1965), with a new preface and postface. The novel includes, in the following order, *La Révocation de l'édit de Nantes* (Paris: Minuit, 1959); *Roberte, ce soir* (Paris: Minuit, 1954); and *Le Souffleur ou le Théâtre de société* (Paris: Jean-Jacques Pauvert, 1960). The first two parts of the trilogy were published in English as *Roberte, Ce Soir and The Revocation of the Edict of Nantes*, trans. Austryn Wainhouse (New York: Grove Press, 1969).

13 Pierre Klossowski, *Le Baphomet* (1965), trans. Sophie Hawkes and Stephen Sartarelli, with a foreword by Michel Foucault (Hygiene, Colorado: Eridanos Press, 1988).

14 Pierre Klossowski, *La Monnaie Vivante* (Paris: Éditions Éric Losfeld, 1970; reissued Paris: Éditions Joëlle Losfeld, 1984).

15 For catalogues of Klossowski's exhibitions, see Catherine Grenier et al., *Pierre Klossowski* (Paris: La Différence/Centre National des Arts Plastiques, 1990); and *Pierre Klossowski* (Paris: Flammarion; Brussels: Ludion, 1996).

16 A comment by Klossowski cited in Johannes Gachnang, 'De la conquête des images', in *Pierre Klossowski* (Paris: Flammarion; Brussels: Ludion, 1996), p. 9.

17 Pierre Klossowski, 'Postface', in Jean Decottignies, *Klossowski* (Paris: Henri Veyrier, 1985), p. 137, emphasis added.

18 For Nietzsche's language of the impulses, see Christoph Cox, 'The "Subject" of Nietzsche's perspectivism', in *Journal of the History of Philosophy* 35, no. 2 (April 1997), pp. 93–115. In English, the only treatment of Nietzsche's conception of the impulses comparable to Klossowski's is Graham Parkes's magisterial work, *Composing the Soul: Reaches of Nietzsche's Psychology* (Chicago: University of Chicago Press, 1994).

19 See Arnaud, *Pierre Klossowski*, pp. 8–9, who cites Augustine, Meister Eckhardt and Teresa of Avila as precursors to Klossowski.

20 Pierre Klossowski, 'Protase et apodose', in *L'Arc* 43 (1970), p. 10. Portions of this essay have been reprinted in Klossowski's *La Ressemblance* (Marseille: André Dimanche, 1984).

21 Pierre Klossowski, *La Ressemblance*, p. 76. Klossowski's theory of the simulacrum has had an immense impact on contemporary French thought. For the most important interpretations, see Michel Foucault, 'The prose of Acteon', in Klossowski, *The Baphomet*, pp. xix–xxxviii; Gilles Deleuze, 'Klossowski, or bodies-language', in *The Logic of Sense*, trans. Mark Lester with Charles Stivale, ed. Constantin V. Boundas (London: The Athlone Press, 1990), pp. 280–301; and Maurice Blanchot, 'Le rire des dieux', in *L'Amitié* (Paris: Gallimard, 1971), pp. 192–207.

22 For Klossowski's theory of the stereotype, see 'On the use of stereotypes and the censure exercised by classical syntax', in 'Protase et apodose', pp. 15–20.

23 Klossowski, *Sade My Neighbor*, p. 14. Cf. 'Protase et apodose', p. 19: 'In the domain of communication (literary or pictorial), the stereotype (as "style") is the residue of a simulacrum (corresponding to an obsessional constraint) that has fallen to the level of current usage, disclosed and abandoned to a common interpretation.'

24 Pierre Klossowski, 'Protase et apodose', pp. 16–19.

25 See P.-B. Grenet, *Ontologie: analyse spectrale de la réalité* (Paris:

Beauchesne, 1963): 'Substance merits the special title of
"*suppôt*" or "hypostasis" or "subsisting subject" insofar as it
totalizes or *integrates* (1) a nature or essence, (2) accidents, (3)
an existence-in-itself.'
26 Leibniz, for instance, employed the term to refer to the
body–soul unity: 'Soul and body compose one and the same
suppôt, or what is called a person' (*Theodicy* I, 59). Pascal used it
to refer to the anatomical unity of the body: 'A man is a *suppôt*;
but if we dissect him, will it be the head, the heart, the stomach,
the veins, each vein, each portion of the vein, the blood, each
secretion of the blood?' (*Pensées* II, 115).
27 For a detailed analysis of Klossowski's theory of the *suppôt*, see
Jean-Pol Madou, *Démons et simulacres dans l'oeuvre de Pierre
Klossowski* (Paris: Méridiens Klincksieck, 1987), pp. 35–41.

Introduction

28   KSA, Vol. 9, p. 484, 11[121], Spring–Fall 1881.

1 The Combat against Culture

29   KSA, Vol. 11, pp. 518–19, 35[24], May–July 1885.
30   KSA, Vol. 10, p. 262, 7[62], Spring–Summer 1883.
31   KSA, Vol. 10, p. 262, 7[62], Spring–Summer 1883.
32   Cf. KSA, Vol. 11, p. 665, 40[65], and Vol. 2, p. 16.
33   KSA, Vol. 13, p. 304, 14[123] = WP, § 685, p. 365.
34   KSA, Vol. 11, p. 49, 25[135], Spring 1884.
35   KSA, Vol. 1, p. 767.
36   Letter to Carl von Gersdorff, 21 June 1871. Schlechta, Vol.
     III, p. 1043 = Middleton, Letter 31, pp. 80–1, translation
     modified.
37   KSA, Vol. 11, pp. 663–4, 40[65], August–September 1885.
38   KSA, Vol. 12, p. 406, 9[121], Autumn 1887 = WP, §
     124, p. 76.
39   KSA, Vol. 11, p. 553, 36[10], June–July 1885.

2 The Valetudinary States at the Origin of a Semiotic of Impulses

40   Letter to Peter Gast, 11 September 1879. Schlechta, Vol. III, p.
     1156 = Levy, pp. 122–4.
41   Letter to Peter Gast, 5 October 1879. Schlechta, Vol. III, p.

1158 = Middleton, Letter 82, pp. 168–9.

42 Letter to Malwida von Meysenbug, 14 January 1880. Schlechta, Vol. III, p. 1160 = Middleton, Letter 83, pp. 170–1.

43 Letter to Doctor O. Eiser, January 1880. Schlechta, Vol. III, p. 1161.

44 Letter to Franz Overbeck, November 1880. Schlechta, Vol. III, pp. 1167–8 = Middleton, Letter 85, p. 174.

45 Letter to Franziska Nietzsche, mid-July 1881. Schlechta, Vol. III, p. 1170 = Leidecker, Letter 29, pp. 81–2.

46 Lou Andreas-Salomé, *Friedrich Nietzsche in seinen Werken* (Dresden: Carl Reißner Verlag, 1924), p. 83.

47 KSA, Vol. 10, pp. 655–6, 24[16], Winter 1883–1884 = WP, § 676, p. 358.

48 KSA, Vol. 10, p. 404, 12[25], Summer 1883.

49 KSA, Vol. 10, pp. 404–5, 12[27], Summer 1883.

50 KSA, Vol. 10, p. 406, 12[33], Summer 1883.

51 KSA, Vol. 10, pp. 406–7, 12[34], Summer 1883.

52 KSA, Vol. 10, p. 407, 12[37], Summer 1883.

53 KSA, Vol. 10, pp. 407–8, 12[38], Summer 1883.

54 KSA, Vol. 11, p. 408, 12[39], Summer 1883.

55 Cf. GS, Vol. 4, p. 40.

56 KSA, Vol. 10, pp. 408–9, 12[40], Summer 1883.

57 KSA, Vol. 12, pp. 534–5, 10[137], Fall 1887 = WP, § 707, pp. 376–7.

58 KSA, Vol. 12, pp. 16–17, 1[28–9], Fall 1885–Spring 1886.

59 KSA, Vol. 12, p. 25, 1[58], Fall 1885–Spring 1886.

60 KSA, Vol. 12, p. 25, 1[58], Fall 1885–Spring 1886.

61 KSA, Vol. 12, pp. 16–17, 1[28], Fall 1885–Spring 1886.

62 KSA, Vol. 13, p. 258, 14[79], Spring 1888 = WP, § 634, p. 337.

63 KSA, Vol. 11, p. 506, 34[253], April–June 1885 = WP, § 493, p. 272.

64 KSA, Vol. 12, pp. 16–17, 1[28], Fall 1885–Spring 1886.

65 Cf. KSA, Vol. 12, p. 315, 7[60] = WP, § 481, p. 267.

66 KSA, Vol. 12, pp. 247–8, 7[1], end of 1886–Spring 1887 = WP, § 666, pp. 351–2.

67 GS, Vol. 12, p. 369, no. 720.

3 The Experience of the Eternal Return

68 Letter to Peter Gast, 14 August 1881. Schlechta, Vol. 3, pp. 1172–4 = Middleton, Letter 90, p. 178, translation modified.

69 KSA, Vol. 9, p. 505, 11[163], Spring–Fall 1881.

70   Cf. *The Gay Science*, trans. Walter Kaufman (New York: Viking, 1974), § 310, p. 248.
71   *Thus Spoke Zarathustra*, Third Part, 'On the Vision and the Riddle', § 2.
72   KSA, Vol. 11, p. 70, 25[214], Spring 1884.
73   KSA, Vol. 9, p. 520, 11[197], Spring–Fall 1881.
74   GS, Vol. 14, p. 130.

4 The Valetudinary States at the Origin of Four Criteria: Decadence, Vigour, Gregariousness, the Singular Case

75   KSA, Vol. 11, pp. 664–5, 40[65], August–September 1885.
76   KSA, Vol. 13, p. 474, 15[114], Spring 1888 = WP, § 909, p. 481.
77   KSA, Vol. 12, pp. 537–8, 10[145], Fall 1887 = WP, § 1009, p. 522.
78   KSA, Vol. 13, pp. 250–1, 14[65], Spring 1888 = WP, § 47, pp. 29–30.
79   KSA, Vol. 13, pp. 252–3, 14[68], Spring 1888 = WP, § 48, pp. 30–1.
80   KSA, Vol. 13, pp. 341–2, 14[157], Spring 1888 = WP, § 778, p. 408.
81   KSA, Vol. 13, p. 456, 15[80], Spring 1888 = WP, § 49, p. 31.

5 Attempt at a Scientific Explanation of the Eternal Return

82   Lou Andreas-Salomé, *F. Nietzsche* (Dresden: 1914), p. 196 ff. = Lou Salomé, *Nietzsche*, trans. and ed. Siegfried Mandel (Redding Ridge, Conn.: Black Swan Books, 1988), pp. 130–1.
83   Letter to Franz Overbeck, early March 1884. *F. Nietzsches Briefwechsel mit Franz Overbeck* (Leipzig: Insel Verlag, 1916), p. 245.
84   KSA, Vol. 13, pp. 300–2, 14[121–2], Spring 1888 = WP, § 688, p. 366.
85   KSA, Vol. 13, pp. 300–2, 14[121–2], Spring 1888 = WP, § 692, p. 369.
86   Source unidentified.
87   GS, Vol. III, p. 560; KSA, Vol. 12, pp. 342–3, 9[8], Fall 1887 = WP, § 462, p. 255, translation modified. In the last line, we have rendered *dressage* [*Züchtung*] as 'training' rather than 'breeding', and so throughout the book.
88   KSA, Vol. 12, p. 343, 9[8], Fall 1887 = WP, § 712, pp. 379–80, translation modified.

89 KSA, Vol. 12, p. 342, 9[7], Fall 1887 = WP, § 687, pp. 340–1.
90 KSA, Vol. 12, pp. 535–6, 10[138], Fall 1887 = WP, § 639, pp. 340–1.
91 KSA, Vol. 13, pp. 257–9, 14[79], Spring 1888 = WP, § 634–5, pp. 337–8.
92 KSA, Vol. 11, pp. 537–8, 34[54–5], Summer 1885 = WP, § 1064, p. 547.
93 Schlecta, Vol. III, p. 775 ff. = WP, § 689, pp. 367–8.
94 KSA, Vol. 12, p. 342, 9[7], Fall 1887 = WP, § 687, pp. 366.
95 KSA, Vol. 12, p. 342, 9[7], Fall 1887 = WP, § 687, pp. 366.
96 KSA, Vol. 12, p. 386, 9[91], Fall 1887.

6 The Vicious Circle as a Selective Doctrine

97 Source unidentified.
98 GS, Vol. 16, p. 199.
99 KSA, Vol. 12, p. 236, 6[9], Summer 1886–Spring 1887.
100 KSA, Vol. 12, pp. 407–8, 9[123], Fall 1887 = Schlecta, Vol. III, p. 530 = WP, § 25, p. 18, translation modified.
101 KSA, Vol. 12, p. 398, 9[107], Fall 1887.
102 KSA, Vol. 11, pp. 699–700, 43[1], Fall 1885.
103 KSA, Vol. 9, p. 570, 11[330], Spring–Fall 1881.
104 Cf. KSA, Vol. 12, p. 366, 9[60], Fall 1887.
105 KSA, Vol. 9, pp. 500–2, 11[156], Spring–Fall 1881.
106 KSA, Vol. 9, pp. 547–8, 11[276], Spring–Fall 1881.
107 KSA, Vol. 12, pp. 413–14, 9[138], Fall 1887 = WP, § 1025, p. 530.
108 KSA, Vol. 12, p. 414, 9[139], Fall 1887 = WP, § 933, p. 492.
109 KSA, Vol. 12, p. 414, 9[139], Fall 1887 = WP, § 933, p. 492. Cf. KSA, Vol. 13, p. 484, 16[6], Spring–Summer 1888, and Schlechta, Vol. III, pp. 527–8.
110 KSA, Vol. 12, p. 416, 9[142], Fall 1887 = WP, § 121, p. 75.
111 KSA, Vol. 12, pp. 87–8, 2[57], Fall 1885–Fall 1886 = WP, § 960, p. 504, translation modified.
112 KSA, Vol. 10, p. 209, 5[1]203, November 1882–February 1883.
113 KSA, Vol. 11, pp. 91–2, 25[309], Spring 1884.
114 KSA, Vol. 13, p. 450, 15[65], Spring 1888 = WP, § 398, p. 215, translation modified.
115 Schlechta, Vol. III, p. 525 = WP, § 521, p. 282.
116 KSA, Vol. 9, p. 527, 11 [221], Spring–Fall 1881.
117 KSA, Vol. 12, pp. 424–6, 9[153], Fall 1887 = WP, § 898, pp. 477–8, translation modified.

118   KSA, Vol. 12, p. 357, 9[44], Fall 1887 = WP, § 901, p. 479.
119   KSA, Vol. 9, pp. 664–5, 16[23], December 1881–January 1882.
120   KSA, Vol. 12, pp. 462–3, 10[17], Fall 1887 = WP, § 866, pp. 463–4.
121   KSA, Vol. 12, p. 458, 10[8], Fall 1887 = WP, § 719, p. 383.
122   KSA, Vol. 12, pp. 424–6, 9[153], Fall 1887 = WP, § 898, pp. 477–8, translation modified.
123   KAS, Vol. 12, pp. 424–6, 9[153], Fall 1887 = WP, § 898, pp. 477–8.
124   KSA, Vol. 13, pp. 45–6, 11[97], November 1887–March 1888 = WP, § 36, pp. 23–4.
125   KSA, Vol. 13, pp. 59–60, 11[123], November 1887–March 1888 = WP, § 24, p. 18.

7 The Consultation of the Paternal Shadow

126   KSA, Vol. 6, p. 264 = *Ecce Homo*, trans. Walter Kaufman (New York: Random House, 1967), 'Why I Am So Wise', § 1, p. 222, translation modified.
127   Schlechta, Vol. III, p. 17.
128   Schlechta, Vol. III, p. 93.
129   KSA, Vol. 6, p. 264 = *Ecce Homo*, 'Why I Am So Wise', § 1, p. 222.
130   Schlechta, Vol. III, p. 65. The reference to the city of Halle in the preceding paragraph appears to be a misreading on Klossowski's part. Nietzsche is referring not to the city of Halle but to the lugubrious *hall* (*Halle*) at Schulpforta, which he subsequently refers to as a 'town' [*Stadt*]. It would have been a detour of around 100 kilometres to reach Naumburg via Halle. I thank Graham Parkes for pointing out this discrepancy.
131   Schlechta, Vol. III, p. 67.
132   Nietzsche, *Historisch-Kritische Gesamtausgabe*, Werke Bd. 2 (München: 1934), pp. 70 ff.
133   Schlechta, Vol. III, p. 110.
134   KSA, Vol. 5, p. 99 = *Beyond Good and Evil*, trans. Walter Kaufman (New York: Random House, 1966), § 150, p. 90.
135   Cf. KSA, Vol. 9, p. 528, 11[525], Spring–Fall 1881.
136   KSA, Vol. 6, p. 326 = *Ecce Homo*, 'Why I Write Such Good Books', '*Human, All-Too-Human*, with Two Sequels', § 4, pp. 287–8.
137   Postcard to Cosima Wagner, early January 1889. Schlechta, Vol. 3, p. 1350 = Middleton, Letter 204, p. 346.

138 Letter to Franz Overbeck, 11 February 1883. *F. Nietzsches Briefwechel mit Franz Overbeck*, p. 198 = Middleton, Letter 110, pp. 206–7, translation modified.

139 *Thus Spoke Zarathustra*, Part Two, 'On Redemption'.

140 Letter to Franz Overbeck, Summer 1883. *F. Nietzsches Briefwechel mit Franz Overbeck*, pp. 222–3 = Middleton, Letter 117, pp. 214–15.

8 The Most Beautiful Invention of the Sick

141 Schlechta, Vol. III, pp. 754 ff. = WP, § 812, p. 430.

142 KSA, Vol. 13, pp. 365–7, 14[182], Spring 1888 = WP, § 864, pp. 460–1.

143 KSA, Vol. 6, p. 351 = *Ecce Homo*, 'Why I Write Such Good Books', '*Beyond Good and Evil*', § 2, p. 311.

144 KSA, Vol. 6, p. 287 = *Ecce Homo*, 'Why I Am So Clever', § 4, p. 246.

145 KSA, Vol. 6, p. 288 = *Ecce Homo*, 'Why I Am So Clever', § 4, p. 247.

146 KSA, Vol. 6, p. 287 = *Ecce Homo*, 'Why I Am So Clever', § 4, p. 246.

9 The Euphoria of Turin

147 KSA, Vol. 13, pp. 139–40, 11[327], November 1887–March 1888.

148 Schlechta, Vol. III, p. 794 = WP, § 1039, p. 535.

149 Schlechta, Vol. III, p. 838 = WP, § 1038, pp. 534–5.

150 Cf. *Antichrist*, § 36.

151 F. Overbeck, zit. mach C. A. Bernoulli, *F. Overbeck u. Franz Nietzsche – Eine Freundschaft* (Jena 1908), Bd 2, p. 216 ff.

152 KSA, Vol. 12, p. 29, 1[75], Fall 1885–Spring 1886.

153 KSA, Vol. 11, p. 58, 25[168], Spring 1884 = WP, § 506, p. 275.

154 Schlechta, Vol. III, p. 868 = WP, § 277, p. 158.

155 Schlechta, Vol. III, p. 911 ff. = WP, § 417, p. 224 (portions of the fragment quoted by Klossowski are not included in the English translation).

156 Schlechta, Vol. III, p. 1254.

157 Karl Strecker, *Nietzsche und Strindberg* (München, 1921), pp. 35 ff. = Levy, pp. 301–2, translation modified.

158 Strecker, *Nietzsche und Strindberg*, pp. 78 ff. = Middleton, Letter 189, pp. 330–1.

159 Strecker, *Nietzsche und Strindberg*, pp. 82 ff. = Levy, pp. 308–10.

160 Strecker, *Nietzsche und Strindberg*, pp. 90 ff. = Middleton, Letter 200, p. 344. 'A single condition: Let us divorce' (in French in the original).

161 *Selected Letters of Friedrich Nietzsche*, ed. and trans. Christopher Middleton (Chicago: University of Chicago Press, 1969), p. 344. In English translation:

> Dearest Doctor:
> I want, I want to be mad!
> I could not read your letter without a severe shock, and I thank you very much indeed.
> 'Better wilt thou live, Licinious, by neither always pressing out to sea nor too closely hugging the dangerous shores in cautious fear of storms.'
> Meanwhile let us rejoice in our madness.
> Fare you well and remain true to your
> Strindberg
> (The best, the highest God)

Middleton notes that the Greek quotation is from an Anacreontic poem; see *Anacreontics*, ed. Isaac Bagg (Boston, 1895), Nos. III and IV, pp. 2–4. The quotation in Latin is from Horace, *Odes* II, X, lines 1–4, Loeb translation.

162 Strecker, *Nietzsche und Strindberg*, p. 93 = Middleton, Letter 200, p. 345.

163 Letter to Georges Brandes, 4 January 1989. Schlechta, Vol. 3, p. 1350 = Middleton, Letter 202, p. 345.

164 Schlechta, Vol. 3, p. 1350 = Middleton, Letter 203, p. 345, translation modified.

165 Postcard to Cosima Wagner, beginning of January 1889. Schlechta, Vol. 3, p. 1350 = Middleton, Letter 204, p. 346.

166 Letter to Jacob Burckhardt, 5 January 1889. Schlechta, Vol. 3, pp. 1351–2 = Middleton, Letter 206, pp. 346–8, translation modified.

167 'Are we happy? I am God, I made this caricature.' From the letter to Jacob Burckhardt, 5 January 1889.

168 KSA, Vol. 12, pp. 401–2, 9[115], Fall 1887.

169 KSA, Vol. 12, pp. 401–2, 9[115], Fall 1887.

170 KSA, Vol. 12, p. 510, 10[94], Fall 1887.

171 KSA, Vol. 13, p. 498, 16[40], Spring–Summer 1888. Cf. *Twilight of the Idols*, 'Skirmishes of an Untimely Man', § 19.

172 KSA, Vol. 6, p. 401 = *Dithyrambs of Dionysus*, trans. R. J. Hollingdale (Redding Ridge, Conn.: Black Swan Books, 1984), p. 59 (last strophe of 'Ariadne's Complaint'). Cf. *Zarathustra*, III, 15, 2.

173 Letter to Cosima Wagner, 3 January 1889.

174 KSA, Vol. 14, p. 473.

175 Cf. Nietzsche, *Oeuvres complètes* (Paris: Gallimard, 1982), Vol. 14, *Fragments Posthumes: Début 1888–début janvier 1889*, p. 381.

176 KSA, Vol. 14, p. 473.

177 KSA, Vol. 11, p. 159, 26[44], Summer–Fall 1884.

178 Letter to Jacob Burckhardt, 5 January 1889. Schlechta, Vol. 3, pp. 1351–2 = Middleton, Letter 206, pp. 346–8.

179 Cf. KSA, Vol. 10, p. 426, 13[1], Summer 1883.

10 Additional Note on Nietzsche's Semiotic

180 KSA, Vol. 11, p. 522, 35[31], May–July 1885 = WP, § 424, p. 229.

Index

absurdity, 119
abyss, 114, 135, 178, 184, 205, 210
action, 35, 51, 67, 99, 105, 134,
    203; action at a distance, 34;
    and reaction, 87
actor(s), 1, 78, 223, 236, 252
actualization, process of, 6, 23,
    235; de-actualization, 57, 80,
    196; re-actualization, 26, 94,
    240, 245, 256
affect(s), affection(s), 13, 48-9,
    101, 146, 150, 167, 208;
    culture of, 14; perspective
    theory of, 106
agent [*suppôt*], xii-xiii, 28, 30-1,
    37-8, 48, 50, 83, 88, 153, 218,
    256, 259-61
agnosticism, 221
aim, 15, 38, 41, 47, 162
alterity, 69
anamnesis, 56-7
anti-Semites, 201, 237, 243, 249
antinomy, 54, 56
aphasia, and science, xix-xx
aphoristic form, 65, 68, 255
Apollo, 87
Ariadne, 30, 187, 197, 238, 240-1,
    243, 245-9
aristocracy, aristocratism, 125, 144,
    146, 150, 152, 158, 161
art, xvii, 9-10, 13-15, 32, 126,
    145, 196, 203; as formation
    of sovereignty, 145; lack of
    in Nietzsche's life, 18-19; and
    simulacra, 134; value of, 8-9
artist(s), 146, 170, 198-9, 202, 223;
    as criminals, 203
asceticism, 18-19, 82, 88
atom, 101, 108-9, 111
authentic, authenticity, 26, 42-3,
    50-1, 87, 118, 145, 169, 178,
    184-5, 221, 223; *see also* depth
autobiography, xv, 173, 249
automatism, automaton, 5,
    50-1, 54
autonomy, 12; of science, 145

Bacon, Francis, 204-6, 248
bad conscience, 167
Balthus, viii
Basel, 20
Bataille, George, vii, 12n
Baudelaire, Charles, 149
beauty, 130, 163
becoming, 56, 58, 90, 104, 106;
    innocence of, 14, 122; no
    language for, 49; vs. change, 91
behavior, 32, 52-3, 68, 80, 86,
    112, 127, 131, 134-5, 139,
    152, 222
being, 44, 56, 66, 72, 85, 101,
    108, 111, 131-2, 137, 139

belief, 123; in the eternal return, 53, 94, 100
Benjamin, Walter, ix
Bismark, 249
body, 15, 23-4, 26, 27, 50, 185, 186, 220; and impulses, 30; and self, 29; higher, 33
bourgeois, 5, 8
brain, 15, 22, 24-5, 30, 32, 221
Brandes, Georges, 226-7, 233-4, 236
Buddha, 132
buffoon, 79, 86, 205; Zarathustra as, 99
Burkhardt, Jakob, 226, 237-8, 239-43, 245, 249

Caesar, 205, 232-4, 248
Cagliostro, 1, 222
calculus, 138
Callois, Roger, viii
capitalism, 171
caste, 151-2, 166
categories, 50-1, 76; of consciousness, 13, 41, 43, 50, 77, 135, 142; of the intellect, 135
causality, 52, 102, 105, 110-11, 122
celibacy, 188
censor, 76, 87, 92, 134
certainty, 45, 204-5
chance, 45, 72, 140
change, 102, 110
Chaos, xv, 33, 41, 43, 50, 65, 114, 135, 139-40, 184-5, 188-9, 216, 224
character, 29
chasm, xv
Christianity, 8-9, 238; and gnosis, 70; and morality, 10, 12, 83, 128
civilization, 9
class, xv
code of everyday signs, xvii, 26, 37, 40-1, 46-7, 52, 62-4, 206
coherence, 258-60
cohesion, 30, 48, 50
communication, 44, 76

Comte, Auguste, 152, 158
concepts, xvi, 217, 254, 257n
conscience, 48
conscious, 47, 141; vs. consciousness, 37
consciousness, 12-14, 26, 34, 37-8, 40-1, 43, 47-8, 50, 53, 102, 116, 235; as terminal phenomenon, 52; of the eternal return, 58
conspiracy, xv-xvi, 80, 121, 145-6, 164, 168-9, 171, 225, 234, 237, 240, 249
continence, 91
continuity, 41, 65, 134
contradiction, principle of, 77, 217
courage, 11, 13
creation, 67, 129, 147, 195; of the world, 239-41, 244, 246
criminals, 128, 202, 205
Crucified; *see* Dionysus
culture, xix, 13, 40-1, 79, 103, 126, 167; anthropo-culture, 140-1; crime against, 9-11; critique of, xvi; culture complex, 106; lived, 8, 157; vs civilization, 144; Western, 77

Dante, Alighieri, 16
Darwinism, 6, 124, 169
decadence, 75, 89, 91, 95, 149, 177, 201; *see also* vigour
decentering, 195
decision, 28
declarations, 37, 49, 261
degeneration, 75, 85-6, 133, 200
Deleuze, Gilles, vii-viii, 12n
delirium, xv-xvii, 22, 86, 97, 164, 205, 217; of thought, 25
democracy, 107, 125, 146, 165
demon(s), 66, 96, 203
depth [*fond*] (of existence), ix-x, 21, 254; as authentic, 50, 184-5; as meaningless, 170; as unexchangeable, 39-40, 184; as unintelligible, 43, 50, 80, 93, 169, 221, 255
Derrida, Jacques, viii

Descartes, Réné, 4
designation(s), 43, 46, 61, 63
desire, 12-13, 34, 72, 83-4
Deussen, 152, 213-14
dialectic, Hegelian, 12
difference, 154, 165
digestion, 35
Dionysus, 65, 87, 92, 191, 222-3,
    236, 238, 240, 246, 248; and
    Ariadne, 247-8; and Crucified,
    57, 233-4, 237, 239, 249
discordance, 103
dissonance, 72
dithyramb, 99
doer and doing, 109
Dostoevsky, Feodor, 203, 239,
    251; *Underground Man*, 224
dream(s), 39-40, 149; pre-
    monitory, 173-4
duration, 43

eccentricity, 214n, 215
economy, 147, 149, 156, 161; and
    the affects, 150
education, 143-4, 163
ego, 38, 42, 109
Eiser, O., 19-20
emotion, 217
end, 43, 52
energ, 105
energy, 25, 101, 105-7, 112-16;
    will to power as, 46
Engadine, 17
epistemology, 106
equilibrium, 26, 88, 101, 103,
    105, 107, 109, 110, 113, 119,
    195, 238
eros, 190
error, 2, 44-6
eternal return, 16, 30, 43, 53-4,
    58-9, 66, 67, 90, 103, 106,
    113, 118, 148-9, 165, 169,
    184, 195, 199, 206, 220, 244;
    and forgetting, 56-7; as *circulus
    vitiosus deus*, 65, 114, 216; and
    politics, 127; images of, 216;
    as simulacrum of a doctrine,
    99; effect of its disclosure, 93;

Hellenic conceptions of, 56,
    213; interpretations of, 123-5;
    series of individualities in, 57-8,
    70, 91, 93, 98, 104, 115, 217
eternity, 29, 57, 68, 70, 72
ethics, 56
Europe, 9, 125, 146, 163
evangelist, 171
event, 51, 107-8, 134
evil, 82-3
evolution, 41, 94, 155
excess, 84, 89
exchange, 76
excitations, 38, 47
exhaustion, 82, 85-6, 88, 92,
    94-5, 101
existence, conditions of, 45-6, 50,
    54, 137-8, 140
experimentation, 9, 34, 125, 137,
    140, 146, 170
experimenter(s), 127-8, 166
expiation, 70
exploitation, 164

fabulation, 66, 139
false, positive notion of, 132
fatalism, 69, 73; and eternal
    return, 71
fatality, 29-30, 172; Nietzsche's,
    176-7, 192
fate, 74, 79, 121, 153, 159, 165,
    206, 254
fatum, 29, 71-2
fecundity, 6, 200
feelings, xvi, 7, 36, 53, 55, 82, 86,
    113, 157, 165, 218; of distance,
    161; eternal return as highest
    feeling, 60, 63, 65; of eternity,
    72; gregarious uniformity of,
    136, 147, 165; of madness,
    92; of power, 101, 110-11; of
    security, 103; of time, 136
fiction(s), 42, 44-6, 50, 102,
    108-9, 111, 129, 132, 199
Flaubert, Gustave, 149
flux (afflux and reflux), 15, 27, 39,
    47, 61-2, 65, 109, 112, 137,
    191, 248

fool, 203
force(s), 9, 15-16, 23, 31-2, 37, 43, 49-50, 101, 103, 108-10, 117, 127, 140; active, 24, 52, 220; centrifugal, 216; corporealizing, 31; dissolving, 24; impulsive, 45, 47; invading, 88, 92; libidinal, 91; of de-assimilation, 150, 166; relations of, 105; repressive, 258; somatic vs. spiritual, 24, 31; surplus, 77, 152, 158, 159, 164
forgetfulness, forgetting, 28, 38, 53, 54, 56-8, 61, 80
forms, 48
fortuitous case (singular case), 7, 69, 71, 80, 94, 115, 117, 141, 146, 151, 154, 170, 189-90, 199, 219-20, 221, 226, 261
Foucault, Michel, vii
Frederick II of Hohenstaufen, 130
freedom, 254, 255
Freud, Sigmund, 37
Fuchs, Carl, 214n

Gandillac, Maurice, viii
Gast, Peter, 18, 22, 93, 226, 233-4
Gautier, Judith, 246
generality, 261
genius, 201, 203
Germany, 249
Gersdorff, 9
gesture(s), 43, 46, 48-9, 53, 100, 134, 224, 225; *see also* histrionics, masks
Gide, André, viii
goal(s), 30, 37, 42, 70, 73, 95, 104-5, 107, 112, 114-15, 121, 134, 147, 155, 170, 209
God, 104-7, 113, 116, 118, 183, 197, 209, 241; as guarantor of identity, 4, 57; as sensorium, 41; death of, 3, 57, 184, 189, 244
gods, 209; multiple, 4, 65
Goethe, 90, 209
good, 82; and evil, 41
grammar, 49

gravity, spirit of, 209
Greece, 184
Greek, state, 8; tragedy, 16
gregariousness, 6, 13, 76, 77, 79, 117, 119-20, 128, 129, 134, 141, 151, 153, 157, 167, 199, 261; *see also* singular
Guattari, Félix, viii
guilt, 10, 11, 14

hallucination, eternal return as, 66
health, 6, 75-6, 80-1, 84, 88, 92, 95, 128, 142, 151, 177, 199-200; *see also* morbidity, sickness
Hegel, G. W. F., 4, 12
Heidegger, Martin, vii
Hellenism, 178
Heraclitus, 7
heredity, 35, 76, 89
hierarchy, 159-61
Hinduism, 152
history, 127, 171; of the self, 29, histrionics, 222, 233, 235-6, 241, 246; of health, 75
Hölderlin, Freidrich, 251
Horace, 233
humanism, 128
humanity, 36, 153; breaking its history in two, 93, 100, 170
humility, 82-3
hunger, 34
hygiene, 26

ideals, 209
identity, xviii, 42, 58; God as guarantor of, 4, 57; individual, 93; loss of, 233; of the self, 29, 56, 73, 184; principle of, xvii, 77, 170, 206, 245
idiosyncrasy, 12, 147
illness; *see* sickness
illusion(s), 45-6, 50, 52
images, xvi, 15, 47, 99, 217
immortality, 71
impotence, 81, 84
impulse(s), x, 2, 26-7, 31, 33-4, 37-8, 44, 46-50, 73, 76, 83,

101, 110, 112, 117, 135, 137, 157, 225, 254-5, 258; body as the fortuitous encounter of, 28; combat of, 50; fluctuations of, 250, 255; generate phantasms, 133; primordial, 103; *see also* intensity; soul, tonality of
inclinations, 48
incommunicable, 77
India, 70
indifference, 61
individual(s), xv, 26, 53, 107, 112-13, 148; and affects, 9, 13; and eternal return, 68-72; and formations of sovereignty, 119-20, 123, 127, 131, 147, 153; as fortuitous, 94, 115, 137, 153; as series of individualities, 91, 93, 98, 140; and species, 76-7, 80, 83, 92, 103, 140, 155, 200, 261; will to power in, 103
industrialization, 5, 128, 145, 148-9, 158, 167, 171
inequality, 11, 13
innocence, 70
insanity, 199
insomnia, 26, 39
intellect, 33, 35, 48, 52, 135, 259-61; as caricature of unreason, 133; as impulse, 254-5
intelligence, 130; intelligibility, 16, 219
intensity, intensities, xix, 37, 47-8, 51, 61, 65, 91, 104, 106, 112, 114, 135, 140, 251; and intention, 70; fluctuations of, 49, 60-2, 218; flux and reflux of, 65; rises and falls of, 6, 61; *see also* impulses
intention, intentionality, xviii, 37, 46, 49, 51, 52, 53, 114, 118, 138, 172; acting without, 140
interiority, 53
interpretation, 51, 61, 86, 107, 114, 117, 129, 172-3, 234
intoxication, 86-7
irony, 239
irresponsibility, 14

irreversibility, 30

Jaspers, Karl, vii, 22
Jesus Christ, 210, 233-4, 249
Jews, 182, 201, 249-50
judgement, 48
justice, 11, 103, 156, 221
justification, 14

Kafka, Franz, ix
Kant, Immanuel, 4-5, 7
Kierkegaard, Søren, vii, ix
kingdom of God, 171
Klee, Paul, ix
knowledge, xvii, 50, 103, 133, 141, 205
Kojève, Alexandre, 12n

La Rochefoucauld, 7
labour, 12
labyrinth, 247-9
Lacoue-Labarthe, Philippe, viii
language, xvii, 14, 24, 30, 41-3, 45-6, 48, 53, 76, 79, 109, 111, 251, 254, 261; German, xiv; institutional, 52-3; *see also* code of everyday signs
laughter, 70, 251
law(s), 108, 138, 140; of eternal return, 57
Leiris, Michel, viii
levelling, process of, 7, 152, 156; *see also* gregariousness
life, 7, 34, 41-2, 45, 54, 80, 102-3, 107, 116, 163, 177, 196, 257n; affirmation of, 94; non-sense of, 53
light, variations of, 251
logic, 129
Louvre, 13
Lowith, Karl, vii
lucidity, xvi, 25, 32, 53, 93, 97, 98, 122, 123
Lyotard, Jean-Francois, viii

Machiavelli, Niccolò, 255
madness, 33, 95, 136, 178, 206, 211

magic, 245
Malthus, Thomas, 142
Manu, laws of, 151
marionette, 86
Marxism, xv
mask(s), 92, 96-7, 191, 223-4, 233;
    see also gesture(s)
master-slave relationship, 11,
    126-7, 148-9, 156, 158
Masters of the Earth, 125, 128,
    146, 148, 171
meaning, 30, 37-8, 41-2, 51-2,
    70, 73-4, 105, 112, 114, 121,
    134, 147, 155, 168, 170, 209;
    constitution of, 218
means, 51-2, 104; and ends, 42-3
mechanism, 101, 106, 110, 114;
    critique of, 108-9
memory, 32, 38, 58, 61, 185
Mendès, Catulle, 246
metamorphosis, 69, 71, 73, 94,
    188
metaphysics, 6-7, 106
metempsychosis, 70
Meysenbug, Malwilda von, 19
migraines, 16, 22, 24, 61
miming, 4, 100, 139
mind, 34-5, 102
modernity, xvi, 75, 145, 156; *see*
    also industrialization
moment, in the eternal return, 95
money, 149, 201
monstrosity, 9, 42, 154, 200,
    204-5, 250
mood(s), xviii-xix, 260
morality, 6, 10, 14, 38, 40, 81,
    83-4, 90, 92, 128, 133, 162,
    204, 219, 245; Christian, 12;
    naturalization of, 106; without
    intention, 140
morbidity, 75-6, 80, 84, 95, 128,
    198-9; *see also* health, sickness
motion, 109
Mozart, Wolfgang A., 200
music, as language of affects, 2-3
muteness, xviii, 31, 76-7, 79, 204;
    absolute, 95, 251
mysticism, 222

mystification, and demystification,
    130-1

Nancy, Jean-Luc, viii
Napolean, 248
nature, humanization of, 44
necessity, 73, 108; and eternal
    return, 57
neighbour, 33, 36
nervous system, 21, 25, 34, 198
neurasthenia, 81
Nietzsche, Elisabeth, 197, 211
Nietzsche, Franziska, 21-2, 197
Nietzsche, Friedrich, works:
    Antichrist, 210, 225, 238, 249;
    Beyond Good and Evil, 122,
    245, 254; *Birth of Tragedy*, 16;
    The Case of Wagner, 225, 227;
    The Dawn, 186; *Ecce Homo*, 86,
    172, 174-5, 189, 203, 204, 207,
    224, 225, 228-9, 234, 236, 239,
    245; 'Euphorion', 181-3, 197;
    The Gay Science, vii, 60, 66,
    68, 122, 158; *On the Genealogy*
    of Morals, 122, 232; *Human*,
    All-Too-Human, 16, 75, 122,
    204; *Nietzsche contra Wagner*,
    234, 238; *Sketch for a Satyr Play*,
    245; *Thus Spoke Zarathustra*, 66,
    68, 99-100, 122, 190-1, 196,
    204, 210, 226; *Twilight of the*
    Idols, 225, 227; *The Wanderer*
    and His Shadow, 186
nihilism, 113, 123, 125, 168, 208;
    active, 94; passive, 94, 132
Nirvanaism, 132
non-sense, 53, 94
norm(s), 77, 199, 257
nothingness, 40, 51, 132

object, 38, 102
obsession, 59, 67, 76, 127, 184
Oedipal schema, 176, 187
organic world, 106, 112, 220, 257;
    and inorganic, 32, 34-5, 43, 45
origin, 13, 28, 38, 104, 138,
    158, 256-8
Overbeck, Franz, 17, 20-1, 93,

94, 97, 170, 188, 191, 193-5,
211-15, 226, 237
overman, 70, 147, 156, 161,
169-70

pain, 25, 28
paranoia, 225-6, 238-9; and the
return of the repressed, 238
Paris, 9, 91, 96
Parmenides, 75
Pascal, Blaise, 255
passion(s), 11, 44, 48, 143; the
'great' passion, 129, 215;
Nietzsche's, 213, 215; relations
among, 89-91
passivity, 98
pathology, xvi, 142
pathos, 1, 220, 254
person, 24, 27-8
perspective, perspectivism, 11, 44,
50, 106, 130, 177, 218
phantasm(s), 8, 13, 16, 47, 67, 72,
92, 133-5, 137-41, 146-7, 164,
169, 196, 223, 251, 259-61;
defined, x-xi,
philistinism, 8
philology, 10, 183, 185-6,
210, 244
philosopher: as a type, 1-2; the
philosopher-imposter, 127,
132, 134, 137, 222
philosophy, 81; as expression of
impulses, 2-5; historians of,
xviii; political, 125
physiognomy, ix, xi, 29, 65, 125,
180; absence of, 224; divine,
66, 235; gregarious, 128; of
Jesus, 233; of the philosopher,
126; of the Masters of the
Earth, 128, 223-4; divine, 65-6,
235; of Cosima Wagner, 248;
of Richard Wagner, 223
physiology, 26, 32, 36, 52-4, 126-
9, 134, 162, 181, 185; applied,
127-8, 146-7; Nietzsche's, 73
planetary management, 160-1,
164, 167
Plato, 130

pleasure, 25, 28, 33, 41, 82, 101,
110-12, 131, 162, 168, 203
Poe, Edgar Allen, 149
Poland, 250
politics, 15, 32, 125-6, 131, 146,
157, 162, 167, 170, 250
possessive article, 70
power, 45, 76, 84, 87-8, 92, 95,
101, 105, 108, 110, 112, 115,
117; relations of, 49; *see also*
will to power
precociousness, 91
preexistence, 69, 70, 94
prejudice, of the sentiments,
121, 254
premeditation, 169, 256
Prometheus, 128
propensities, 48
propositions, 62
psychiatry, xviii, 38, 40
purification, 70
purpose, 41-2, 51-2, 104, 147

quality, critique of, 44; and
quantity, 15

race, 62, 91, 163, 198, 203;
Nietzsche's, 250; of masters,
146, 163, 166
reality, xix
reality principle, xvii-xviii, 104,
121, 134, 137, 139, 141, 144,
146, 150, 170, 200, 235
reason, 24, 27, 102; sufficient, 110
redemption, 69
Rée, Paul, 16, 187, 188-91, 194
regularity, 103
relaxation, 61
religion, 3, 19, 70, 81, 106,
136, 202
repulsion, 34, 47, 49, 259-61
resignation, 82-3
resistance, 87; and non-resistance,
199
ressentiment, xix, 87, 202
revaluation, 125, 147, 177, 201;
Revaluation of All Values, 225
Rilke, Ranier Maria, viii-ix

Rohde, Erwin, 16, 187, 188, 213
Russia, 161

Sade, Marquis de, viii, xv, 130
saint, as type, 203
Salomé, Lou A., 23, 91, 94, 95-9,
    186-91, 192, 195-6, 212, 248
schizophrenia, 239
Schopenhauer, Arthur, 102
Schulpforta, 178-9, 181
science, xviii, 5, 32, 41, 79, 93,
    99, 111, 127, 134-5, 136-9,
    141-2, 144, 146, 185, 239, 245;
    autonomy of, 145
security, 4
selection, 202; Darwinian, 169;
    natural, 124
self, xiii, 26, 31-3, 35-6, 57, 62-6,
    114; multiplication of, 66
semiotic, 138; of consciousness,
    50; of impulses, 50
sensation, 34-5
senses, 89, 109
serenity, 25, 216
series; *see* eternal return
servitude, 9, 13, 34, 54, 115, 119,
    126, 157, 164, 172
Shakespeare, 204-6, 223, 248
sickness, 23, 28, 75, 81, 151,
    186, 199-200; *see also* health,
    valetudinary states
sign, of the eternal return, 64, 66;
    of vicious circle, 105
sign(s), 31, 38, 44, 46-8, 50, 52,
    61-2, 219, 251, 261; and their
    abbreviation, 44, 48-50; *see also*
    code of everyday signs
signification, 40, 61-2, 65, 95,
    117, 225
silence, 13, 31, 37, 39, 41, 43, 49,
    70, 252; *see also* muteness
Sils-Maria, 16, 66-7, 69, 72, 80,
    93, 98-100, 124, 213, 216
simulacrum [*Trugbild*], 99,
    125, 130, 133, 135, 137,
    139-40, 142, 223; defined,
    x-xi; the reproduction of
    phantasms, 133;

simulation, 50, 138, 234
singular, x, 6, 76-7, 79, 93,
    119-20, 128, 151, 154, 199;
    singular case, *see* fortuitous case;
    see also gregariousness
slavery, 8, 11; role of, 156-7
sociology, 104, 106, 126, 145
soul, x, 71, 102; tonality of, x,
    xviii, 60, 63-4, 66, 71, 93, 100,
    112, 114; *see also* impulses
sovereignty, 12, 76, 250; form-
    ations of [*Herrschaftesgebilde*],
    104, 106, 118-19, 125, 166
space, 109
species, xv, 7, 44-5, 79-80, 103,
    130, 140-1, 154-5, 200, 261
speech, 76, 95, 110, 188, 224-6,
    232, 260
Spinoza, Baruch, 4-5, 7, 102
spirituality, spiritualization,
    106-7, 113-14
spontaneity, 50-1, 54, 157
stereotypes, xi-xiii
sterility, 145, 200
Stimmung, 56-8, 63, 65
Stirner, 153
strength, 75, 82, 199
Strindberg, August, 170, 226,
    239, 227-34
strong, of the future, 162-3
subject, 38, 48, 101, 102
subjectivism, 139
sublimation, 203-4
substance, 35; critique of, 44, 136
suffering, 25, 96-7, 99
symptoms, 75, 80, 84, 101

taste, 2-3, 136-7, 144, 193
teaching, xviii
technology, 110, 157
temporality, 110, 185
theology, 118, 170
therapeutics, 23
Theseus, 247
thing, 109
thinking, xvi, 38, 49, 53, 62, 257;
    act of, 75; and suffering, 23
thought, xv, xvii, 34, 36, 44,

49-50, 102; and behavior, 4;
highest, 65; spontaneity of, 51
Thousand and One Nights, A, 66
time, 69; as irreversible, 67
tonality; *see* soul
trace(s), 26, 31, 47, 61-2, 114,
256, 258
tragedy, 183, 246
training and selection, 121, 125-6,
128, 149, 151, 156; training vs.
taming, 152
Tribschen, 196, 238, 240, 245
Tristan, 248
truth, 2-5, 102, 208; as error, 45,
135-6; and falsity, 44, 48
types, typology, 77, 86, 127, 129,
140, 147, 161, 166

unconscious, 38, 41, 47, 50, 77,
141; vs. unconsciousness, 37
unconsciousness, 37-8, 40-1, 54
understanding, 40
unexchangeable, ix, 76-7, 93,
166, 201
unintelligibility, 67, 76, 79, 100,
133-4, 151, 185, 199
unity, unities, 34, 37-38, 44, 48-9,
91, 109, 138

valetudinary states, 32, 75, 99; *see
also* sickness
value(s), 75, 119, 155, 160,
209, 257
vicious circle, 30, 53, 64, 66, 72,
80, 98, 103, 128, 152, 155-6,
160, 171
Vienna, 96
vigour, 75, 95, 107, 187, 199; *see
also* decadence
violence, 95, 101, 114-15, 117,
119-20, 129, 153, 155-6
Virgil, ix, 249
virtue, Christian, 83; virtue-
imperative, 157, 163, 166-7
Voltaire, 130, 248

Wagner, Cosima, 187, 196-7, 222,
226, 237, 238, 240, 245-6, 248

Wagner, Richard, 16, 87, 185-8,
196-7, 204, 222-3, 238, 245-6;
Parsifal, 92
wave, image of, 61-2
weak, the, 201-3; weakness, 82,
199
will, 38, 47, 50, 52, 57, 61, 64,
69, 73, 88, 102, 112, 260; to
unconsciousness, 54
will to power, 12, 45-6, 56, 83-4,
88, 95, 101-5, 107-8, 110, 112,
117, 130, 135, 137, 199, 244,
254-5; paradox of, 105-6
willing, 36-7, 43, 53, 58, 67; and
non-willing, 37
Wittgenstein, Ludwig, ix
women, 79, 173, 188-9, 199, 202,
222, 227, 231
words, 15, 217
world, 64; true vs. apparent, 41
writing, 6, 15, 19, 38, 182

Zarathustra, character of, 36, 65,
67, 99-100, 192, 204, 210; as
prophet, 99
Zola, 229-30

Made in the USA
Las Vegas, NV
26 May 2021